Microsoft® Copilot™ Studio
Quick Start

Microsoft® Copilot™ Studio Quick Start

Learn to Create and Deploy Personalized AI Solutions

Jared Matfess

WILEY

Copyright © 2025 by John Wiley & Sons, Inc. All rights reserved, including rights for text and data mining and training of artificial intelligence technologies or similar technologies.

Published by John Wiley & Sons, Inc., Hoboken, New Jersey.
Published simultaneously in Canada and the United Kingdom.

ISBNs: 9781394333707 (paperback), 9781394333721 (ePDF), 9781394333714 (ePub)

No part of this publication may be reproduced, stored in a retrieval system, or transmitted in any form or by any means, electronic, mechanical, photocopying, recording, scanning, or otherwise, except as permitted under Section 107 or 108 of the 1976 United States Copyright Act, without either the prior written permission of the Publisher, or authorization through payment of the appropriate per-copy fee to the Copyright Clearance Center, Inc., 222 Rosewood Drive, Danvers, MA 01923, (978) 750-8400, fax (978) 750-4470, or on the web at www.copyright.com. Requests to the Publisher for permission should be addressed to the Permissions Department, John Wiley & Sons, Inc., 111 River Street, Hoboken, NJ 07030, (201) 748-6011, fax (201) 748-6008, or online at http://www.wiley.com/go/permission.

The manufacturer's authorized representative according to the EU General Product Safety Regulation is Wiley-VCH GmbH, Boschstr. 12, 69469 Weinheim, Germany, e-mail: Product_Safety@wiley.com.

Trademarks: Wiley and the Wiley logo are trademarks or registered trademarks of John Wiley & Sons, Inc. and/or its affiliates in the United States and other countries and may not be used without written permission. Microsoft and Copilot are trademarks or registered trademarks of Microsoft Corporation. All other trademarks are the property of their respective owners. John Wiley & Sons, Inc. is not associated with any product or vendor mentioned in this book. *Microsoft® Copilot™ Studio Quick Start* is an independent publication and is neither affiliated with, nor authorized, sponsored, or approved by, Microsoft Corporation.

Limit of Liability/Disclaimer of Warranty: While the publisher and author have used their best efforts in preparing this book, they make no representations or warranties with respect to the accuracy or completeness of the contents of this book and specifically disclaim any implied warranties of merchantability or fitness for a particular purpose. No warranty may be created or extended by sales representatives or written sales materials. The advice and strategies contained herein may not be suitable for your situation. You should consult with a professional where appropriate. Further, readers should be aware that websites listed in this work may have changed or disappeared between when this work was written and when it is read. Neither the publisher nor author shall be liable for any loss of profit or any other commercial damages, including but not limited to special, incidental, consequential, or other damages.

For general information on our other products and services or for technical support, please contact our Customer Care Department within the United States at (800) 762-2974, outside the United States at (317) 572-3993 or fax (317) 572-4002. For product technical support, you can find answers to frequently asked questions or reach us via live chat at https://support.wiley.com.

Wiley also publishes its books in a variety of electronic formats. Some content that appears in print may not be available in electronic formats. For more information about Wiley products, visit our web site at www.wiley.com.

Library of Congress Control Number: 2025940679

Cover image: © CSA-Printstock/Getty Images

Cover design: Wiley

SKY10120355_070325

This book is dedicated to Professor John S. Gray, former chair of the Multimedia Web Design & Development program at the University of Hartford.

About the Author

Jared Matfess is a Solutions Architect at AvePoint, specializing in helping organizations maximize the value of their investments in Microsoft technologies. He is a coauthor of *Microsoft 365 Copilot at Work: Using AI to Get the Most from Your Business Data and Favorite Apps* (John Wiley & Sons, Inc., 2024). Jared holds certifications from both Microsoft and AWS and was recognized as a Microsoft MVP from 2016 to 2022, and again in 2025. He earned a bachelor's degree in Interactive Information Technology from the University of Hartford, an MBA from the University of Massachusetts Amherst, and a master's degree in Computer Information Systems from Boston University.

About the Technical Editor

Norm Young is a Power Platform Solution Architect at AvePoint, where he guides clients in the strategic adoption and governance of the Power Platform. With two decades of experience spanning manufacturing, higher education, and the computer software sector, Norm brings a wealth of practical knowledge to the table. His expertise in Microsoft analytics, collaboration, and low-code platforms empowers teams to succeed with Microsoft technologies. A five-time Microsoft MVP (Business Applications & M365), Norm is passionate about sharing his insights through speaking and blogging. He's dedicated to making complex concepts accessible and helping readers navigate the ever-evolving world of Microsoft solutions.

Acknowledgments

First and foremost, I have to thank my wife, May, for her patience, support, and for wrangling Tobias and Gus during the long nights and stressful weekends when I disappeared into writing mode. No matter how much I tried to balance work, life, and writing, it always seemed like work and writing got the bulk of my attention. Gus gets an honorable mention for snoring quietly in his bed through countless Saturday mornings, and the Foo Fighters for keeping the vibe alive when I needed it most.

A big thank you as well to Norm Young, my tech editor and partner on this project. Norm not only ensured everything was technically accurate, but also helped me navigate the world of Power Platform, a key part of building agents in Copilot Studio.

I'd be remiss if I didn't also thank the broader Microsoft community, including the Microsoft employees and MVPs I leaned on for both moral and occasional tech support. Mike Maadarani, Tom Daly, Marc Anderson, Christian Buckley, Manpreet Singh, Todd Klindt, Jason Himmelstein, Kanwal Khipple, Richard Harbridge, Ray Loyola, Jason Rivera, Stacy Deere, and a whole host of others—thank you for always being there.

And to my friend of over a decade, Heidi Lamar—thank you for everything you do. I hope you enjoy your retirement in 7 years, but until then, I'll see you for coffee at Rebel Dog.

Finally, thank you to *you*, the reader. Whether you're deep into your tech career or just getting started, I'm honored you picked up this book. And if you happen to be reading this quietly in the corner of a Barnes & Noble, like I used to over 25 years ago, I hope this sparks something that carries you forward.

Contents at a Glance

Foreword		xxi
Chapter 1	Navigating the Copilot Ecosystem	1
Chapter 2	Introduction to Copilot Studio	29
Chapter 3	Publishing Your Copilot Agent	71
Chapter 4	Microsoft 365 Copilot Declarative Agents	91
Chapter 5	Planning ALM for Your Copilot Agents	119
Chapter 6	Deep Dive into Agent Templates	143
Chapter 7	Real-World Use Cases and Inspiration	171
Chapter 8	Building an Autonomous Agent	197
Chapter 9	Optimizing and Measuring Your Agent	245
Chapter 10	Copilot Studio and Azure AI Foundry: Better Together	267
Appendix	Agent Flows	291
Index		297

Contents

Foreword		**xxi**
Chapter 1	**Navigating the Copilot Ecosystem**	**1**
	What Is GenAI?	2
	How Does GenAI Work?	3
	GenAI Key Terms and Definitions	3
	The Risk of Bias in GenAI	4
	OpenAI Brings GenAI to the World	4
	ChatGPT Gains Excitement	5
	ChatGPT Data Leaks	5
	Microsoft's Strategic Investment in OpenAI	6
	Retrieval-Augmented Generation	7
	Azure OpenAI RAG Pattern	8
	Enterprise Adoption of the RAG Pattern	9
	Microsoft M365 Copilot	10
	The Rise of the Copilots	12
	Copilot, aka Bing Chat Enterprise	12
	Microsoft's Copilot Portfolio	13
	Copilot for Sales	14
	Copilot for Service	16
	Copilot for Security	17
	Copilot in Microsoft Viva	19
	Viva Goals	19
	Viva Engage	20
	Viva Amplify	21
	Viva Roadmap	22
	Additional Copilots	22

xvi   Contents

	Aligning Copilots with Company Personas	24
	Introducing Copilot Studio	25
	Conclusion	26
Chapter 2	**Introduction to Copilot Studio**	**29**
	Copilot Studio's Core Audience	29
	Citizen Developers Overview	30
	Citizen Developer Challenges	31
	The Role of IT	32
	Copilot Studio: The Platform	33
	Copilot Studio Prerequisites	33
	Accessing Copilot Studio	34
	Power Platform Environments	35
	Microsoft Dataverse	36
	Dataverse Core Components	37
	Environment Management	39
	Creating Your First Agent	39
	Adding Knowledge Sources	42
	Testing Your Copilot Agent	47
	Copilot Studio Topics	50
	Conversational Boosting with GenAI	52
	Modifying Your User Experience with Topics	55
	Lights, Camera, Actions!	57
	Conclusion	69
Chapter 3	**Publishing Your Copilot Agent**	**71**
	Channels	71
	Publishing Your Agent to Teams + Microsoft 365	74
	Publishing Your Agent	79
	Testing Your Agent in Microsoft Teams and M365 Copilot	86
	Conclusion	90
Chapter 4	**Microsoft 365 Copilot Declarative Agents**	**91**
	The Spectrum of Copilot Agents	91
	M365 Copilot Agents	92
	Declarative Copilot Agents	93
	The Agent App Package	93
	App Manifest	93
	App Icons	94
	Declarative Agents Manifest	94
	Plugin Manifest	95
	Configuration Options	96
	The AI Orchestrator	96
	Creating a Declarative M365 Copilot Agent with the Copilot Studio Agent Builder	97
	Configuring Your Agent	98
	Setting Instructions	99

Configuring Knowledge 101
Actions and Capabilities 103
Starter Prompts 104
Creating Your Agent 105
Adjusting Sharing Permissions 106
Application Manifest: Manifest.json 108
The DeclarativeAgent_0.json File 110
Code Versus Configuration 112
Test Driving Your Agent 112
Updating Your Declarative Agent 114
Copilot Studio Agent Builder Limitations 115
Data Storage 115
Application Lifecycle Management 116
User Experience 116
When to Use Declarative Agents 117
Conclusion 118

Chapter 5   **Planning ALM for Your Copilot Agents**   **119**
The ALM Framework 120
Requirements Gathering 120
Design 121
Development 121
Testing 122
Deployment 122
Maintenance and Retirement 123
ALM Summary 123
Power Platform Environments 123
Environment Strategy 124
Environment Costs 124
Managed Environments 125
Managed Environments Considerations 127
Solutions 127
Creating a Solution 129
Exporting a Solution 132
Importing a Solution 135
CI/CD Pipelines 140
Conclusion 141

Chapter 6   **Deep Dive into Agent Templates**   **143**
Prerequisites 144
Selecting Our Agent Template 145
Citizen Services Template 146
Knowledge Sources 146
Topics 147
Apply for a Service Topic 148
Data Collection Topic and Adaptive Cards 149

xviii **Contents**

Road Closures Topic	154
Conversational Boosting Topic	155
Summarizing Topics	157
Building Our Agent from the Citizen Services Template	157
Updating Knowledge Sources	158
Updating Topics	159
Testing Your Agent	166
Conclusion	169

Chapter 7 Real-World Use Cases and Inspiration 171

Agents in the Contact Center	171
The Scenario	172
Technical Setup	173
Testing the Contact Center Agent	175
Contact Center Charlie Agent Summary	176
Agents in the Public Sector	176
Technical Setup	176
Testing Our Shared Mailbox Agent	182
Summary of the Shared Mailbox Agent	185
Agents in Human Resources	186
Technical Setup	186
Testing Your Heidi from HR Agent	194
Summary of the Updated Heidi from HR Agent	195
Conclusion	195

Chapter 8 Building an Autonomous Agent 197

Autonomous vs. Semi-autonomous Agents	197
Considerations for Autonomous Agents	198
How Microsoft's Autonomous Agents Work	198
Autonomous Agent Use Case	199
Microsoft Form Configuration	200
Salesforce Sales Cloud Setup	201
Configuring Your Agent	202
Enabling Orchestration	203
Creating a Trigger	204
Configuring your Trigger	207
Setting Up Knowledge Sources	213
Creating Actions	218
Creating Inputs	220
Formatting Variables	221
Getting the Account ID	222
Creating a Condition	224
Creating a Contact	226
Creating an Opportunity	227
Associating Your Opportunity to a Contact	228
Configuring "Run as" User	231
Configuring the Create Lead Action	232

	Configuring Your Agent Instructions	235
	Testing Your Agent	236
	Publishing and Monitoring	242
	Conclusion	242
Chapter 9	**Optimizing and Measuring Your Agent**	**245**
	Prerequisites	245
	Agent Analytics	246
	Optimizing Your Agent for Cost	248
	Enhancing User-Focused Agent Performance	251
	Quick Replies	251
	Starter Prompts	253
	Capturing User Feedback	255
	Conclusion	265
Chapter 10	**Copilot Studio and Azure AI Foundry: Better Together**	**267**
	Azure AI Search	268
	Optimizing for Cost	269
	Creating Your Azure SQL Database	269
	Creating a Table and Loading Data	274
	Provisioning Azure AI Search	276
	Configuring Your Agent for Azure AI Search	286
	Testing Your Agent	288
	Conclusion	289
Appendix	**Agent Flows**	**291**
Index		**297**

Foreword

"I wonder what will happen if I push this button."

If you're reading this, you're probably one of the curious ones. The bold ones. The "let me see how this works under the hood before I use it" kind of human. Welcome. You're my people.

We are standing at the beginning of our third great tech rodeo: the first, offline to online; the second, on-prem to cloud and mobile; and now, the era of AI.

This is not the time to sit back and let others have all the fun. This is your moment to lean in, run all the experiments, and yes—get a little uncomfortable. Because in the age of AI, those who understand how to *work* with it—not just use it—will shape the next generation of tech, business, and community.

Now let's be honest—AI is not magic. It's not a crystal ball. And Copilot isn't some kind of wizard in the cloud (though that would be fun). It's a *reasoning engine*. It helps you dynamically understand your world and make plans based on context, data, and intent. It doesn't "know" you until you teach it. It doesn't "remember" you unless you build memory into the experience. And it won't make your workflows better unless *you* have clarity on what "better" actually looks like.

This book is about that *clarity*.

Copilot Studio is not just a toolset—it's your launchpad for building agent-based systems that can think, adapt, and scale with you. It's where orchestration, context, connectors, and automation come together. And if those words sound scary, don't worry. You already know this. If you've ever used Power Automate, built a connector, or stood in front of your exec team defending why we *don't* need another rogue Excel tracker—congrats, you're ready.

But let's talk about responsibility.

The AI systems we build reflect the data and intent we feed them. They're only as inclusive, ethical, and safe as we make them. This means you—yes, *you*—are not just a maker, or a developer, or a Power Platform pro. You are now a curator of AI experiences. And with that comes a new kind of power—and a new kind of accountability.

I want you to think of this era not as "AI will take our jobs," but as "you, using AI well, will evolve your job." Your job has evolved; you're not doing the same things you were doing 5 years ago, right?

Just like DevOps wasn't a thing 20 years ago, "AI engineer" and "AI power user" are roles that are now not only real but in high demand. We're not replacing—we're upgrading. And you get to define what that means in your world.

If you're overwhelmed, that's fine. I run a wine cave, own a fashion line, write books, ship products at Microsoft, and build AI demos. I don't believe in burning down the house to start over. I believe in adding to your comfort zone—one tool, one use case, one weird-but-useful experiment at a time. Build a bot for your side hustle. Create a planning agent for your family vacation. Use Copilot Studio to solve a real problem in your life—and then scale it.

This book will give you the practical tools, architectures, and mindset shifts to do just that.

So buckle up, friends. This is not your first rodeo—but it may be your most impactful.

Let's go do the thing!

—Dona Sarkar
Director of Tech | Microsoft AI, Copilot and Agents
Fashion designer. Storyteller. AI troublemaker.

Reader Support for This Book

Companion Download Files

The book mentions some additional files, including code listings. These items are available for digital download from www.wiley.com/go/copilotstudioqs.

How to Contact the Publisher

If you believe you have found a mistake in this book, please bring it to our attention. At John Wiley & Sons, we understand how important it is to provide our customers with accurate content, but even with our best efforts an error may occur.

In order to submit your possible errata, please email it to our Customer Service Team at wileysupport@wiley.com with the subject line "Possible Book Errata Submission."

Microsoft® Copilot™ Studio
Quick Start

CHAPTER 1

Navigating the Copilot Ecosystem

Information technology (IT), as an organizational function, has the primary purpose of enabling business counterparts to implement solutions that improve productivity at the task and business process levels. For the past decade, IT leaders have been under incredible pressure to deliver business value while also being charged with continuing to drive down costs. For every new wave of technological innovation, IT leaders must navigate the fine line between embracing the hype and delivering tangible ROI.

Generative AI (GenAI) has forced an almost "gold rush" mentality within the IT industry, with consultants and independent software developers (ISVs) alike working hard to bring forward the next wave of innovation. Microsoft has made significant investments in GenAI through its Azure AI Studio service, which enables organizations to safely and securely develop their own GenAI applications, as well as its Copilot brand of GenAI-as-a-Service offerings, which are being built-in to its entire portfolio of applications. Satya Nadella, Chairman and Chief Executive Officer (CEO) of Microsoft, has been quoted as saying:

> We are the Copilot company. We believe in a future where there will be a Copilot for everyone and everything you do. Microsoft Copilot is that one experience that runs across all our surfaces, understanding your context on the Web, on your device. And when you're at work, bringing the right skills to you when you need them. Just like, say today you boot up an operating

> system to access applications or a browser to navigate to a Web site, you
> can invoke a Copilot to do all these activities, and more—to shop, to call,
> to analyze, to learn, to create. We want the compiler to be everywhere
> you are.
>
> redmondmag.com/articles/2023/11/16/
> nadella-ignite-2023-keynote.aspx

This chapter will begin with a quick primer on GenAI and Microsoft's role in maturing this technology over the past few years. We will then step through Microsoft's Copilot brand of products to better understand its strategy of transforming how people work by introducing artificial intelligence (AI) into their workflow. Finally, we will end with a high-level overview of Copilot Studio and how it will enable citizen developers and IT professionals to drive even greater business value by combining a low-code application development platform with GenAI.

What Is GenAI?

If you are unfamiliar with the term, GenAI is a type of AI that focuses on creating content by analyzing and learning patterns from large datasets. Examples of content GenAI can create include text, images, code, and audio. Additionally, GenAI can analyze existing content and provide you with feedback based on questions you ask it. For example, you could write an email and then ask it for suggestions on how to rewrite it for tone, clarity, or brevity. It will then analyze both the content you provided and its dataset to provide you with recommendations in natural language, meaning text.

GenAI is on the same trajectory as other large disruptive technologies, such as the graphical user interface (GUI), the Internet, and the iPhone. Unlike other technologies, such as robotics process automation (RPA), monolithic enterprise resource planning platforms, or event-driven architectures, what makes GenAI appealing is how it blends creativity with computation using the most powerful interface that exists: language.

GenAI blends creativity with computational power, enabling people to draft compelling narratives, design complex visuals, write code, and even create business strategies in a fraction of the time it once took. The technology is intuitive and adaptable, making it accessible to a wide range of users—from seasoned professionals to those without technical expertise. Its ability to personalize interactions, learn from context, and continuously improve makes GenAI a powerful tool for enhancing productivity, boosting innovation, and driving meaningful engagement across industries.

How Does GenAI Work?

At a high level, GenAI works through a combination of machine learning and then through the development of neural networks, which are a type of AI modeled after the human brain. Machine learning is when you feed in large amounts of data into a computer application, and it begins to create patterns to organize the data. Neural networks are an architecture within AI that include a series of interconnected nodes organized into various layers. These nodes, often referred to as *neurons*, are computational units that process information by performing mathematical operations on inputs, applying a weight (to emphasize importance), and passing the result through an activation function to determine the output. Like humans, GenAI models are trained with enormous amounts of data. While humans are trained over decades, GenAI models are trained over months with large datasets and computing infrastructure.

Like the human brain, as information flows through these interconnected nodes within the neural networks, it is transformed—but by mathematical functions. What is often viewed as being "GenAI magic" is a combination of being trained on a very large amount of data and the organization of this data in a way that can identify patterns and structures. At the end of the day, GenAI does an amazing job of predicting your desired output to the question you have asked it because it has been trained on a tremendous amount of data.

GenAI Key Terms and Definitions

While this book isn't meant to be a deep dive into GenAI, there are some key terms that are helpful to understand:

- **GenAI models:** Models are designed to create new data from machine learning patterns. The output could be text, images, music, etc.

- **Large language models (LLMs):** An LLM is a type of GenAI model that has been specifically trained on human language and can be used to create new content or summarize existing content.

- **Training data:** Data is the key to GenAI, as it is what feeds the GenAI models. Training data typically consists of large datasets, which include text, images, audio, etc. For LLMs specifically, the training data is human language in the form of text.

- **Pattern recognition:** This is where the model analyzes all the data you have trained it on and begins to identify patterns and structures that will be leveraged for content creation or content summarization.

- **Content creation:** This is where the model applies what it has learned and attempts to generate new content that mimics the style and structure of the training data it was provided when it responds to a user prompt.

The Risk of Bias in GenAI

When people talk about being careful about bias with GenAI, it is because the models are only as good as the data they are trained on. To provide a practical example, if you were building a model on baseball statistics and only provided statistics of the Boston Red Sox defeating the New York Yankees, the model would be biased toward the Boston Red Sox being the more dominant team. If you asked it who will win an upcoming game between the two teams, it would more than likely propose the Boston Red Sox based on its data. However, when you include all the matchups, the model might be biased toward the New York Yankees, since historically they have won more of the games between the two teams.

When you apply this same concept to people, the consequences can be even more drastic. For example, it has been proven that some ethnicities are statistically more prone to certain diseases. Therefore, it is important to have a wide set of training data for AI applications that are meant for health care use cases. If you train data only on a particular ethnicity, you may miss out on some of the potential nuances. Combined with a potential over-reliance on AI, this could lead to a situation where a clinician might miss a diagnosis even though they have access to this incredibly powerful AI application. The consequences of being over-reliant on technology that is wrong can have dire consequences, thus the need to plan for a comprehensive responsible AI strategy to help minimize these risks.

The technology industry and many data scientists are especially careful to point out the potential risks of bias that can happen with AI. Therefore, the need to obtain or create diverse datasets reflective of the various types of people, ethnicities, cultures, etc. is important to ensure that AI is for everyone, not just a subset of people. This risk is even more problematic given that the user experience of interacting with GenAI is very conversational in nature. In addition, the confidence with which LLMs provide responses is rather convincing, even when those answers are incorrect answer. The popularization of engaging with LLMs through conversation was catapulted into the spotlight through OpenAI's ChatGPT.

OpenAI Brings GenAI to the World

While OpenAI did not invent GenAI, it was able to bring it to the mainstream with its launch of ChatGPT in November 2022. ChatGPT was able to amass a user base of over 100 million users in less than a year, far quicker than any other technology to date. ChatGPT rapidly surpassed the adoption of commercial AI assistants such as Amazon's Alexa, Google's Echo, and Microsoft's Cortana by providing what seems like infinite expertise. ChatGPT's user experience, both then and now, is simple, with a basic chat-based user interface that is forgiving of typos and grammatical errors.

ChatGPT Gains Excitement

People began asking ChatGPT everything from how to make certain food dishes to recommendations for fuel-efficient vehicles to providing programming code to build responsive websites. You can even ask ChatGPT philosophical questions, such as *"What is the meaning of life in three sentences,"* and it will provide an answer, such as *"The meaning of life often revolves around finding purpose, creating connections, and embracing the journey. It's about making an impact through love, growth, and kindness while learning from experiences. Ultimately, life's meaning is unique to each person, shaped by their values, passions, and aspirations."* The magic of this interaction between human and machine really lies in the simplicity of being able to have a conversation with technology and having it understand the intricate nuances of language and culture.

As people continued to interact with ChatGPT, businesses started to think through how they might be able to incorporate this powerful new capability into their products and services. The buzz was all around identifying GenAI use cases that would help to unlock new revenue streams; however, there also began to be a growing concern about what OpenAI was doing with both the prompts that people were sending to its popular ChatGPT service and its responses.

ChatGPT Data Leaks

As businesses started to leverage this new capability, they found themselves in a situation where people inadvertently exposed their organization's sensitive data to a capability that feeds on knowledge. One of the early instances of this risk becoming a reality was when Samsung workers inadvertently leaked company secrets by using ChatGPT to assist with fixing source code.[1]

Additionally, they found instances where an employee used ChatGPT to summarize meeting minutes into a presentation. While today, the idea of having a meeting platform like Microsoft Teams or Zoom capturing meeting minutes and then summarizing them into action items, bullets, etc. might be considered common, this was incredibly impactful at the time. It combined the two things that most business professionals dislike: attending meetings and producing meeting summaries. This was perhaps one of the earliest examples of applying GenAI technology to streamline a business process, and it was a very relatable use case. As a reminder, this was still the early days of GenAI, when everyone was collectively learning how this technology worked in almost real time.

---

[1] techradar.com/news/samsung-workers-leaked-company-secrets-by-using-chatgpt.

This story became national news and set off a flurry of activity around how to enable a secure ChatGPT service that wouldn't expose company secrets to OpenAI. An additional challenge during the early years was OpenAI itself. It originally started as a nonprofit research organization when it organized in 2015, but then became a for-profit company structured as a "capped profit" organization. In many ways, with the almost overnight success of ChatGPT, OpenAI was thrust into the spotlight without having time to thoughtfully plan and scale to meet the needs of large enterprise customers. Just as we were all collectively learning about GenAI, OpenAI was learning about what it takes to become a company. Sam Altman, the Co-founder and CEO of OpenAI, has been very forthcoming of the potential societal impact of AI, which is reflective in the company's mission and incorporation. He also recognizes that the valuation of OpenAI is not in the models of today but in the continued research that will inevitably unlock potential we can barely even imagine in the future.

> **OpenAI's goal is to create general-purpose artificial intelligence that benefits all humanity.**
>
> *Sam Altman, Co-founder and CEO of OpenAI*
> `community.openai.com/t/the-possibilities-of-ai-`
> `interview-with-sam-altman-openai/733526`

Microsoft's Strategic Investment in OpenAI

Microsoft has been an early investor in OpenAI, and its initial 1 billion US dollar investment in OpenAI may be one of the most strategic moves made under Satya Nadella's tenure as CEO. After over 13 years of lagging behind Amazon Web Services (AWS) in the pursuit of providing cloud services, Microsoft's investment in OpenAI helped it leapfrog over the other hyperscalers. This gave Microsoft early access to OpenAI's models and helped it to architect its own service to help securely deliver enterprise-ready GenAI services well before its competition.

NOTE The term *hyperscalers*, which has been around since the 1990s, simply refers to large-scale datacenters that are able to deliver massive amounts of computing resources typically delivered through cloud computing.

In early January 2023, Microsoft announced Azure OpenAI as a new service that would allow you to provision instances of OpenAI's LLMs, including GPT-3, ChatGPT, and Codex models, all within your own Azure subscription. This was pivotal in helping organizations looking to experiment early with GenAI build their own ChatGPT-like solution within an existing cloud Azure subscription, either in an existing or new "landing zone."

A *landing zone* includes best practice configurations for security, networking, access management, and provisioning within your cloud environment. It allows organizations to isolate cloud resources, manage multiple environments (e.g., development, testing, and production), and scale as needed. This architecture provides the same level of controls and separation—or greater—than is available in a typical on-premises datacenter. The benefit is that your landing zone is completely virtualized and can be provisioned and deprovisioned using Infrastructure as Code (IaC) templates instead of managing physical hardware.

Azure OpenAI was a key enabler in helping organizations avoid any murkiness around how OpenAI handled prompt data and whether they were training their LLMs with this data. Thus, it ushered in an era of CompanyGPT experiments to placate the C-Suite that IT teams were evaluating this new capability while also working to minimize any business risk associated with exposing proprietary business data to one of the fastest-adopted consumer-facing IT services in history.

As businesses continued to experiment, they found that while having access to an LLM trained on billions of data parameters was incredible, the real potential value comes from combining this new capability with their own business data. However, one of the challenges of developing an LLM trained on business data was the sheer compute, power, and technical knowledge required. Hyperscalers such as Microsoft have the advantage of near-infinite computing resources at their disposal, along with the capital needed to perform this task. Building LLMs was not feasible for most organizations, but luckily a new pattern of leveraging the power of LLMs with business enterprise data emerged: retrieval-augmented generation.

Retrieval-Augmented Generation

Retrieval-augmented generation (RAG) hit the mainstream in 2020 in a paper titled "Retrieval-Augmented Generation for Knowledge-Intensive NLP Task,"[2] authored by several members of Meta (formerly Facebook). The concept was developed to improve the accuracy of responses produced by LLMs by pulling in external data sources as part of the response, instead of them responding solely based on their training data.

As shown in Figure 1.1, the core elements of the RAG architecture include the following:

- **Retrieval:** This is where you are querying an external data source based on the user request.

---

[2] arxiv.org/pdf/2005.11401

- **Augmentation:** This is where you are combining the response from the external data query with the user prompt and sending both of those together to the LLM for processing.
- **Generation:** This is where the LLM analyzes both the user prompt and the additional context (the "augmentation") and then provides a response back to the user.

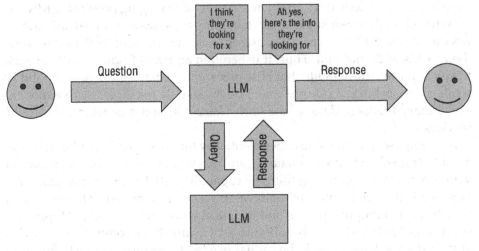

Figure 1.1: The core elements of RAG

The RAG approach enables you to gain the benefits of LLMs, which includes their reasoning and understanding skills. When you combine this capability with your business data, you are providing the LLM with additional context, which is also referred to as *grounding*. This grounding, in theory, should help the LLM predict a response that is closer to your anticipated outcome then if it were solely based on the training data alone. Additionally, this helps address one of the challenges with LLMs: they don't necessarily provide you with the reasoning or source behind their answer unless prompted to do so.

Azure OpenAI RAG Pattern

The architecture was relatively straightforward and required minimal resources to build. First, you would configure Azure Cognitive Search (later renamed Azure AI Search) to crawl defined Azure Blob Storage, Azure SQL databases, Azure applications, and other data sources. Upon completion of crawling your data sources, it would create an index that you could query from your chat application.

Your chat application would take a user prompt and perform an Azure Cognitive Services keyword search against your business data, which would return a subset of the data based on the additional parameters you may have specified. It would then pass that response, along with the original user prompt, to Azure OpenAI, reason over the data, and present the response back to the user.

An alternative to this architecture was to pass the user prompt to Azure OpenAI and then describe the type of data in your index, as well as potential keywords to look for. You would then take the modified prompt and perform a keyword search using Azure AI Search, passing that data to Azure OpenAI to reason over. Finally, you would return Azure OpenAI's response back to the user, along with the reference source file that it derived its response from. Typically, the developer would include an additional visual cue in the response to ensure that the user verifies the response provided by AI. Figure 1.2 illustrates an example of this RAG pattern in Azure OpenAI.

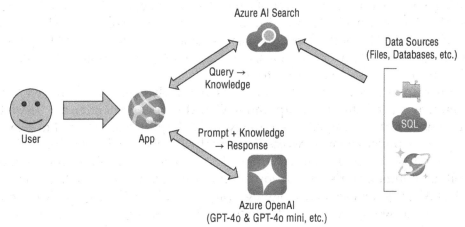

Figure 1.2: The Azure OpenAI RAG pattern
Source: Pablocastro (2023) / Microsoft

Enterprise Adoption of the RAG Pattern

This architecture became highly adopted across both custom GenAI applications developed in house and many off-the-shelf platforms being sold by software companies. Building custom LLMs is an incredibly expensive endeavor of scaling up large amounts of computing power and vast sets of training data to feed the model. Outlaying large amounts of capital without knowing precisely the effectiveness of the model is a risky endeavor.

However, the RAG pattern combined the power of GenAI and business data, while also checking the box of ensuring that your solution had some elements of responsible AI built in. This responsible AI check is satisfied by the LLM not providing a direct answer based on training data but rather citing the source

Chapter 1 ■ Navigating the Copilot Ecosystem

from where its response originated from. While it certainly wasn't foolproof, it at least provided the file reference for its answer, allowing the user to "check AI's work." This pattern's validity became cemented even further when Microsoft announced its upcoming new GenAI offering, Microsoft 365 Copilot (M365 Copilot).

Microsoft M365 Copilot

Microsoft's announcement of M365 Copilot in March 2023 represented yet another significant evolution in its service offering by becoming one of the first vendors to promise GenAI-as-a-service within its existing SaaS offering. Microsoft Office has been the market leader in the productivity suite category, and the idea of being able to leverage the power of ChatGPT-like functionality within its core application suite made the promises of GenAI even more relevant to business professionals. Microsoft named this new AI sidekick—which would help you with your tasks, answer questions, and engage in conversations—"Copilot." And the rest will someday be history.

Microsoft's investment in OpenAI was incredibly beneficial, as it gave the company a head start in incorporating GenAI into its SaaS offerings several months before its competition. Initially, M365 Copilot was released to select customers under an Early Access Preview (EAP) model, whereby you had to commit to a set 300 licenses for a year. This allowed Microsoft to control the rollout, minimizing risk to its reputation if users encountered shortcomings. The EAP program included assigning a Microsoft Cloud Architect to assist and oversee the deployment, as well as to help collect feedback to better inform the product team about what customers were experiencing through actual usage. This very risk-averse approach is actually something you can observe with the product itself.

As shown in Figure 1.3, M365 Copilot's architecture is an example of the RAG pattern discussed earlier. The user prompt is first sent to Copilot, which then performs a retrieval against the Microsoft Graph + Web sources. The Copilot service then sends that augmented payload to the LLM. The LLM then sends a response back to it, which it evaluates against the Microsoft Graph and Microsoft Purview for a compliance check. Finally, the response is sent back to the user. This additional compliance check before displaying the response back to the user is an example of Microsoft recognizing the needs of large enterprises to log activity and prevent malicious use of technology. This is a consistent theme with all of Microsoft's GenAI offerings: to design with security and compliance in mind.

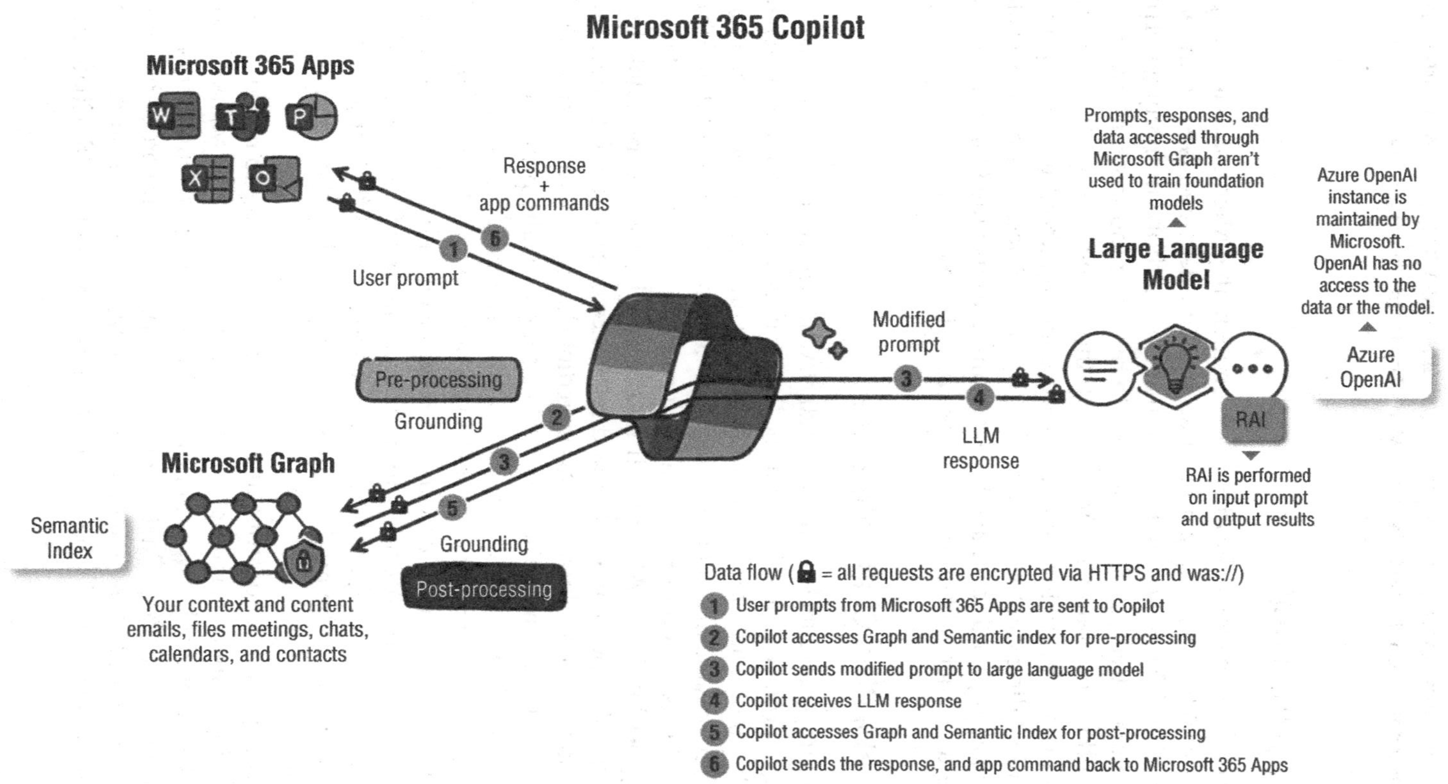

Microsoft 365 Copilot

Microsoft 365 Apps

Response + app commands

User prompt

Pre-processing

Grounding

Microsoft Graph

Semantic Index

Your context and content emails, files meetings, chats, calendars, and contacts

Post-processing

Grounding

Modified prompt

LLM response

Prompts, responses, and data accessed through Microsoft Graph aren't used to train foundation models

Large Language Model

RAI

RAI is performed on input prompt and output results

Azure OpenAI instance is maintained by Microsoft. OpenAI has no access to the data or the model.

Azure OpenAI

Data flow (🔒 = all requests are encrypted via HTTPS and was://)

1. User prompts from Microsoft 365 Apps are sent to Copilot
2. Copilot accesses Graph and Semantic index for pre-processing
3. Copilot sends modified prompt to large language model
4. Copilot receives LLM response
5. Copilot accesses Graph and Semantic Index for post-processing
6. Copilot sends the response, and app command back to Microsoft 365 Apps

Figure 1.3: The M365 Copilot architecture

Source: Angela Byers (2024) / Microsoft

Chapter 1 ▪ Navigating the Copilot Ecosystem

> **NOTE** This book is a companion to *Microsoft 365 Copilot at Work: Using AI to Get the Most from Your Business Data and Favorite Apps* (ISBN: 978-1-394-25837-6), which goes into greater detail about how to leverage M365 Copilot in your company.

The Rise of the Copilots

Microsoft marketing took to heart Satya's comment that Microsoft is the "Copilot company" and began naming all products with integrated GenAI under the name "Copilot." Microsoft marketing has been a thorn in many enterprise IT professional's lives, as they continue to rename products mid-cycle, causing the need to continuously include both the current and previous name in conversations to ensure that both parties are talking about the same product. For example, "Bing Chat Enterprise" has been renamed to simply "Copilot." As more existing products have been renamed to use the Copilot branding, customers and Microsoft employees alike have been confused.

Copilot, aka Bing Chat Enterprise

Microsoft Bing was launched in June of 2009, when Steve Ballmer was the Chief Executive Officer. Google was by far the leader in terms of Internet search back then, with Yahoo and China's Baidu being the only other competition at the time. Google was the market leader in Internet search to the point that "Google something" was synonymous with performing an Internet search. Previous search engines like MSN, AOL Search, and even Ask Jeeves were unable to ever keep up with the speed, reliability, and relevance of a Google Internet search.

Additionally, Google's business was incredibly lucrative, as advertisers flocked to it and paid large sums of money to have their results promoted for their desired keywords. Google's Internet search business still brings in over 50% of Google's parent company Alphabet's revenue, even with the expansion into other products such as YouTube, Google Cloud, Google Pixel phones, and Google Home devices. Microsoft's foray into the Internet search business had a mix of altruism in "improving the Internet search experience," but in reality, there was a lot of money to be made in stealing away market share from Google's Internet search business.

Microsoft spent an enormous amount of money trying to market Bing, as well as forcing it upon their employees to help market it. After years of trailing Google, in July of 2023, it was announced that enterprise customers would receive AI-powered "Bing Chat Enterprise" as part of their core M365 service. This offering would allow users to perform "AI-powered searches," which were meant to combine the best of Internet search results with ChatGPT-like

AI reasoning. For example, when you asked a question, you might receive an answer directly from the LLM if the answer is within its training data, or alternatively, a RAG-based search would be performed, and you would be provided with a reference for where the answer was found. While Bing's relevance and ranking still lagged Google, the incorporation of GenAI within the search experience was a differentiator, at least for a period.

This new offering would be covered under the existing Microsoft commercial data protection agreement. This ensured that Microsoft would not have access to the prompts or responses, which removed the concern that it would be harvesting this data to further train its LLMs. Bing Chat Enterprise also had enterprise controls that you could manage through your M365 Administrator console. The requirement to be covered under the commercial data protection agreement is that a user would need to access `bing.com/chat` with a Microsoft Entra ID to ensure that the session was covered under the commercial data protection agreement.

However, the name Bing Chat Enterprise did not last long. On November 15, 2023, just two weeks after M365 Copilot became Generally Available, Microsoft decided to rename this new offering to "Copilot." This name change, while innocent enough, was a significant contributor to confusion around which Copilots bore an additional cost and which ones were included as part of current licensing agreements. Additionally, with this change, the homepage for Bing Chat Enterprise transitioned to `copilot.microsoft.com` and included a new toggle to flip between "Web" and "Work" for customers with an M365 Copilot license, as shown in Figure 1.4.

Interacting with the "Web" version of Copilot only returned Internet results, whereas interacting with "Work" meant you would have access to your enterprise data sources, such as documents in Microsoft Teams and OneDrive. To add even additional confusion, Microsoft's marketing renamed the "Work" mode of interacting with Copilot to "BizChat." However, just like anything else with Microsoft marketing, there's a good chance that name could be changed again.

Microsoft's Copilot Portfolio

Before we dive into the main topic of this book, Copilot Studio, it is important to have a baseline understanding of Microsoft's other offerings. As we will discuss later, the main value proposition for Copilot Studio is that it enables you to build additional functionality for an existing copilot product or to create a standalone copilot agent that can be deployed to a number of supported communication channels. So, for now, let's step through some of Microsoft's featured copilot products.

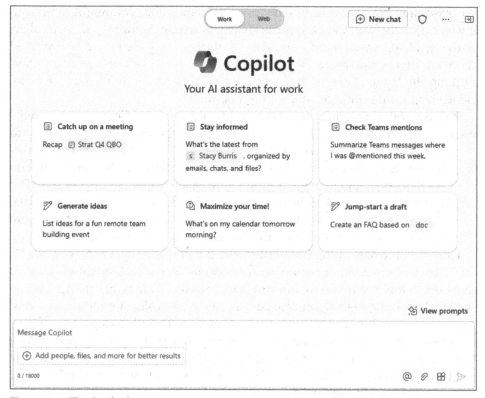

Figure 1.4: The Copilot homepage

Copilot for Sales

Copilot for Sales is an exciting AI product focused on individuals in sales-oriented roles. While M365 Copilot was focused on enabling knowledge workers to be more productive, the value proposition for Copilot for Sales is its integration with Customer Relationship Management (CRM) software, including both Dynamics 365 Sales & Marketing and Salesforce's Sales Cloud product. There's no question that Salesforce is the most dominant CRM in the marketplace today, with over 25% of the total market share, and their own investment in AI as part of its Einstein technology. Microsoft's support of Salesforce's CRM product is a prime example of Satya Nadella seeing an opportunity to serve a larger audience.

> **NOTE** Copilot for Sales is another example of how a product can have more names than it has years of being on the market. What started out as "Viva Sales" became "Sales Copilot" and then finally "Copilot for Sales."

The Copilot for Sales functionality is available in both Microsoft Teams and Outlook and includes the following features:

- **AI-assisted email generation:** Copilot can help draft an email and optionally reference information from a recent Teams meeting to help provide additional context.

- **Accessing Customer Relationship Management (CRM) objects from Outlook:** While within an email, Copilot will help pull up any associated CRM data, including the Account, Contact, and Opportunity objects based on the participants in the email conversation.

- **Updating CRM from Outlook:** In addition to having Copilot reference CRM data, you can also update key fields for an Opportunity or Contact record directly within Outlook, in addition to being able to save an email to that Opportunity record.

- **Opportunity summary:** Copilot will summarize the key updates for a given opportunity and provide what it believes is the next steps are to help close that opportunity.

- **In-Call insights:** Copilot will provide sales tips and pull up relevant information during Microsoft Teams calls to help coach your sellers toward winning an opportunity.

- **Call analysis:** Copilot will summarize the key points from a meeting that can be used in a recap email, suggest tasks based on the conversation flow, and highlight keywords mentions, along with sentiment during the call.

- **Sales automation:** Automatic provisioning of channels in Microsoft Teams enables the internal team to collaborate on proposals, contracts, etc., while also creating an external sharing channel to collaborate with your customers securely.

- **Sharing of adaptive cards in Teams messages:** To help reduce application context switching, you can share an opportunity, account, or contact record directly within Microsoft Teams and maintain any security trimming in the backend CRM.

Microsoft's vision for Copilot for Sales is enabling your sellers to stay in the applications they use daily to stay connected with your customers: Microsoft Teams and Outlook. AI helps pull relevant CRM data into the flow of work, thus removing the additional context switching. It also serves as a coach to your sellers, providing actionable insights and potential next steps to help continue driving opportunities forward.

There is a licensing consideration to be aware of when using Copilot for Sales. Copilot for Sales has a dependency on the user also being licensed to M365

Chapter 1 ▪ Navigating the Copilot Ecosystem

Copilot. This would be applicable even if you have a Dynamics 365 Enterprise license, which includes a Copilot for Sales license as part of the bundle. It can be purchased as an add-on to an existing M365 Copilot license, or you can purchase them together as a bundle. At the time of writing, the list price of the combined M365 Copilot & Copilot for Sales bundle is the same as if you were to purchase them separately.

NOTE Always be sure to confirm licensing with an Authorized Microsoft Reseller, your Microsoft Account Team, or the licensing guide, which you can consult at `microsoft.com/licensing/docs/view/Licensing-Guides`.

Copilot for Service

Copilot for Service follows many of the same patterns as Copilot for Sales, including the same licensing model, presentation through Microsoft Teams and Outlook, and interoperability with the Dynamics and Salesforce CRM platforms. While both offerings are targeted at improving the customer experience, Copilot for Service focuses on after-sale service activities such as case resolution, collecting and processing customer feedback, identifying potential upsell opportunities, and handling warranty claims or return/exchange activities.

The target persona for Copilot for Service includes individuals who work in your Contact Center or help support Customer Service and even Customer Outreach activities. Some examples of where Copilot for Service can help improve the overall customer service experience include:

- Assisting with creating customer outreach emails based on their interaction history with your company
- Summarizing a customer case using AI to help a customer service representative get up to speed faster with the history and recommended next steps
- Quickly confirming policies and procedures associated with a given activity (e.g., warranty coverage, return policies)
- Assisting customer service representatives to understand their current workload through natural language—for example:
  - Show me all my active cases.
  - Show me all my escalated cases.
  - Show me all my cases due tomorrow.
- Enabling managers to quickly understand the health of their business through natural language prompts—for example:

- What cases missed their service-level agreement (SLA) in the past week?
- Show me active escalated support tickets for "Heidi Lamar" in the past 30 days.
- Show me the high-priority support tickets for Deepak's Dairy in the past 15 days.

Customer service groups are constantly under pressure to improve the service quality across multiple KPIs, including net promoter score, customer satisfaction scores, first contact resolution, response time, ticket volume, resolution time, agent productivity, etc. The goal is to ensure that customers stay loyal to the company through positive experiences across the value chain. Copilot for Service's goal is to help improve these scores and retain customers through AI-generated insights and personalization.

> **NOTE** Additional information about Copilot for Service, including pricing and implementation details, can be found at `microsoft.com/en-us/microsoft-365/copilot/copilot-for-service`.

Copilot for Security

Copilot for Security is another role-based AI technology targeted at IT professionals responsible for cybersecurity tasks such as threat detection and analysis, incident response, threat hunting, and user activity monitoring. While M365 Copilot focuses heavily on the ability to create content, the real value of Copilot for Security is in its ability to parse large amounts of data and provide critical insights quickly. Microsoft has included the Copilot experience across its security portfolio of applications, including:

- **Microsoft Defender Extended Detection & Response (XDR)**
  - Assists with summarizing security incidents, including assessing the impact, providing recommendations for how to address, and then assembling the post-response activity report for tracking remediation efforts
  - Enables security professionals to assess risk through natural language to provide insights around potential security issues or vulnerabilities
- **Unified SOC Platform**
  - Assesses emerging threats and provides AI-driven insights
  - Streamlines investigation and response activities through AI-driven summarization and recommendations

Chapter 1 ▪ Navigating the Copilot Ecosystem

- ▪ Enables security analysists to complete tasks through natural language, which Copilot translates to Kusto Query Language (KQL) for processing

- ▪ **Microsoft Purview**
  - ▪ Enables visibility across multiple solutions and layering in applicable compliance and regulatory requirements
  - ▪ Summarizes alerts across multiple channels to help prioritize where to focus based on business impact

- ▪ **Microsoft Entra**
  - ▪ Accelerates investigations of identity-related issues through natural language and by providing AI-driven recommendations to improve security posture
  - ▪ Finds gaps in current policies, generates workflows, and arrives at root causes faster

- ▪ **Microsoft Intune**
  - ▪ Remediates endpoint issues with what-if analysis and through AI-driven analysis of the potential problems and resolution actions
  - ▪ Assists with translating business intent into actionable configuration and policies using natural language

Microsoft's value proposition for Copilot for Security is that it enables IT security professionals to focus on the most important signals that are being generated through their enterprise security portfolio. It also removes some of the barriers that perhaps have prevented organizations from tapping into additional in-house talent to assist with incident response activities, including removing the need to know how to construct Kusto Query Language (KQL) for platform queries. Finally, given that Microsoft is one of the largest IT security companies, with a yearly $1 billion investment, organizations can benefit from the learnings of these investments to better enhance their own security posture.

Copilot for Security differs from the other copilots Microsoft has brought to market because it does not have a per-user, per-month subscription model. Copilot for Security is licensed via a pay-as-you-go model. You are paying for the computing capacity to perform analysis of the various log files across Microsoft Security. This model is similar to a typical cloud computing model, where you provision resources and then pay for the time they execute transactions in the cloud. Microsoft recommends a minimum of three Security Compute Units (SCUs) to begin experimenting with Copilot for Security. These units carry a per-hour charge that is included in your monthly Azure bill along with any additional cloud infrastructure in your subscription.

While not a firm requirement, Microsoft also recommends that customers who are planning on using Copilot for Security also have Microsoft Sentinel SIEM service provisioned along with Microsoft Defender for Endpoint (MDE) Plan 2 (P2), which is an advanced endpoint security solution that includes features like automated investigation and remediation, advanced threat prevention, threat and vulnerability management, and threat hunting capabilities. So, when considering moving forward with Copilot for Security, you will want to factor in all the additional cloud computing costs and potential ancillary licensing costs associated with this cutting-edge service.

> **NOTE** Additional Copilot for Security pricing details can be found at `azure` `.microsoft.com/en-us/pricing/details/microsoft-copilot-` `for-security`.

Copilot in Microsoft Viva

Microsoft Viva is not a single product but rather a digital employee experience platform focused on tools and technologies to improve the employee experience. While much of M365 focuses on productivity and collaboration, Microsoft Viva focuses on employee growth, learning, well-being, and connectedness to others. It is made up of several individual products that come together to help round out the experience. It is probably no surprise that certain modules have been prioritized with Copilot functionality to help provide additional value in Microsoft Viva.

> **NOTE** Microsoft Viva licensing is complicated, as there are some features included in your base M365 license and others require a separate add-on license. It is best to review the licensing comparison table found at `microsoft.com/en-us/` `microsoft-viva/pricing`.

Viva Goals

Microsoft Viva Goals is a goal alignment solution that uses the popular objectives and key results (OKR) framework to help connect people to an organization's strategic priorities. It helps employees understand the impact of their work and how it aligns with the company's mission and drives business results. Setting these goals can be a bit challenging, which is where Copilot in Viva Goals comes in handy. You can collaborate with Copilot as part of your initial goal-setting process to brainstorm appropriate OKRs based on your company's strategic vision. For example, you could ask Copilot, "Please help me generate OKRs for bringing a new GenAI product to market," and it will assist with creating objectives and then key results that would roll up underneath each objective, as shown in Figure 1.5.

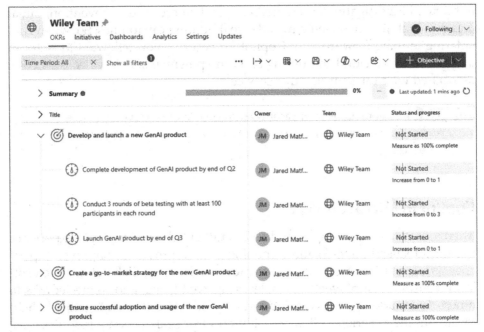

Figure 1.5: Copilot-generated OKRs

Viva Engage

Viva Engage is a social collaboration platform focused on employee engagement, knowledge sharing, corporate communications, and building communities within an organization. It also helps establish a channel for leaders to connect with employees at all levels of the organization through constructive dialogue. This two-way communication channel helps leaders keep their finger on the pulse of the organization while identifying high-potential individuals. For larger organizations with lengthy hierarchies, this also helps more junior employees feel part of something bigger than just their team or function.

> **NOTE** In February of 2023, Yammer was rebranded as Viva Engage and given a new set of features to help drive interest and support the niche customers who had already invested in the platform. Users can leverage Copilot in Viva Engage through their home feed, storyline, community feed, and campaign pages. An example use case might be a communications manager or senior leader who wants to share an update with the company. For example, see Figure 1.6, where I asked Copilot to assist with creating a post announcing the release of this book. It created a draft for a brief message and included fun emoticons to enhance the post.

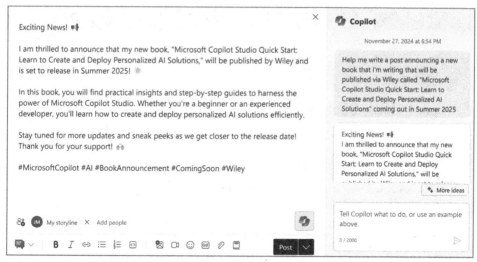

Figure 1.6: Copilot in Viva Engage

> **NOTE** To leverage Copilot in Viva Engage, you will need both a Viva Engage license (purchased as part of Microsoft Viva Suite or Microsoft Viva Employee Communications and Communities) and an M365 Copilot license.

Viva Amplify

Viva Amplify is another solution in the Viva Suite designed to help communications professionals create, manage, and publish campaigns to engage employees across multiple channels. It centralizes communication processes, offering tools for campaign management, writing guidance, and analytics to measure the impact of messages. These communications are authored in modern SharePoint pages and then disseminated through email, SharePoint Sites (via SharePoint news), and also Microsoft Teams. Communications professionals can then measure which channel was most effective.

The Copilot experience in Viva Amplify is centered around helping communicators refine their messages. When drafting a new communication as part of a campaign, you can use Copilot to help "Auto rewrite" or adjust the tone of your communication, as shown in Figure 1.7. This functionality helps communicators refine their messages to make them more accessible to the target audience. A potential communications strategy might be to create multiple versions of the same communication for managers, individual contributors, and executives. They could start with the initial draft communications and then leverage Copilot to help refine the tone per target audience.

Chapter 1 ■ Navigating the Copilot Ecosystem

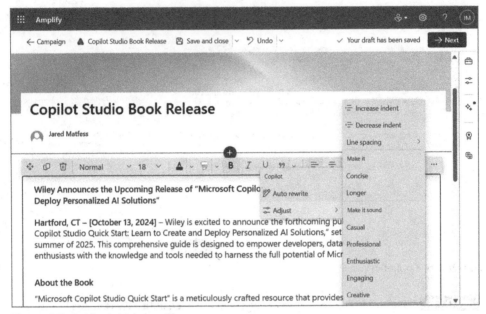

Figure 1.7: Copilot in Viva Amplify

Viva Roadmap

These are just a couple of examples of Microsoft integrating Copilot within the Microsoft Viva Suite, with many more features included in the roadmap. Known targets include Viva Glint, with planned functionality that enables Copilot to analyze employee feedback and survey data to unlock critical insights and identify outliers in the dataset. It will be very interesting to see how Microsoft addresses the licensing requirements across experiences and whether there are any concessions made to help boost the adoption of M365 Copilot.

Additional Copilots

The intent of this book isn't to go deep into all of Microsoft's Copilot offerings but rather to provide a high-level overview so you can start to see some of the emerging patterns for what is being brought to market. There are several additional copilots, including:

- **GitHub Copilot:** Microsoft acquired GitHub back in 2018, giving it access to one of the world's largest developer platforms, including all of its open-source software. This served as training data for GitHub Copilot, which is GenAI within popular integrated development environments (IDEs), such as Visual Studio, Visual Studio Code, Neovim, and JetBrains IDEs. GitHub Copilot can both suggest code and act as a pair-programmer, along with being able to analyze existing code and, in natural language, provide an explanation for what it does.

- **Copilot for Finance:** Another role-specific offering, Copilot for Finance, is targeted at streamlining tasks like quote-to-cash processes, credit and collections, risk management, and compliance activities. In addition, it can help enable executives and managers who need real-time insights into business performance and strategic decision-making based on financial data.

- **Copilot in Azure:** Microsoft has developed a Copilot that's focused on your Cloud team and can assist with tasks such as summarizing bills, providing recommendations to optimize cost based on activity, receiving recommendations of services based on your business use case, or navigating the Azure portal using natural language.

- **Copilot in Microsoft Power Platform:** Similar to the Copilot in Azure, Microsoft has introduced GenAI into its key Power Platform applications, such as PowerApps, Power Automate, Power BI, and AI Builder. This enables makers to create compelling business solutions using the power of natural language. Example use cases include:

  - **Power Automate:** Describing a workflow to help solve a business problem, with Copilot creating the initial logic as a starting point for you to iterate on

  - **Power Automate:** Creating PowerApps, including the design, layout, fields, etc., to help create exciting low-code business applications

  - **Power BI:** Automatically creating reports, generating actionable insights, and designing dashboards using the power of natural language

With Microsoft focused on being the Copilot company, keeping up with the pace of its innovation can be incredibly challenging. For IT budget owners feeling extreme pressure from the business to reduce costs, navigating these various Copilot offerings and developing a strategy for enabling innovation while also controlling costs can be challenging. There is also likely pressure from your executives, the board, and even business stakeholders to understand where you are from an AI strategy perspective, which offerings might be coming, and when.

The consumerization of AI in solutions with similar capabilities to ChatGPT will continue to make it difficult for IT leaders to keep the demand at bay. Therefore, it is essential to plan and communicate your AI strategy to help inform your stakeholders and help you plan the financial investment required to enable these new capabilities. As part of that planning, you must factor in the people within your organization as part of a mapping exercise to determine who gets which copilots or other AI offerings.

Aligning Copilots with Company Personas

The approach you will want to take to organize this AI boom is first to take an inventory of the personas within your organization. The reality is that not everyone is going to need every copilot. There are some departments whose function and personnel will align to a particular body of work, and you will want to understand their primary business functions and begin aligning which copilot might deliver value. Through a persona mapping exercise, you will likely develop something similar to Table 1.1, which outlines the persona, potential products, and highlighted use cases or business outcomes you hope to drive.

Table 1.1: AI/Copilot persona mapping

PERSONA/DEPARTMENT	PRODUCT	USE CASES
Developers	GitHub Copilot	■ Increase developer productivity ■ Improve code quality ■ Help support junior developers through AI assistance
Knowledge workers (marketing, communications, legal)	M365 Copilot	■ Improve the quality of documents ■ Provide an intelligent recap of virtual meetings ■ Improve enterprise search
Customer service representatives	Copilot for Service	■ Reduce case resolution time ■ Provide enhanced customer service
Sales reps or alumni relations (university)	Copilot for Sales	■ Streamline customer sales activities ■ Provide AI coaching to improve presentation skills ■ Enable sellers to spend more time working with customers
Cybersecurity professionals	Copilot for Security	■ Help reduce the risk associated with security incidents ■ Improve the security posture of your organization ■ Focus on the most critical threats

Once you have finished the persona mapping exercise for your organization, you may find some personas are not represented, or some use cases may not be satisfied by current out-of-the-box capabilities. For those personas and use cases, you can fall back on traditional IT analysis techniques to solve business problems and align technology solutions by:

- Understanding the business problem
- Gathering business requirements
- Assessing current system capabilities
- Researching and proposing solutions

As part of the researching and proposing solutions step, you may also consider build verses buy scenarios. Since you have already attempted to map use cases against Microsoft's existing portfolio, from an analysis of what you might be potentially "buying," you would be looking at other third-party products and the functionality they provide.

Assuming that you believe the business use case would benefit from a custom AI-related solution, there are two questions for you to consider:

- Is this solution something you would build as a standalone product, such as a fit-for-purpose copilot targeted at a particular persona?
- Would the solution have a better user experience if the functionality were made available through an existing Copilot product?

If you answered yes to either question, then the approach for building this solution might be a good use case for Microsoft's Copilot Studio.

Introducing Copilot Studio

Copilot Studio is not a standalone copilot like many of the other copilots we've reviewed thus far. It is a low-code application platform positioned to serve two purposes:

- **Extend first-party Copilots:** Similar to any enterprise software package, you can build specific customizations unique to your business for Microsoft's existing copilot products, such as M365 Copilot, Copilot for Sales, and Copilot for Service. For example, you could build a Copilot Agent that extends Microsoft 365 Copilot to pull your PTO balance or to return policies and procedures information from a preset list of SharePoint sites.
- **Build standalone Copilot agents:** There may be scenarios where the user might not be using a first-party copilot, such as external customers or your frontline workers. Copilot Studio allows you to develop standalone copilot agents that can help to assist them with tasks. Some examples include a copilot agent to assist customers with navigating your website or to assist your frontline workers with submitting safety incident reports from the factory floor. These agents can be published across several different channels to help deliver a custom experience for your target userbase.

Copilot Studio is part of Microsoft's Business Applications Solution area and can integrate with core elements of Microsoft's Power Platform portfolio of applications, as shown in Figure 1.8. The Power Platform also helps to ensure that the solutions developed can connect to other line-of-business applications through a mix of low-code and professional-code solutions.

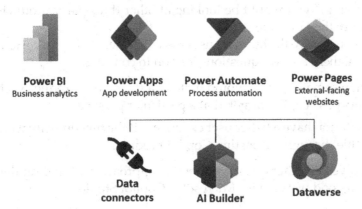

Figure 1.8: Microsoft Power Platform

In the next chapter, we will explore Copilot Studio in detail, including the licensing prerequisites, how to access it, and the key elements of building your own custom copilot. Later in the book, we will walk through extending M365 Copilot with additional functionality, also configured using Copilot Studio.

Conclusion

Microsoft's copilot ecosystem is growing by the day, all powered by its strategic partnership with OpenAI. Satya's direction of Microsoft is to be the copilot company and build a future with a copilot for everything you do. In this chapter, we went over a high-level overview of GenAI and how it catalyzed AI-driven innovation. We stepped through Microsoft's investment in OpenAI and its impact on shaping the products and solutions that Microsoft is bringing to market. We then studied Microsoft's numerous copilots, their target personas, and key use cases that drive business value.

We then discussed how to map Microsoft's copilots to personas in your organization in a "when to use what" type manner. Finally, the key topic of this book, Copilot Studio, was introduced, and you learned where it fits in the current landscape. Now that you have been acclimated to Microsoft's various copilots, let's dive into Copilot Studio.

CHAPTER

2

Introduction to Copilot Studio

The launch of Copilot Studio in April 2024 marked an exciting time in AI-driven innovation. While the market is rich with low-code application platforms, Copilot Studio marked the start of copilots helping you create new copilots. For fans of the *Terminator* movie series, it almost feels like the warning of Skynet and an eventual doomsday are happening right before our eyes, with copilots creating copilots and eventually becoming self-aware. Hopefully, there will be a John Connor just like in the movie series to help save us from Judgment Day.

In this chapter, we will step into the book's main topic, Copilot Studio. We'll start with who should use Copilot Studio and for what purpose and then talk about the role of citizen developers in this new era of copilots. Next, we will review the Copilot Studio user interface and some key planning steps for your custom copilot. Finally, we'll cover some foundational topics around designing a conversation flow, actions, connectors, and environments.

Copilot Studio's Core Audience

Copilot Studio, as mentioned before, is a low-code application platform that can be used to either create a new copilot or to extend an existing Microsoft-developed copilot. The platform is meant for "everyone" to be able to have the ability to create their own copilots with little to no code. In fact, Microsoft has

Chapter 2 ■ Introduction to Copilot Studio

even integrated a copilot within the Copilot Studio platform to help you do just that. There is even a natural language interface that allows you to describe the features and functionality that you are looking to develop, which will be converted into a prompt, and Copilot Studio will start to build out the initial logic for that experience. This really lowers the barrier to entry in terms of the technical skills and knowledge to build your own custom copilot.

The question that many organizations are facing is, "who is going to be creating all these copilots?" The answer is not simple because every organization is different. The product marketing suggests that anyone can use Copilot Studio to build their own copilot; however, the practicality of a Fortune 50 CEO creating a custom copilot between board meetings seems a bit far-fetched. So, the questions still remain: Who is the target audience for Copilot Studio? Who is going to create all these copilots?

To help answer these questions, we should start with what it means to be a low-code application platform. Microsoft has worked to lower the barrier to entry for professionals to begin developing their customizations using Copilot Studio. Copilot Studio is targeted at both IT professionals with experience building business applications, as well as a new type of business professional also referred to as *citizen developers*.

Citizen Developers Overview

The term "citizen developers" is often used when discussing low-code application development. Citizen developers are typically individuals who do not have formal IT backgrounds and don't reside within an organization's IT department but are still supporting the development or maintenance of technology solutions. These individuals have strong business domain knowledge and are closest to the problem being solved with technology. Their level of technical expertise will likely vary by the organization and each person's work experience. Sometimes, these folks start as power users for a particular application and then can grow their responsibility to be its citizen developers.

Some of the benefits of enabling citizen developers in your organization include:

- It accelerates innovation by empowering employees to work outside the typical constraints of yearly IT projects and budget planning cycles.

- It offers potential cost savings by shifting development or maintenance costs outside of IT and into the respective business units.

- It provides for enhanced collaboration between business and IT by removing the friction of request prioritization or lack of budget.

- Solutions built using low-code application platforms can more easily be moved to professional code or third-party solutions since their core business logic is demonstrable in a live environment.

Citizen developers tend to have a deeper understanding of the business needs, data requirements to satisfy those needs, use cases, edge cases, and overall end-to-end processes, so their solutions are more applicable to real-world workflows. IT can still own the greater platforms, but citizen developers can own part of the extensibility of these platforms to make them more relevant to their end users. When large projects are required to reduce scope to meet target budgets and timelines, citizen developers can help build out that extra personalization capability that will ensure greater adoption of the end solution.

This panacea of business and IT professionals working in perfect harmony to usher in the next wave of technology sounds wonderful. However, citizen developers and the applications they create can also create a set of new challenges for you to manage.

Citizen Developer Challenges

One of the challenges with citizen developers is that they often do not have any background in IT. Therefore, they may lack an understanding and appreciation for best practices in application development. Some examples include not having separate environments or instances of an application to test changes before making them available to everyone in "production." This can create a situation where citizen-developed applications become business-critical but do not fit the typical multitiered environment approach, which enables safe development, testing, and release cycles to help minimize any business disruptions. When bugs are reported, if the development is done in production, this could compound the issue, potentially causing a business outage with financial implications.

There can also be challenges if the solution is non-performant because the citizen developer is unfamiliar with techniques for performance tuning. Their calls to external systems might not be developed with performance in mind. They could have circular logic or other configurations that cause the application to take longer to run over time. As solutions become more technically complex, this could lead to IT needing to provide unplanned support for the build-out of certain business applications.

Another challenge could be the proliferation of applications with similar functionality across the enterprise. With application development being performed across various business silos, it can be challenging to avoid re-creating the wheel repeatedly across your organization. From an overall business cost perspective, you may incur costs many times more than if you centralized a portion of the development. However, the same situation could arise even when you have IT resources to perform this development if they are not collaborating and working as a single team.

While none of these challenges are insurmountable, they require planning to introduce citizen development to your organization. One of the best approaches to minimize risk is through education. Helping business developers understand the value of specific IT processes is a great way to ensure they are armed with the proper knowledge to support their business area. When framed as techniques to minimize risk, after-hours support, or potential financial implications, people will likely be receptive to learning how to deliver business value while reducing business risk.

> **NOTE** Recently, Microsoft has adopted the term "maker" instead of "citizen developer" to refer to people who "make applications." I believe this is done to help illustrate that anyone can be a maker and that the role doesn't require specialized developer training. Going forward, we will use the term "maker" to conform with current Microsoft messaging.

The Role of IT

IT professionals may view Copilot Studio as a threat to their work. If business users can develop their applications, then what is IT's role in this new paradigm? Who needs IT application specialists if the future of application development lies in a mix of AI and citizen developers solving all the business challenges? This removes the need to wait for projects to be funded by IT, and it allows the business to have greater control over their direction and more agility to respond to market changes that have business impacts. Going down that same path of reasoning could lead to even greater existential thoughts about the future of humans and work.

Despite all of these advanced capabilities that are being incorporated into tools we use, the reality is that the role of IT is not going away; rather, the work that employees do may change. IT professionals will still be responsible for the core systems and the infrastructure, whether it's on-premises or in the cloud. They will also be responsible for the enterprise compliance requirements, such as identity and access management, integrations with other line-of-business applications and enterprise data reporting tools, and the general architecture of the platforms. These are concepts that do require a more advanced understanding of technology to ensure overall availability, reliability, and scalability to meet the needs of the business.

This existential threat to job security and potential displacement by technological advancement is not a new concept. On the manufacturing floor, there has been a consistent need to modify and sometimes reinvent the role of humans in the business process based on technological advancements and investments in automation. There's even a term for this constant back-and-forth struggle: the *productivity paradox* or the *automation paradox*. It reflects the ongoing cycle in which technological advances drive efficiencies, and humans then adapt, redefine, and reimagine their roles to create new forms of value within the evolving landscape.

> This touches on another often-discussed topic: artificial general intelligence (AGI). AGI is a type of AI that can understand, learn, and apply knowledge across a wide range of tasks at a level comparable to or exceeding human intelligence. Unlike AI technologies such as Copilot, which are designed for specific tasks (like language translation, content creation, or content summarization), AGI can perform any intellectual task that a human can. We are starting to see the early stages of this new emerging capability as Microsoft has evolved from focusing on copilots to also introducing Copilot agents, which are able to perform tasks independently of direct human guidance. AGI warrants its own book, as it raises both deep technical and philosophical questions to explore.

Copilot Studio: The Platform

If you have previously used Microsoft Power Virtual Agents to build an intelligent chatbot, then you already have some understanding of Copilot Studio. Microsoft took the foundation of Power Virtual Agents and then layered on additional AI capabilities to help bring Copilot Studio to market. There are some references to Power Virtual Agents throughout the platform, so don't be surprised if you encounter them along the way.

Copilot Studio is completely web-based, meaning all your development occurs within the browser. When I say development, it is a configuration-based pattern where you select objects to add to the authoring canvas and then update the parameters for those objects to ultimately build out your application workflow. There are some elements of code, but they follow more of a formula-based approach, similar to what you might use within Microsoft Excel to format and manipulate data.

Just because Copilot Studio is low-code does not mean that the solutions developed are not enterprise-ready or scalable. Solutions developed using Copilot Studio fit neatly into your existing Microsoft Entra ID identity infrastructure; data is encrypted in transit and at rest; there is logging to help assist with troubleshooting; and it can integrate with full-code solutions such as Azure Functions, call APIs, and ultimately perform many of the same functions as professional-code solutions.

Copilot Studio Prerequisites

Before diving directly into Copilot Studio, let's discuss some of the prerequisites for using it. First, you will need access to an M365 tenant with appropriate individual user licenses (Business Premium, E3, E5, A3, A5, etc.). This provides

Chapter 2 ■ Introduction to Copilot Studio

baseline access to Microsoft's various M365 services. Second, there are a couple of core licenses you will need to build Copilot agents, which include:

- **Copilot Studio Tenant License:** This is a license that your Microsoft 365 Global Administrator or similar role would acquire for your tenant from the M365 Admin Center. It is not assigned to an individual user but rather to your Microsoft 365 tenant.
- **Copilot Studio User License:** This license should be assigned to individual users who need access to Copilot Studio to create and manage agents.

> **NOTE** Detailed information about Copilot Studio licensing can be found on Microsoft's website at `go.microsoft.com/fwlink/?linkid=2085130`.

Where you intend to deploy your Copilot agent will factor into the potential licensing needs for your solution. For example, if you want to develop an M365 Copilot agent, you'll also need an M365 Copilot license in addition to your existing Microsoft 365 license. If you are extending Copilot for Service or Copilot for Sales, you will also need licenses for those, in addition to an M365 Copilot license.

Next, you should be aware of the costs associated with developing a Copilot agent. If you think of copilots as intelligent chatbots, the licensing paradigm might make a bit more sense. Copilot agents are billed on a per-message basis. This means that when you send a message to the copilot, that is considered one message. When the agent responds with an answer, this counts as a message, so you're now at two messages.

To add an additional layer of complexity, if answering your question requires leveraging a feature called *generative answers*, then it would count as two messages, bringing the total for the conversation to three total messages. We'll discuss generative answers later in this chapter, as well as ways to optimize your custom copilot to maximize the business impact while also maintaining your costs. At this time, Copilot Studio licenses are either sold packages of 25,000 messages per month, at a cost determined by your local currency and Microsoft Enterprise Agreement, or they are sold in a pay-as-you-go licensing model similar to other cloud-based services. If you opt for the package of messages, the capacity is pooled across the entire tenant but must be assigned to an environment to enable Copilot Studio features for agents in that environment. We'll cover Power Platform environments and how they work next.

Accessing Copilot Studio

There are two ways to begin building Copilot agents using Copilot Studio: the Agent Builder Experience, which we will cover in the next chapter, and the full Copilot Studio experience. To access Copilot Studio, open your preferred browser, navigate to copilotstudio.microsoft.com, and authenticate with your Microsoft Entra ID (formerly Azure Active Directory ID). Once authenticated, you should be brought to the Copilot Studio homepage, as shown in Figure 2.1. This is going to be your central home for managing copilot agents.

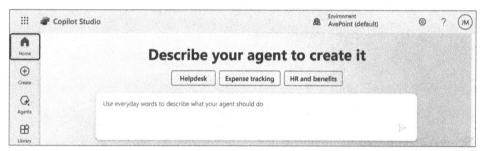

Figure 2.1: The Copilot Studio homepage

> **NOTE** While your IT admins negotiate with Microsoft for licensing, you can self-service request a 30-day trial for Copilot Studio at aka.ms/TryCopilotStudio. You can also extend the trial for an additional 30 days.

Power Platform Environments

When you click the Environment list in the top-right corner of the Copilot Studio UI, you will see a drop-down menu like Figure 2.2. This menu shows all the Power Platform environments available in your tenant. A Power Platform environment allows you to store, manage, and share your organization's data, apps, and workflows. It serves as a container to separate different sets of data, applications, and customizations, and it's essential for managing resources and security. To help with larger tenants that may have dozens or even hundreds of environments, there is also a filter menu for you to more easily navigate to find your desired environment. You can start to type the name of the environment you are looking for, and the menu will filter the list of environments based on your input.

Environments provide you with a logical level of separation to help separate applications that might have different roles, security requirements, or target audiences. Depending on your tenant, you may have a lot of environments, or you may just have a default environment, which will be denoted with the word "default" in parentheses.

Chapter 2 ■ Introduction to Copilot Studio

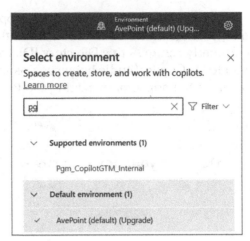

Figure 2.2: Power Platform environments

Microsoft Dataverse

Microsoft Dataverse is a cloud-based, low-code scalable application and data platform. Sometimes, people think that Dataverse is just a cloud-based database, but it is much more than that. Dataverse brings together various types of data and business rules to help applications and processes work seamlessly while keeping everything secure and compliant. It is the central data platform behind many of Microsoft's business applications, including Dynamics 365, Power Platform, and Power Automate. The purpose of an application and data platform is to help remove some of the typical silos that exist within the enterprise to help better serve the individuals who are looking to make decisions based on enterprise data.

When I refer to silos, I'm specifically talking about:

- **Productivity data:** Email, Teams meetings, SharePoint sites, Microsoft Teams, and Exchange groups
- **Line-of-business data:** Platforms that run the business, including customer relationship management (CRM), enterprise resource planning (ERP), product lifecycle management (PLM), supply chain management (SCM), and e-commerce platforms
- **Unstructured data:** Documents and images in file shares, OneDrive, SharePoint, Teams, and other cloud storage services
- **Analytical data:** Data stored in data warehouses, data lakes, dashboards, and reports

The value of Dataverse is making it simple to keep your business data organized, accessible, and secure across different teams and applications. It allows you to store all your business information in one place, making it easy to pull up what you need when you need it without having to dig through multiple systems. With Dataverse, you can create applications and automate tasks quickly so your team can focus on what matters most, helping the business move faster and work smarter.

Dataverse Core Components

Microsoft Dataverse is built on five core components that work together to streamline data management:

- **Security:** This is where you set authentication and authorization for your application, fully integrated with Microsoft Entra ID, which allows you to enforce role-based security, perform auditing, and tap into additional capabilities such as Intune Conditional Access policies and multifactor authentication.

- **Logic:** You can create logic at the data layer, including duplicate record detection, execute business rules and workflows, connect to other systems through plug-ins, and run jobs.

- **Data:** This enables you to organize data into structured models with validation rules to ensure accuracy, while also enabling easy connections between related information. Dataverse also integrates seamlessly with Power BI, allowing business users to create insightful reports and dashboards for real-time, data-driven decision-making.

- **Storage:** This is the aggregation of structured and unstructured data, including files, blobs, and relational databases. It also includes the supporting log files associated with those data sources.

- **Integration:** This enables seamless connections with both Microsoft and external systems, supporting powerful workflows and data movement. It includes webhooks for real-time data updates across platforms, application lifecycle management (ALM) for managing app versions and deployments, data export for sending information to external analytics or storage solutions, and Azure DevOps integration for streamlined development and deployment processes.

As shown in Figure 2.3, all of these components come together to deliver an end-to-end application and data platform solution.

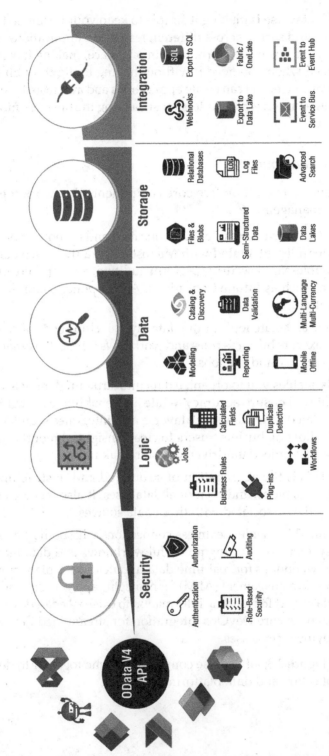

Figure 2.3: Microsoft Dataverse architecture

Environment Management

Microsoft Dataverse can also serve as the storage layer for your environments in the Power Platform. While it's not mandatory for all Power Platform configurations, a common scenario is to have a Dataverse instance per environment. However, Copilot agents created with Copilot Studio do require Dataverse. Additionally, as you are thinking about maintaining good ALM for Copilot agents, you will want to plan for development, staging, and production environments, which require you to have storage capacity allocated to your tenant.

Power Platform storage capacity is allocated based on user licenses, with additional storage added as more users are licensed. Each license includes database, file, and log storage, providing a shared pool for your organization. You can purchase add-ons for each type (database, file, and log) in 1 GB increments through the Microsoft 365 Admin Center or your usual procurement process if you need more storage.

NOTE Information about Power Platform storage licensing can be found at learn.microsoft.com/en-us/power-platform/admin/capacity-storage.

Creating Your First Agent

Now that you understand Power Platform environments and Microsoft Dataverse, let's create a custom copilot using natural language to describe its purpose and utility. Once again, navigate to copilotstudio.microsoft.com. At the top of the screen, you'll see a chat window, as shown in Figure 2.4, titled Describe Your Copilot to Create It. As mentioned at the beginning of this chapter, one of the exciting features about Copilot Studio is that there's a copilot to help you with developing your own custom copilot agent. It also includes some prompt starters, such as Helpdesk, Expense Tracking, and HR and Benefits, as examples of the types of custom copilots that you might be interested in developing for your users.

Figure 2.4: Describing your custom copilot

Chapter 2 ▪ Introduction to Copilot Studio

This functionality helps lower the barrier to entry for creating your own custom copilots. Using natural language, you can describe the purpose of the copilot using business- and outcome-focused language. For example, you could enter the following prompt:

"Please help me create an IT Help Desk copilot that will answer common questions such as how to reset my password, how to request software to be installed on my computer, and when my laptop is due for a refresh."

Enter this text into the chat window and then press the paper arrow icon in the right-hand corner to start the configuration process for your new custom copilot. You will then be redirected to a screen, as displayed in Figure 2.5, that will further the conversation about configuring your copilot.

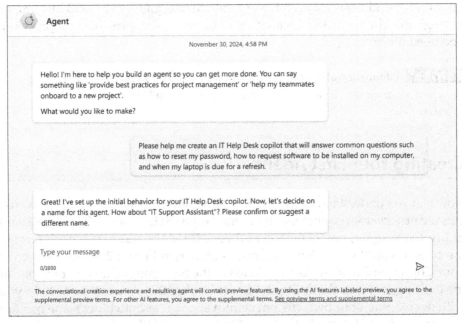

Figure 2.5: Initial Copilot configuration

For my example, the next question I'm posed is, *"Great! I've set up the initial behavior for your IT Help Desk copilot. Now, let's decide on a name for this agent. How about "IT Support Assistant"? Please confirm or suggest a different name."*

You can either choose to accept the name provided by Copilot, or you can choose to give it your own name. For example, you can call your Copilot Agent "Zoë." Copilot will confirm the name change, as shown in Figure 2.6. Additionally, if you compare Figures 2.5 and 2.6, you will notice that the name will change in the upper-left corner of the Copilot Studio UI to reflect the updated name for your copilot.

The next question I'm posed is, *"Next, let's refine the instructions for Zoë. What should be emphasized or avoided in Zoë's responses?"*

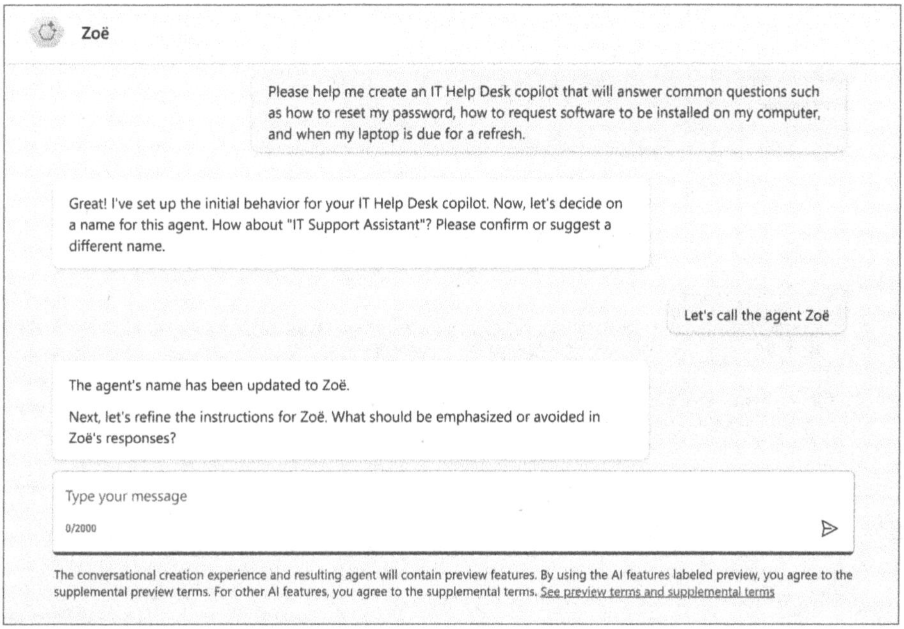

Chapter 2 ▪ Introduction to Copilot Studio   41

Figure 2.6: Naming your Copilot agent

This next question by the Copilot Studio configuration process asks you to establish what is referred to as the *system prompt* for the large language model (LLM). The system prompt sets the AI's initial behavior and tone, guiding it on how to respond. In other words, it's a set of instructions that defines the assistant's personality, capabilities, and how it should handle specific scenarios. This is also where you can establish an initial set of guardrails to ensure that your copilot does not respond to requests that it is not an authoritative source for.

For this example, you might respond with the following:

"Please only respond to questions where you find a supporting document for your answer. Avoid any responses where you do not have a supporting document. Maintain a positive and business-professional tone. Please clarify when you are confused or do not know what the person is asking. Remember that you reflect the person's experience with the IT department, so you want to be very helpful and approachable."

Notice that I'm providing it with technical boundaries in terms of only responding where it finds a source document and user experience parameters in terms of the tone of its response. This is natural language being used to help establish the system prompt or the set of instructions that will be provided to the AI to help it understand the appropriate ways of responding back to a user request.

After sending that set of instructions, you will receive a confirmation of the instructions, as shown in Figure 2.7. It then asks where it should find information. Remember, we are following the RAG pattern discussed in Chapter 1.

Chapter 2 ■ Introduction to Copilot Studio

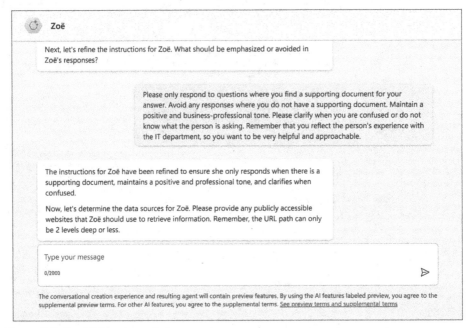

Figure 2.7: Establishing boundaries

Adding Knowledge Sources

Knowledge sources in Copilot Studio play an important role in supporting the RAG pattern; they provide a reliable foundation of data that enhances your copilot's responses. Copilot Studio supports the data sources outlined in Table 2.1 out of the box for your custom copilot.

Table 2.1: Copilot Studio Knowledge Sources

TYPE	DESCRIPTION	LIMITS	AUTHENTICATION
Public Website	Searches the query input on Bing; only returns results from provided websites	Four URLs (e.g., wiley.com)	None
Documents	Searches documents uploaded to Microsoft Dataverse and returns results from the document contents	Limited by Microsoft Dataverse file storage allocation	None

TYPE	DESCRIPTION	LIMITS	AUTHENTICATION
SharePoint	Connects to a SharePoint Site Collection or Site and uses the Microsoft Graph Search to return results	Four SharePoint Sites (URLs) per generative answers topic node	User's Microsoft Entra ID
Microsoft Dataverse	Connects to the connected Dataverse environment and uses the RAG technique in Dataverse to return results	Two Dataverse knowledge sources (and up to 15 tables per knowledge source)	User's Microsoft Entra ID
Enterprise data using Microsoft Graph connectors	Connects to Microsoft Graph connectors where Microsoft Search indexes your organization's data	Two per custom copilot	User's Microsoft Entra ID

In our example, this custom copilot is not trained on any organizational data; instead, we are leveraging its understanding of language and reasoning to evaluate data that will then be sent to it. For the sake of simplicity, we will continue configuring this first copilot to leverage an externally available website; however, this does not mean we can't access other data sources. Later in this chapter, we will discuss Copilot connectors, which are really Power Platform connectors behind the scenes. This opens our copilots for several different use cases and supported data sources.

Remember that in addition to leveraging this copilot within the authoring experience to complete configuration on your behalf, you can also ask it for help. For example, you can ask, "*Any tips for adding websites?*" As shown in Figure 2.8, you will receive guidance around identifying reliable sources, using APIs, etc. As a reminder, when you are building your Copilot agent, you can ask Copilot to help clarify settings or provide recommendations. The assistant role of these copilots is to help you with all sorts of tasks, including the development of Copilot agents.

Let's provide our copilot with an externally facing IT website as its data source. Many organizations maintain this information within their intranet on SharePoint Online, WordPress, or other CMS platforms. However, universities tend to maintain this information externally; therefore, I am going to provide Copilot with the following URL for its data source: `it.utah.edu`.

44 Chapter 2 ■ Introduction to Copilot Studio

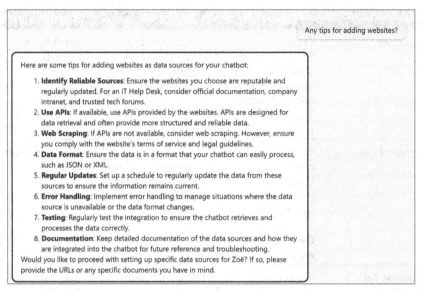

Figure 2.8: Adding websites

Copilot responds, as shown in Figure 2.9, with the update, *"The data source 'https://it.utah.edu' has been added for Zoë. Zoë is now ready to be created. Do you have any further refinements?"*

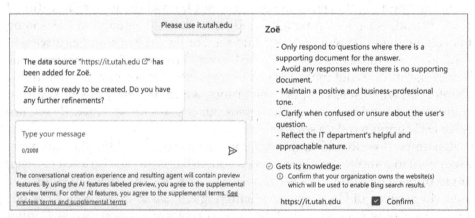

Figure 2.9: Adding a data source

You are likely asking yourself what further refinements you want to add. Some examples include:

- **Personalization:** Allows you to set preferences such as preferred language, tone, or specific areas of interest.

- **Integration:** Integrates with other tools and systems, such as CRM, ticketing systems, and knowledge bases, to provide more comprehensive support.
- **Error handling:** Implements clear and helpful error messages when the chatbot encounters issues.

Please note that you do not have to provide any of these additional refinements at this time. Now, as we provided the copilot with instructions for how this new one should work, you might have noticed that your input was being captured in a window on the right side of the screen, as shown in Figure 2.10. It captures the default language (which you can change through the UI), the intent of the copilot, its name, and the data sources it will get its responses from. Let's go ahead and check the Confirm box next to the it.utah.edu data source, as shown in Figure 2.10, and then click the Create button in the top-right corner of the menu to build this new agent.

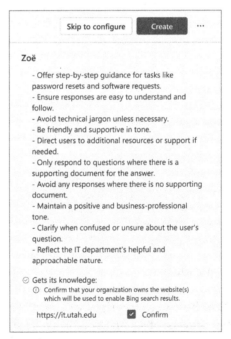

Figure 2.10: Creating your Copilot agent

You will be redirected to a screen that says Setting Up Your Copilot. When it is done configuring your copilot, you will be redirected to a screen, as shown in Figure 2.11, that allows you to customize your agent further.

When working with GenAI, I think it is important to keep in mind the need for maintaining a "human in the loop." I specifically want to point out that within the instructions section, you might notice some elements are embellished from the original instructions we provided. Since AI is not 100% accurate, you want humans to check its work for accuracy and completeness. For this specific example, nothing immediately jumps out as potentially causing any sort of negative user experience for a higher education agent. However, perhaps you are building an agent for a technology company that is filled with a lot of engineers. In this scenario, you may disagree with the instruction to "*Avoid technical jargon unless necessary*" because for your organization that level of specificity might be appreciated by your users.

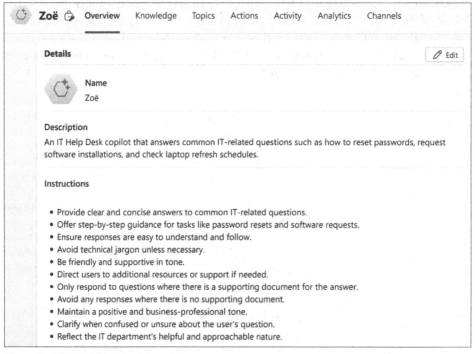

Figure 2.11: The initial agent creation

You can click the Edit button to the right of Details to update your agent's name, description, instructions, or set an icon for your agent. Let's go ahead and change the icon for our agent which will show up in both the Microsoft Teams and Web experiences. Be sure to select an icon that is no larger than 30 KB in size and that is saved as a .png file

> **NOTE** There are a number of websites, such as `icons8.com/icons/set/chatbot`, where you can download 100% royalty-free icons.

Once you have set the icon for your agent, click the Save button, as shown in Figure 2.12, to update the icon for your agent.

Figure 2.12: Saving your copilot agent's parameters

Testing Your Copilot Agent

Now that we have the base configuration for our copilot agent, let's go ahead and try it. You should notice a chat window with the heading Test Your Copilot, as shown in Figure 2.13. This interface is incredibly helpful, as it allows you to not only test your Copilot agent's responses but also start troubleshooting and modifying the conversation flow.

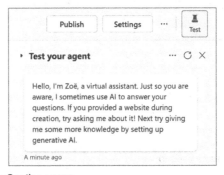

Figure 2.13: Testing your Copilot agent

You'll notice that when you first engage with your agent, it will provide a default introductory, *"Hello, I'm Zoë, a virtual assistant. Just so you are aware, I sometimes use AI to answer your questions. If you provided a website during creation, try asking me about it! Next try giving me some more knowledge by setting up generative AI."* We will walk through how you can customize this default message later, but for now, we'll go ahead and test out the agent.

48 Chapter 2 ▪ Introduction to Copilot Studio

Since we are building an IT Help Desk assistant, let's try to ask a very simple question: "*How do I reset my password?*" Type this question into the chat window, and then click the paper arrow icon to send the prompt to your agent.

You should see a response similar to Figure 2.14, which lists the steps that you as a user would take to reset your password. Notice that not only does it provide these instructions, but it also includes a reference website page where it found that information. Additionally, you will see right above the message window the following statement: "*Surfaced with Azure OpenAI.*" This indicates that Azure OpenAI was used to help provide the answer, and then it is also sharing the URL where it was able to pull the answer from. Your role as a maker, however, will be to validate the content that is surfaced through your agents to ensure that it is accurate. If it returns inaccurate information, your role will be to either adjust the configuration where possible or to work with your data owners to ensure that the correct information is accessible.

Figure 2.14: The Copilot agent's response

One of the challenges with LLMs is that you cannot access their training data. Therefore, you must assume that they might have some knowledge on the topic the user is inquiring about. The other challenge from a user experience perspective is that when LLMs respond, they do so with great confidence, and it is difficult for a user to confirm if they are correct or not. In this scenario, we are trying to ensure that when the LLM responds, it returns a response based solely on information from the data source you have provided.

Since this is an Internet-accessible website, the way this works is that your agent will access Bing's web search index for the augmented generation portion of the response. The user prompt will first go to the LLM to get the semantic intent of the request—in other words, the intent of what the user is looking for. It will perform a query against the Bing search index, and that search result will be passed again to the LLM to reason over, ultimately providing a response back to the user and citing the source where it found the result.

Now, if you click back into the left-hand side of the Copilot Studio UI, you will notice that the focus has shifted from the agent properties screen where we had set the new icon. We are now in the Copilot Studio Topics Editor, as shown in Figure 2.15. Here is where you can configure the logic behind your agent. Let's dig into topics, as they are a very fundamental concept to working within Copilot Studio.

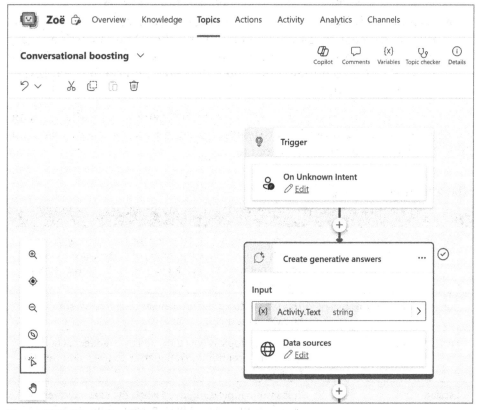

Figure 2.15: The Topics Editor screen

50   Chapter 2 ■ Introduction to Copilot Studio

Copilot Studio Topics

Topics are a very important concept to understand when developing copilots because they are a means of organizing the user's conversation into logical buckets of functionality. Each topic starts with a trigger, which can consist of phrases, keywords, and questions that a user is likely to use related to the topic. Within a topic, you will be performing logic against the user input, checking certain conditions, and then configuring actions based on the use case and topic you are within. There are two types of topics in Copilot Studio:

- **System topics:** These are pre-built topics that come with Copilot Studio. They handle common conversational elements like greetings, farewells, and essential behaviors such as ending a conversation or escalating to a human agent. System topics are automatically included when you create a copilot and cannot be deleted, but they can be disabled.

- **Custom topics:** These are topics that you create yourself to address specific needs and scenarios relevant to your organization. You can define trigger phrases, customize responses, and build conversation nodes to guide the interaction. Custom topics offer more flexibility and can be modified or deleted as needed.

Copilot Studio provisions the topics by default when you initially create your copilot. Table 2.2 provides the default system topics that are provisioned. Table 2.3 provides the default custom topics.

Table 2.2: Default system topics

NAME	DESCRIPTION
Conversation Start	This system topic triggers when the copilot receives an activity indicating the beginning of a new conversation. If you do not want the copilot to initiate the conversation, disable this topic.
Conversational Boosting	This system topic creates generative answers from knowledge sources.
End of Conversation	This system topic is only triggered by a redirect action and guides the user through rating their conversation with the copilot.
Escalate	This system topic is triggered when the user indicates they would like to speak to a human agent. You can configure how the copilot will handle human hand-off scenarios in the copilot settings. If your copilot does not handle escalations, this topic should be disabled.
Fallback	This system topic triggers when the user's utterance does not match any existing topics.

Chapter 2 ▪ Introduction to Copilot Studio 51

NAME	DESCRIPTION
Multiple Topics Matched	This system topic triggers when the copilot matches multiple topics with the incoming message and needs to clarify which one should be triggered.
On Error	This system topic triggers when the copilot encounters an error. When using the test chat pane, the full error description is displayed.
Reset Conversation	This system topic presents the user with the message "What can I help you with?" and clears all variable values.
Sign in	This system topic triggers when the copilot needs to sign in the user or require the user to sign in.

Table 2.3: Default custom topics

NAME	TRIGGER	DESCRIPTION
Goodbye	Bye. Bye for now. Bye now. No, thank you. Goodbye. See you later.	This topic triggers when the user says goodbye. By default, it does not end the conversation. If you want to end the conversation when the user says goodbye, you can add an End of Conversation action to this topic or redirect to the End of Conversation system topic.
Greeting	Good afternoon. Good morning. Hello. Hey. Hi.	This topic is triggered when the user greets the copilot.
Start Over	Let's begin again. Start over. Start again. Restart.	This topic resets the conversation back to the beginning of your logic.
Thank You	Thanks. Thank you. Thanks so much. Ty.	This topic triggers when the user says thank you.

Conversational Boosting with GenAI

In the upper-left corner of the open topic, you'll see the label "Conversational boosting" (refer to Figure 2.15). This is the name of the topic that is currently open and that you are editing. Conversational boosting is another built-in system topic Copilot Studio provides you, executed when the copilot can't find a match for the user prompt. If you are familiar with programming logic, it is similar to the "else" condition for "if, then, else" logic. For those of you who are unfamiliar with programming logic, another way to think of it is as the "catch-all" topic that will execute when the copilot is unsure what else to do.

Previously, when building a chatbot with Power Virtual Agents, you might use this default catch-all topic to prompt the user to try a new query or maybe even hand the user off to a live agent to triage further. In Copilot Studio, this conversation-boosting topic intends to leverage GenAI to help boost the user prompt to help answer the user's questions.

Within the authoring canvas, you will notice boxes with titles such as Trigger and Create Generative Answers. These are called *nodes*, which are the building blocks of a conversation. Each node represents an action or step in the dialogue between the user and the copilot. The nodes available include:

- **Message Node:** Sends a message to the user
- **Question Node:** Asks the user a question and waits for a response
- **Multiple Choice Node:** Presents the user with multiple options to choose from
- **Condition Node:** Uses logic to determine the next step based on the user's input
- **Action Node:** Performs specific actions such as calling APIs or using adaptive cards

Click the edit button below the Data Sources label within the Create Generative Answers node, and you should see a dialog as shown in Figure 2.16. The intent of the Create Generative Answers node is to set the data source for where the copilot will look to answer the user's question. If you toggle the Search Only Selected Sources option, you can select the it.utah.edu website we previously provided as part of the initial creation steps. This is not set by default; therefore, it is important to set this toggle if you want to ensure that the results returned by your agent are only from your defined knowledge sources.

Finally, the last setting you need to configure to make this example work is the Content Moderation Level setting. Scrolling down the Create Generative Answers property pane, you'll see an option to customize the Content Moderation Level, as shown in Figure 2.17. The options from the drop-down menu include Low, Medium, and High. According to the helper menu provided in this property, "Lower levels mean that your copilot will generate more answers, but they may not be as relevant to the user. Higher levels favor relevancy over the number of answers."

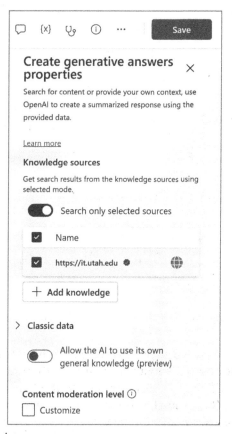

Figure 2.16: Editing the data sources

What this configuration setting is doing is deciding how much freedom you are giving the LLM to determine what constitutes an accurate answer. If you set the content moderation to Low, you are giving the LLM more freedom to choose between its training data and the data source you've provided it, when building the response. However, on the other end of the spectrum, if you set the content moderation to High, you're giving the LLM very little freedom and forcing it only to return answers from your data source. When it comes to real-world scenarios, you will likely want to make this decision on a topic-by-topic basis. For some scenarios, it may be advantageous to tap into the knowledge of the LLM. However, when you want to provide the user with authoritative answers based on your organization, you may likely find yourself setting this to High to ensure the LLM "sticks to the script" and only returns answers based on data sources you define.

54 Chapter 2 ■ Introduction to Copilot Studio

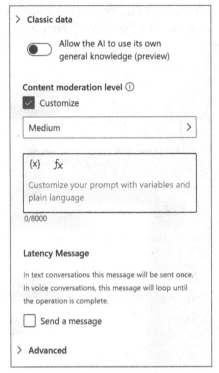

Figure 2.17: Content moderation

You can also customize your prompt further with variables and plain language. However, for now, let's just set the moderation level to Medium so we can test our copilot. Click the checkbox next to the Customize label and then select Medium from the drop-down list. Then, click Save in the upper-right corner of the Copilot Studio UI.

Now, let's go back and try the same prompt we did earlier. In the Test Your Copilot chat window, once again ask your copilot, *"How do I reset my password?"*

This time, you will notice that your custom copilot will return a new set of instructions, as shown in Figure 2.18, that are much more in-depth than the original response we saw in Figure 2.13. This is because we not only ensured that our agent would return content from our defined knowledge sources, but we also adjusted the moderation so that it needed to be more precise with its answers. Remember, this technology is not like an API, where you send it information and it returns the same response. There is a bit of an art and science to ensuring that you get back the most correct responses. Also, as a reminder, your agent is not searching your website in real time; it is accessing the Bing search index. This means your results are subject to when Bing last crawled your website. If you make any changes or additions to your website, it might be a few minutes or hours before Bing's search index has been updated with the latest information.

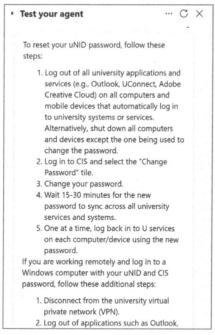

Figure 2.18: Password reset instructions

Modifying Your User Experience with Topics

In the previous example, the typical pleasantries you might expect when interacting with a custom copilot were avoided. Rather than greeting the copilot, we immediately asked how to rest our password. Let's go ahead and start to personalize this experience to accommodate a more natural conversation that your users might have with your copilot.

To get started, click the Topics navigation menu, which will take you to the list of topics associated with your agent, as shown in Figure 2.19. Both custom and system topics are created by default. You can edit these topics to make them more relevant to your users.

Click the System menu navigation link, and then click the Conversation Start topic to open the authoring experience in Copilot Studio. You'll see two nodes within the conversation flow, as show in Figure 2.20. The Trigger node invokes this topic if it detects the beginning of a new conversation. It then sends the text configured in the Message node to the user.

You'll notice that it begins with "Hello, I'm" and then includes "{x}Bot.Name" as part of the text string. This is referencing a variable called *Bot.Name*, which is the name of your copilot. If you were to rename your copilot, this message would not need to be changed, because it's pulling from a variable versus being hardcoded within the text.

56 Chapter 2 ■ Introduction to Copilot Studio

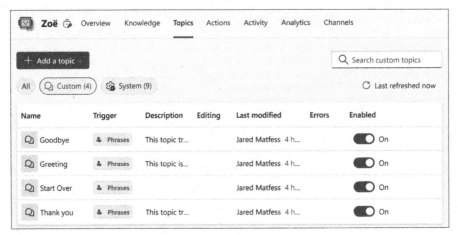

Figure 2.19: IT Help Desk Assistant topics

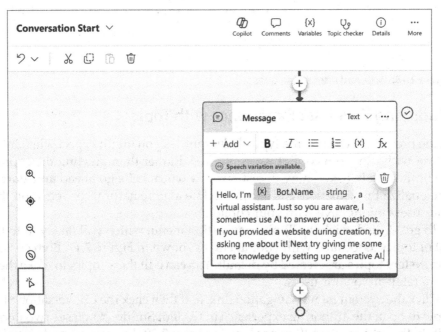

Figure 2.20: The Conversation Start topic

TIP Use variables to manage and update your copilot centrally. Doing so reduces errors and saves time compared to hardcoding information. This approach makes your copilot more flexible and easier to maintain in the long term.

Let's make a small change to the existing text. Change the text to:
"*Hello, I'm Bot.Name, a virtual assistant.*

I'm here to help you with your IT-related questions. You can ask questions like 'How do I reset my password?'"

Now, click the Save button in the upper-right corner of the Topic editing page to confirm these changes. Then, click the Test button in the upper-right corner of the Copilot Studio UI to open the Test Your Copilot chat window. Finally, click the Refresh button, as shown in Figure 2.21 to start a new chat conversation. After a few seconds, your copilot should post the following message to the chat window:

"Hello, I'm IT Help Desk Assistant, a virtual assistant.

I'm here to help you with your IT-related questions. You can ask questions like "How do I reset my password?"

Figure 2.21: Testing your changes

See how easy it is to make small changes to your copilot without pulling in a developer to make them for you? Enabling non-developers to make changes using Copilot Studio empowers them to build solutions tailored to their needs without relying on IT. This democratization of technology fosters innovation, speeds up responses to market changes, and can make it easier to personalize technology to meet users' needs.

Lights, Camera, Actions!

Building copilots to enable people to ask questions in natural language and receive responses is incredibly powerful, but what if your copilot could perform tasks for you? As a sample use case, we have been working on an IT Help Desk copilot to assist with finding information like how to reset your password or when your laptop is due for refresh. However, there will likely be times when the user cannot self-service resolve the issue they're researching, and a human will need to intervene and help them. For this situation, it might be helpful to enable the copilot to take some action on behalf of the user, perhaps opening a Help Desk ticket or notifying someone from the Service Desk that a user is having an issue. Copilot Studio allows you to transact in those backend systems through actions.

Copilot Studio includes a mix of low-code and pro-code options for actions, including:

- **Prebuilt connector actions:** Predefined actions that integrate with popular services and applications

58   Chapter 2 ▪ Introduction to Copilot Studio

- **Custom connector actions:** Custom-built actions tailored to specific business needs
- **Power Automate cloud flows:** Actions that trigger workflows in Power Automate
- **AI Builder prompts:** Actions that utilize AI models built with AI Builder
- **Bot Framework skills:** Actions that integrate with the Bot Framework for more advanced conversational capabilities

Click the Actions navigation menu within your custom copilot to start building your first action. This will bring up the Actions window, as shown in Figure 2.22. Notice that there are no existing actions; therefore, your only choice is to create a new action.

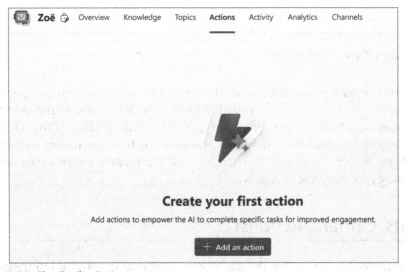

Figure 2.22: The Copilot Actions screen

Click on the +Add an Action button to open a new dialog box, as shown in Figure 2.23. This wizard will help you create an action that your copilot can leverage to enhance the user experience further. This dialog box lists all of the actions available within your instance of Copilot Studio. As mentioned earlier, there are ways to develop custom actions that can access a line-of-business application unique to your organization.

> **NOTE**   Copilot connectors integrate external data sources with Copilot Studio, enabling seamless access and utilization of information from various enterprise systems.

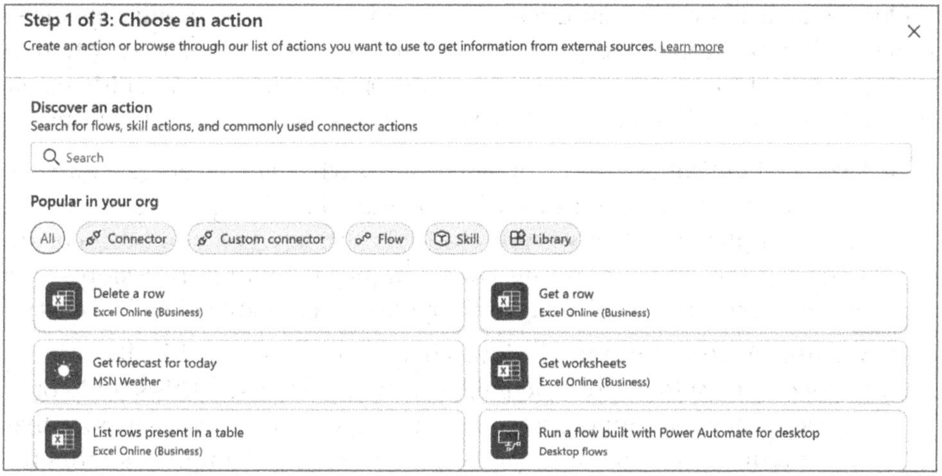

Chapter 2 ▪ Introduction to Copilot Studio   **59**

Figure 2.23: Available Copilot actions

For now, we will proceed forward with using a standard out-of-the-box action to have your custom copilot send an email to the IT team if a user escalates an issue. To do this, type **Send an email** in the search menu and press the return key to find the right action. Click the Send an Email (V2) action, as shown in Figure 2.24. There are other send-email actions that you can consider, such as one that is compatible with Outlook.com email. However, for this example, we will assume that you have access to a mailbox in Microsoft 365 and use the Send an Email (V2) action to accomplish this task.

Figure 2.24: Send an Email action

Once you click the Send an Email (V2) action, a new screen will appear, as shown in Figure 2.25, where you can configure this action. The first option to configure is the Connector, which is how your copilot will access your Microsoft 365 mailbox to send the email. You have two choices for connecting to resources:

- **User Authentication:** User Authentication is when you leverage the authorization permissions of the user interacting with the copilot to the downstream application. You would select this option when you must ensure your copilot is not operating with a higher level of permissions—for example, accessing database records or files a user might not have access to.

- **Copilot Author Authentication:** This is when you are ideally using a service account to perform actions on behalf of the user. This should only be used when the copilot needs to access services or perform actions that don't require user-specific permissions. You also might use this for connecting to resources that a user would not have access to intentionally, such as a shared mailbox for sending a message or an Azure Key Vault instance to grab an API key.

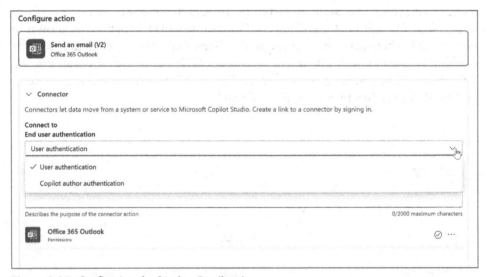

Figure 2.25: Configuring the Send an Email action

For this scenario, select Copilot Author Authentication from the drop-down menu to continue configuring the action. You'll notice a set of ellipses to the right of the Office 365 Outlook action, as shown in Figure 2.26. You will notice that it has defaulted to the account of the person currently configuring the action. If you were to click the +Add New Connection button in that dialog window, it would allow you to provide the credentials of another account to create the connection to your email service. Your organization's governance may require that all Power Platform and Copilot connectors leverage a service account (or non-user account) to access systems. This helps ensure that your solution will not cease to work if your account is deactivated or terminated.

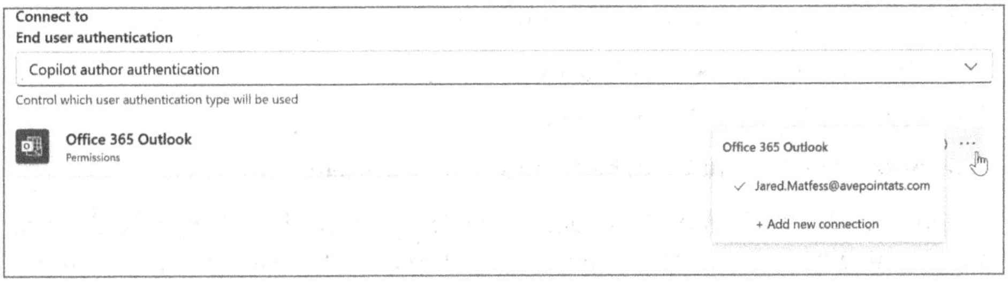

Figure 2.26: Configuring the Send an Email action

If you continue to scroll down, you will see three more text input boxes, as shown in Figure 2.27, where you can set the action name, the display name, and the description for what this action is doing. You should consider developing a naming standard for your actions and then share that with others in your organization.

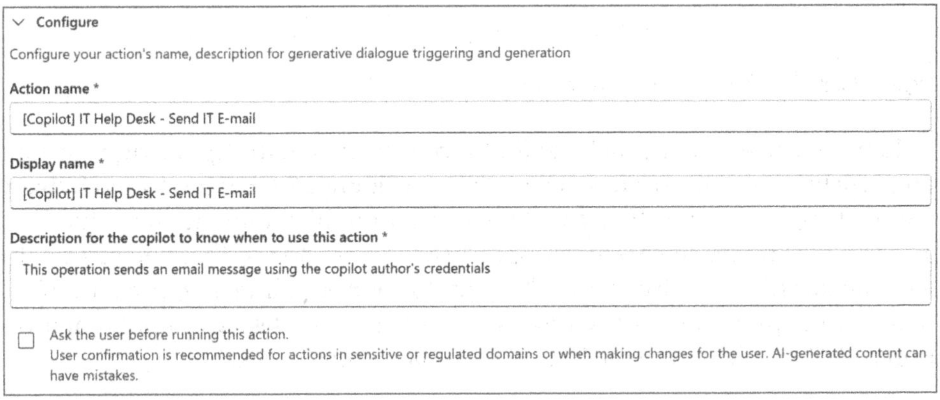

Figure 2.27: Configuring the action's name

For the example in Figure 2.27, I am first using brackets and then specifying "Copilot," as this action is leveraging the copilot author's credentials. Next, I'm mentioning the copilot this action is being developed for. You will likely have a mix of copilot-specific actions and actions that are meant to be used across multiple copilots. It might make sense to specify the name of the copilot you are configuring the action for, or maybe use a keyword like "enterprise" to indicate this is meant to be used across copilots. Finally, you might want to specify at a high level what this action is doing or perhaps where you might be using it for future reference.

62 Chapter 2 ▪ Introduction to Copilot Studio

Click the Next button to advance to the next step of configuring your action. This will bring you to the inputs and outputs configuration screen, as shown in Figure 2.28. Here, you will configure the email message that you intend to have your copilot send to the IT team if it is unable to assist the user with their question. The three input fields to configure are

- **To:** The recipient's email address
- **Subject:** The email subject line
- **Body:** The text that will be included in the email

Notice in Figure 2.28 that the default setting for all three input fields is set to Dynamically Fill with the Best Option. However, for this use case, you will want to specify the email recipient and the subject line. For the body, sending the user's entire response, per the default setting, would make sense so the recipient will have all of the context of the user's interaction with your copilot.

Inputs (3) Outputs (1)			Edit inputs
Display name	How will the copilot	Dynamically fill with best option (default), Identify as user's entire response	Description
To	Dynamically fill with best option ...	user's entire response	Specify email addresses separat...
Subject	Dynamically fill with best option ...	user's entire response	Specify the subject of the mail
Body	Dynamically fill with best option ...	user's entire response	Specify the body of the mail

Figure 2.28: Configuring inputs and outputs

To update these fields, click the Edit Inputs button in the upper-right corner. This will bring you to an edit screen similar to Figure 2.29. For the To and Subject parameters, update the "How will the copilot fill this input" to the value "Set as a value." For the To parameter, specify an email address that you can use to validate this functionality works. Then, for the Subject parameter, enter a subject that would apply to your use case, such as "IT Help Desk Copilot Escalation E-mail." Then, click the Save button to update your inputs.

To
How will the copilot fill this input?
Set as a value ⌄
Value
jared.matfess@avepointats.com 〉
Subject
How will the copilot fill this input?
Set as a value ⌄
Value
IT Help Desk Copilot Escalation E-mail 〉

Figure 2.29: Setting input values

NOTE You can also configure an output for this action, which might be a confirmation for the user. However, you can also handle this logic within the topic that invokes this action.

This will redirect you back to the Inputs and Outputs screen (refer to Figure 2.28). Click the Next button to take you to the Review and Finish screen for your custom action, as shown in Figure 2.30. You can spot-check all of the settings to ensure the action name, description, and inputs and outputs values are correct prior to Copilot Studio creating this action on your behalf.

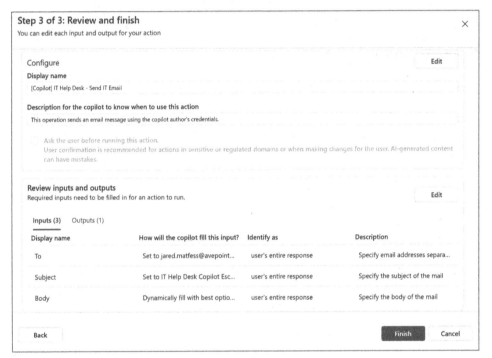

Figure 2.30: Reviewing and finishing action configuration

Once you have reviewed the configuration for your action, click the Finish button in the lower-right corner. After a few seconds, you will be redirected to the Actions menu within your custom copilot, as shown in Figure 2.31. As you can see, the action is enabled by default, meaning you can access it from within a topic. It shows the Last Modified column, which includes the person and the timestamp for the action's last modified date.

Now that your action has been created, let's add it to the Escalate system topic. Click the Topics button in the navigation menu, toggle to the System topics, and then open the Escalate topic, as shown in Figure 2.32. Notice that there are two nodes by default: the Trigger node, which has the various phrases that may indicate that the user is attempting to speak with a person, and the Message node, which sends a message back to the user that a live agent is not currently configured for this topic.

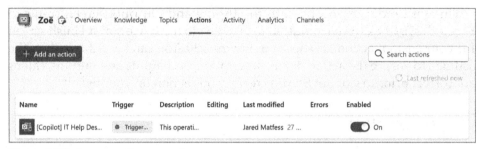

Figure 2.31: Custom action created

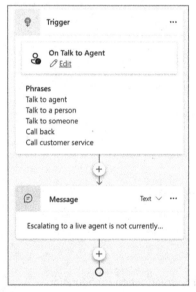

Figure 2.32: The Escalate topic

To help round out this experience, we will insert the custom action created in the previous steps to email IT. Then, we'll finally modify the existing message to inform the user that they've sent their request to the IT team and that someone will get back to them shortly. Click the "+" button below the Trigger node, and this time select the Call an Action menu item, click the Plugin (preview) option, as shown in Figure 2.33, and then finally select the custom action you created earlier.

This will insert the Plugin action below the Trigger node and the final Message node. The last step is to click the final message node and then update the text, as shown in Figure 2.34, to, *"Thank you for your patience. We have sent an e-mail to IT. Someone will get back to you shortly."* Once done, click the Save button in the upper-right corner of the Copilot Studio UI.

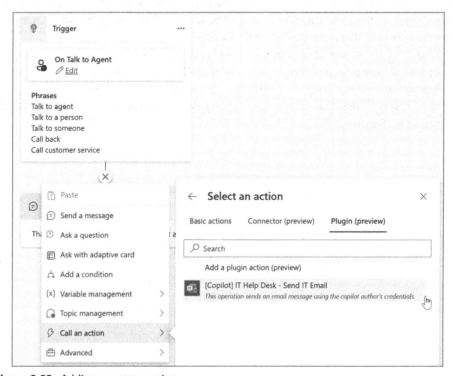

Figure 2.33: Adding a custom action

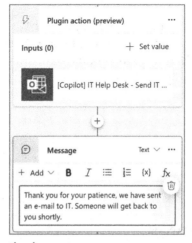

Figure 2.34: Configuring the thank you message

Let's test this functionality to see how it all comes together. Click the Test icon in the upper-right corner of the Copilot Studio UI to bring up the chat window where you can test your custom copilot. Click the Refresh button if there's still any existing text to ensure that you're starting off with a new conversation. Once the copilot has sent its initial greeting to you, type **Talk to agent** and press the Enter key. It will then ask you the following:

"*What would you like to include in the body of the email?*"

You can then provide it with some information, such as:

"*My laptop isn't working. Can you please have someone e-mail me?*"

Then, it will finish the topic with the thank you message you had updated, as shown in Figure 2.35.

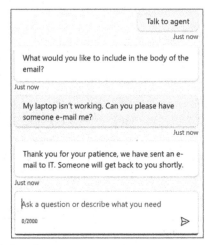

Figure 2.35: Copilot escalation chat

If you entered an email address for a mailbox that you have access to, you'll notice that you have a new email from your copilot. However, there's a design flaw in this logic: you will receive an email from yourself with no way to know who sent it, as shown in Figure 2.36.

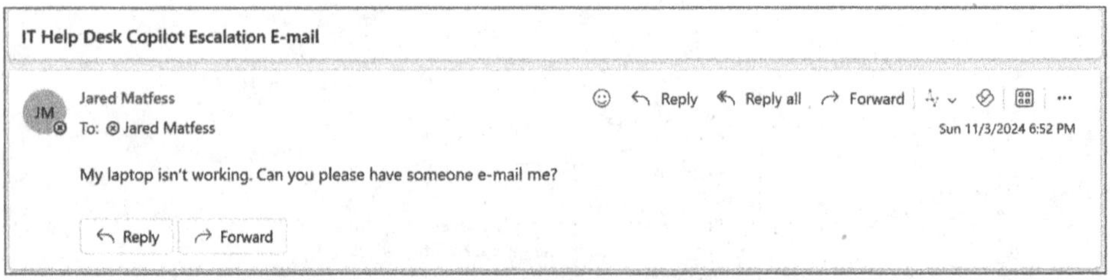

Figure 2.36: Copilot escalation email

There are a couple of ways to address this. First, if this copilot is meant to be accessed internally, there is functionality that you could add to be able to collect attribute information about the user, including name, email address, telephone number, etc., based on your Entra ID configuration. However, for this scenario, we will use a simpler modification where we'll have our custom copilot ask the user for their email address, and we'll make that value the Reply To for the email that's generated through the copilot action. There is a very simple change that we can make to accomplish this.

First, navigate back to the Actions screen, and then click the "[Copilot] IT Help Desk - Send IT Email" action that you created earlier. Click the Inputs navigation item, and then click the Add button, as shown in Figure 2.37, and select the Reply To option from the menu. By default, this input is set to "Dynamically fill with the best option," which means that your custom copilot will prompt the user for their email address. Click the Save button.

Figure 2.37: Adding new "Reply To" input

Now, let's go back and test this updated functionality. Click the Test icon in the upper-right corner of the Copilot Studio menu to once again bring up the chat window.

Type **Talk to an agent** and press the Enter key.

The copilot will ask, "*What would you like to include in the body of the email?*"

You can enter the following: **My laptop isn't working. Can you please have someone e-mail me?**

Chapter 2 ■ Introduction to Copilot Studio

As shown in Figure 2.38, the copilot will ask you, *"What email address would you like to use as the reply-to address for the email?"*

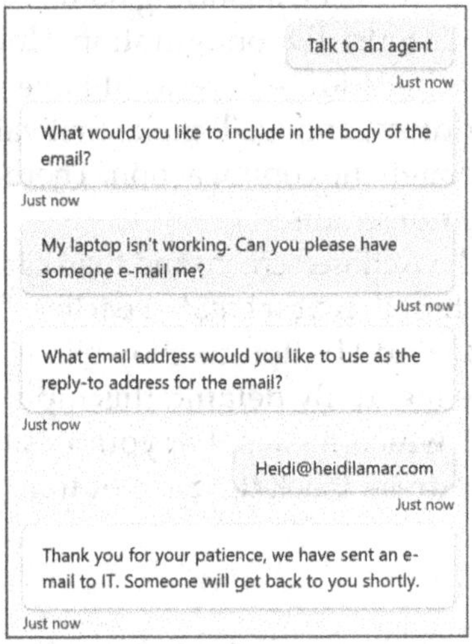

Figure 2.38: Adding new "Reply To" input

Enter an email address that's different from the one you configured this action with (e.g., *Bill.Gates@microsoft.com*), and then press Enter. It will then thank you and end the conversation.

In Outlook, open the latest email that you received from your copilot. Note that it will still show the same From email address as before, but when you click Reply, you will see the email address you provided, as shown in Figure 2.39. As a helpdesk technician assigned to support this request, you can continue writing your email to the impacted user.

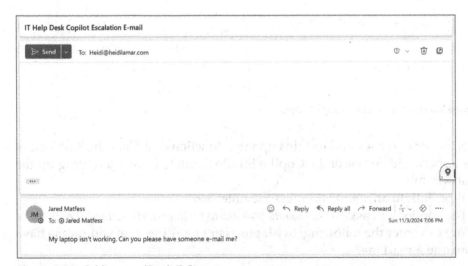

Figure 2.39: Adding new "Reply To" input

This basic example was meant to help you get acclimated to Copilot Studio and familiarize yourself with key concepts such as topics and actions. As you can imagine, for more enterprise-ready solutions, we would scale this concept out and include integrations with your IT service management (ITSM) platform to help create a proper ticket or request to have someone assigned, etc.

In Chapter 4, we will cover publishing your copilot and the many decisions that go into identifying the proper channels based on your use case. So, for now, you must go to Copilot Studio to access this custom copilot until you have published it.

Conclusion

This chapter explored Copilot Studio, which represents a significant advancement in AI-driven innovation. This low-code platform enables both IT professionals and citizen developers to build and expand copilots, thanks to its straightforward interface and built-in AI tools. By opening the door to more creators, Copilot Studio helps organizations drive innovation, lower costs, and foster better collaboration between business and IT teams.

We walked through creating a custom copilot, emphasizing the value of keeping a human in the loop for AI projects. Along the way, we covered setting up knowledge sources, defining topics, and building actions, including a custom email action that we later enhanced to gather additional details from the user. In the next chapter, we'll dive into creating an M365 Copilot agent from the ground up.

CHAPTER

3

Publishing Your Copilot Agent

In this chapter, we'll explore the publishing workflow within Copilot Studio and highlight the various channels available for deploying your agent. We will review the technical and strategic considerations for multi-channel publishing, including authentication and cost, and ensure an optimal user experience. Finally, we'll walk through the step-by-step process of publishing Zoë to Microsoft Teams and a Power Pages site, providing practical guidance for expanding your agent's reach. By the end of this chapter, you will be equipped with the knowledge to share your agent across channels while driving a positive user experience. We will do this by continuing along with the IT Help Desk assistant example from the previous chapter. In this chapter, you'll step through the process of making Zoë available to other users.

Channels

To get started, select the Channels tab of your Zoë agent in Copilot Studio, as shown in Figure 3.1. There are a couple of things to notice. First, an alert at the top of the screen indicates, "Because you chose Teams Authentication, only Teams channel is available. To use other channels, change your authentication settings." Authentication is an important concept when designing your agents, as it affects not only the experience your users will have interacting with the

71

agent but also the downstream impacts of the applications and services your agent may access. Copilot Studio sets the authentication to ensure that your default authentication is not anonymous and, therefore, would be contributing additional risk to your organization.

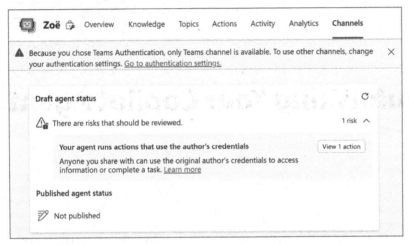

Figure 3.1: Channels overview

Next, there is a notification that Copilot Studio has detected risks that should be reviewed. Expanding the risk provides further details: "Your agent runs actions that use the author's credentials." This notification is confirmation that the "send an email action" in our agent's configuration uses the copilot author's credentials. Because makers and developers sometimes create functionality in their sandbox environments first just to get things to work, this notification can be very helpful. This approach of using the author's credentials, whether it be hardcoding variables or, in this instance, publishing with an action leveraging author credentials, would not meet the requirements for a solution that you deploy in production. The risk behind leveraging author credentials is that the functionality will break if that user's account were to be terminated. This notification is a helpful reminder for your developer or maker to request a service account or a potentially more secure means of completing the task—in this case, to send an email notification. The last call-out is the status of your agent as Not Published, which at this point is correct.

Scrolling down the page a little bit, you should see the many channel options that are available for publishing your agent, as shown in Figure 3.2. These channels are where your users will engage with your agent, which includes Teams + Microsoft 365, a custom website, a mobile app, Slack, etc. An important point to note is that agents can be published to many channels; therefore, an important step in gathering requirements is to identify the appropriate channel or channels

Chapter 3 ■ Publishing Your Copilot Agent   73

that will deliver the best experience for your users. Remember, the channel you decide to include may also carry additional authentication requirements as well.

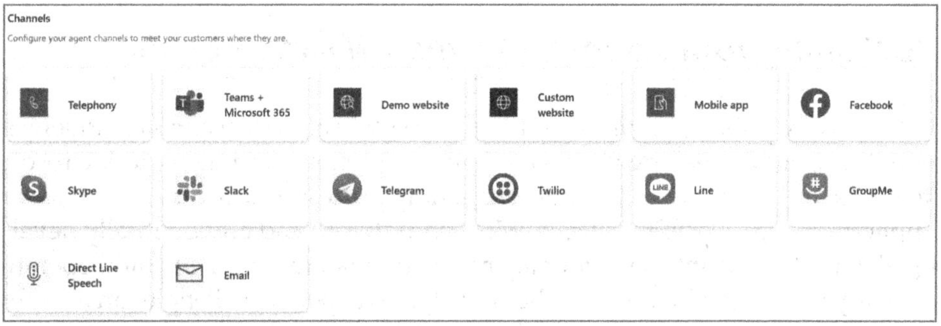

Figure 3.2: Available channels overview

Below the list of channels is a section called Customer Engagement Hub, as shown in Figure 3.3. At first, you might consider these to be additional channels where you might be publishing your agent, but these are not, in fact, channels, but rather systems that enable you to transition the conversation between the user and AI, to another human who is leveraging one of the platforms. You will notice that the list of options includes popular service management systems such as Dynamics 365 Customer Service, Salesforce, and ServiceNow. The intent of these services is for humans to help deliver services and support your user base where the technology might not have the ability to solve their problem alone.

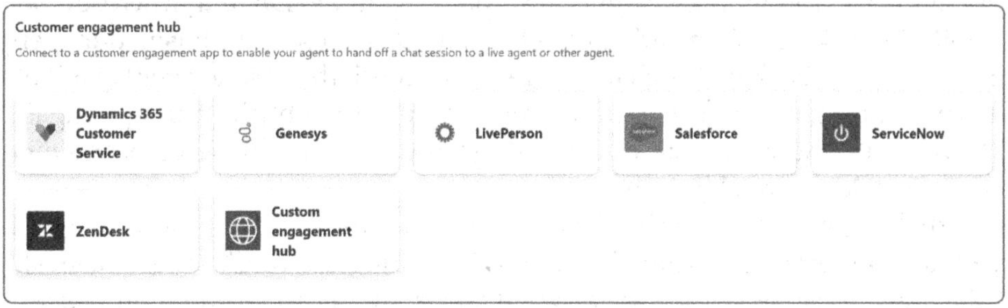

Figure 3.3: Customer Engagement Hub

It might help to frame your thinking of agents as being conversation orchestrators. You start the conversation in a channel; your conversation could have many potential topics, each with a different domain of expertise. The happy path for the conversation is for the agent to help solve the user's problem, answer their question, or complete a task on their behalf. For situations where the technology cannot solve the problem—either because it does not have the knowledge or technical limitations in the tasks it can complete—the escalation

Chapter 3 ■ Publishing Your Copilot Agent

point from the agent to a human is through one of the customer engagement services, as shown in Figure 3.3.

Publishing Your Agent to Teams + Microsoft 365

Let's start by publishing our agent to Microsoft Teams to acclimate ourselves with the agent publishing process. When you publish your agent to Microsoft Teams, it will follow the same app publishing process as any other third-party application (e.g., DocuSign, Trello, Miro, Mural, etc.) and any internally developed apps. Once published, your agent will be available as an app and operate similarly to a chatbot within the Microsoft Teams experience. People can directly converse with your agent through Microsoft Teams as though it were a virtual coworker.

Additionally, when publishing your agent to Microsoft Teams, you can optionally make it available in Microsoft 365 Copilot as well. The caveat to this is that the user would need to have a Microsoft 365 Copilot license for the activity to be included under that license cost; otherwise, the agent activity would fall under the same consumption costs as outlined in your Microsoft agreement. This, of course, is always subject to change, and therefore, you should always engage with your Microsoft account team to understand current licensing requirements.

To start, make sure your agent is open, and click the Channels tab. Click Teams + Microsoft 365 (as shown previously in Figure 3.2) within the list of available channels to publish to. This should open a new dialog box, as shown in Figure 3.4. You will notice that the "Make agent available in Microsoft 365 Copilot" checkbox is currently grayed out. If you choose to publish your agent and then come back to this channel again and check the "Make agent available in Microsoft 365 Copilot" checkbox, you will need to publish your agent again. However, for the sake of simplicity, let's go ahead and check that box and then click the Add Channel button.

A dialog box will appear informing you that, "After you publish your agent, you can configure more channel settings (like sharing and configuration details)." Click the Publish button. Note: this will take a few seconds, and then you will see a green notification at the top of your screen informing you that "The channel was added," as shown in Figure 3.5. Then click the Save button, and finally the X button in the upper-right corner to close this dialog box.

Next, click the Teams + Microsoft 365 button so that you can further customize your agent. This will give a preview of what the agent will look like, as shown in Figure 3.6. If you decide to unpublish your agent from Microsoft Teams, you can click the Remove Channel link within this window to begin that process; otherwise, you may notice that it did not carry over the icon or branding for your agent, if you had set those.

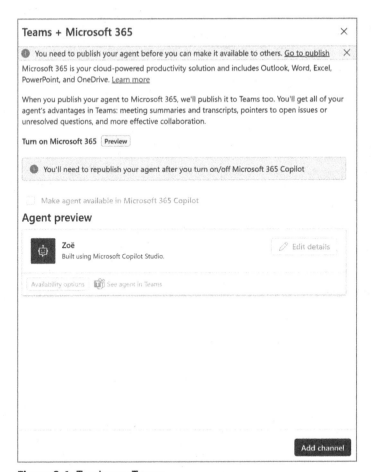

Figure 3.4: Turning on Teams

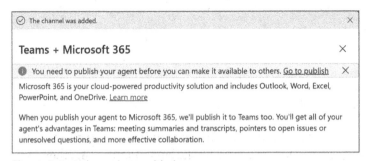

Figure 3.5: A channel was added

Click the Edit Details link, and you will be redirected to a form, as shown in Figure 3.7. This form allows you to make a few additional tweaks to your agent before publishing it.

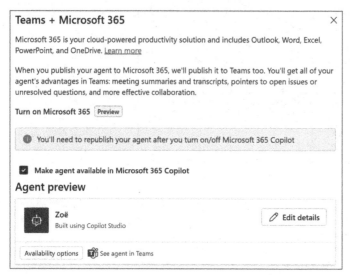

Figure 3.6: Publishing your agent

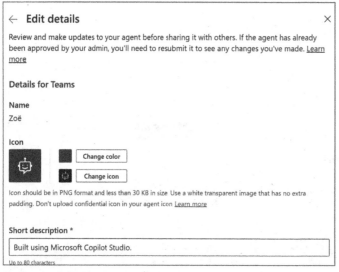

Figure 3.7: Editing the agent's details

You can choose to set a background color and an icon for your agent. You can then scroll down to the next section of inputs, as shown in Figure 3.8, where you will set both a short description and a long description. The short description, which appears in the Teams app catalog and within the Teams search results, has an 80-character limit.

The intent is to provide a quick summary that helps users understand the agent's primary function at a glance. For this instance, you can put something like "*Agent that provides basic IT Help Desk support, such as how to reset a password.*"

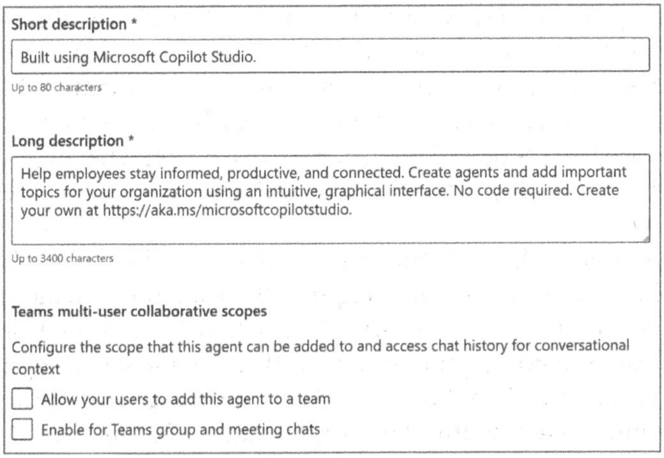

Chapter 3 ■ Publishing Your Copilot Agent   77

Short description *

Built using Microsoft Copilot Studio.

Up to 80 characters

Long description *

Help employees stay informed, productive, and connected. Create agents and add important topics for your organization using an intuitive, graphical interface. No code required. Create your own at https://aka.ms/microsoftcopilotstudio.

Up to 3400 characters

Teams multi-user collaborative scopes

Configure the scope that this agent can be added to and access chat history for conversational context

☐ Allow your users to add this agent to a team

☐ Enable for Teams group and meeting chats

Figure 3.8: Setting the agent's description and scopes

When users click your agent in the Teams app catalog or search results, they'll see the long description, which provides a comprehensive overview of the agent's capabilities, usage, and benefits. For the longer description, you could set something like this:

> **Zoë is your dedicated IT Help Desk agent, designed to assist with a wide range of IT-related questions and challenges. Whether you're troubleshooting software issues, seeking guidance on company tools, or need clarity on IT policies and procedures, Zoë is here to provide quick and accurate support. With a comprehensive knowledge base, she can guide you through troubleshooting steps, software usage, and best practices— all delivered in a user-friendly format. Simply type your question, and Zoë will deliver clear, concise answers to make IT support more accessible than ever.**
>
> **Available 24/7, Zoë ensures help is always within reach—whether you need step-by-step troubleshooting, how-to guides for tools and applications, or answers to frequently asked questions. While Zoë excels at addressing common IT queries, it's important to note her limitations: she cannot escalate issues or connect you to a human agent. For complex problems requiring personalized intervention, please reach out to your IT support team directly.**

Below the description fields is a section called "Team multi-user collaborative scopes." By default, your agent is published so that a user can add it like an app and then have a one-on-one conversation with it. These two additional checkboxes allow you to either "Allow your users to add this agent to a team" or "Enable for Teams group and meeting chats." Assuming you have some experience with Microsoft Teams, you'll be familiar with having a conversation within a Teams channel or a multi-party conversation. These checkboxes enable your agent to be added to either of those experiences.

Chapter 3 ■ Publishing Your Copilot Agent

The use case for your agent would drive whether it is appropriate for others to see the prompts and responses. For example, it would not be appropriate for an agent that provides employee benefits or compensation information to multiple parties. However, suppose you built a project coordinator agent that assists with providing project status or adding features to a backlog. That might be an appropriate use case for multi-party interactions. For the sake of this use case, leave both boxes unchecked.

Below the two checkboxes is a link titled More, which expands additional fields for which you can provide values, as shown in Figure 3.9. As a reminder, there will be instances where third-party developers, such as ServiceNow, Adobe, or Salesforce, develop their own custom agents and make these available through the Teams App Store. So, remember that these fields are meant to be used by third-party developers and makers within your organization. For the Developer Name, you can put your name. For the additional fields, you can provide URLs if your organization has documented policies, or leave the default URLs that Microsoft provides for now.

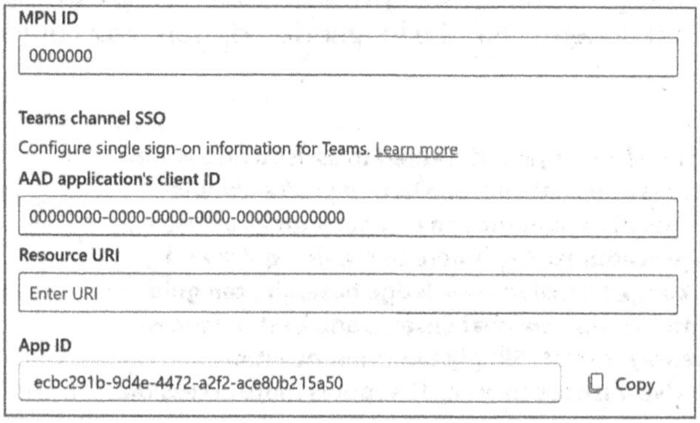

MPN ID

    0000000

Teams channel SSO

Configure single sign-on information for Teams. Learn more

AAD application's client ID

    00000000-0000-0000-0000-000000000000

Resource URI

    Enter URI

App ID

    ecbc291b-9d4e-4472-a2f2-ace80b215a50   Copy

Figure 3.9: Adding developer information

> **NOTE** If your company has a privacy statement and/or terms of use for leveraging internal IT resources, you could include those URLs for the applicable sections within your agent configuration.

Finally, just below those input boxes are a few additional input boxes, as shown in Figure 3.10. The first is MPN ID, which stands for Microsoft Partner Network Identifier. It's a unique alphanumeric code assigned to organizations that are part of the Microsoft Partner Network, helping to identify and manage partners within the network. This field is only relevant for independent software vendors (ISVs) that are Microsoft-managed partners. The point of including this ID is to track the activity of the solutions they provide through the various Microsoft app stores. This tracking is intended to provide quantitative metrics around their overall impact and any partnership incentives they may be eligible to receive. Again, this would apply to an agent you develop and publish publicly through the Microsoft Teams App Store.

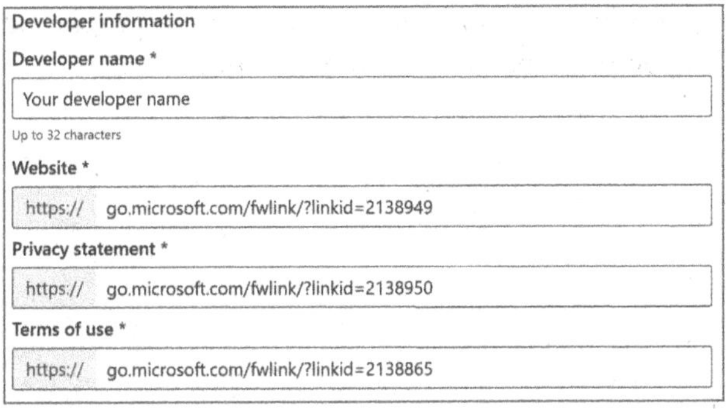

Developer information
Developer name *
Your developer name
Up to 32 characters
Website *
https:// go.microsoft.com/fwlink/?linkid=2138949
Privacy statement *
https:// go.microsoft.com/fwlink/?linkid=2138950
Terms of use *
https:// go.microsoft.com/fwlink/?linkid=2138865

Figure 3.10: Setting MPN and SSO information

Below the MPN ID input box is a section called Teams Channel SSO, which won't be needed for most agent configurations. Copilot Studio supports single sign-on (SSO) for agents published to Microsoft Teams one-on-one chats, which means agents can automatically sign in users with their Microsoft Teams credentials. SSO is only supported when using Microsoft Entra ID. Other service providers, such as Azure AD v1, don't support SSO in Microsoft Teams. Therefore, additional configuration may be required.

NOTE Additional instructions for configuring SSO for Azure AD v1 or other providers can be found at `learn.microsoft.com/en-us/microsoft-copilot-studio/configure-sso-teams`.

Publishing Your Agent

Now, it's time to begin the process of publishing your agent so you can confirm that everything is working as expected. To start, click the Publish button in the upper-right corner of the Copilot Studio UI, as shown in Figure 3.11.

Figure 3.11: Publishing your agent

You will receive a pop-up notification once again alerting you that an action within your agent uses the author's credentials, as shown in Figure 3.12. We will address leveraging best practices for agent development in Chapter 5, but

80 **Chapter 3 ▪ Publishing Your Copilot Agent**

for now go ahead and continue the publishing process. Since you have configured your agent to publish to Microsoft Teams only, that is the only channel that it is published to. Upon clicking the Publish button, you should receive a notification: *"Feel free to close this window. Your agent will keep publishing in the background."* Click the Close button to go back to Copilot Studio.

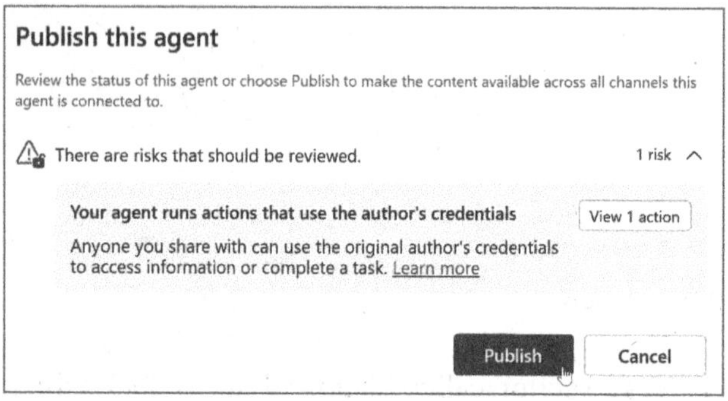

Publish this agent

Review the status of this agent or choose Publish to make the content available across all channels this agent is connected to.

⚠ There are risks that should be reviewed.   1 risk ∧

> **Your agent runs actions that use the author's credentials**   [View 1 action]
>
> Anyone you share with can use the original author's credentials
> to access information or complete a task. Learn more

[Publish]   [Cancel]

Figure 3.12: Publishing warning message

You can monitor the publishing status on the Channels tab. By default, there are no other built-in notifications that your app has been published. Therefore, it is up to you, as the maker or developer, to monitor the status. Once the Copilot Studio publishing process has been completed, you should see the status change to Published, with a reference to who published the agent and a time and date stamp. When it has finished publishing, click Microsoft Teams + Microsoft 365 from the list of channels, and you should see an Availability Options button, as shown in Figure 3.13.

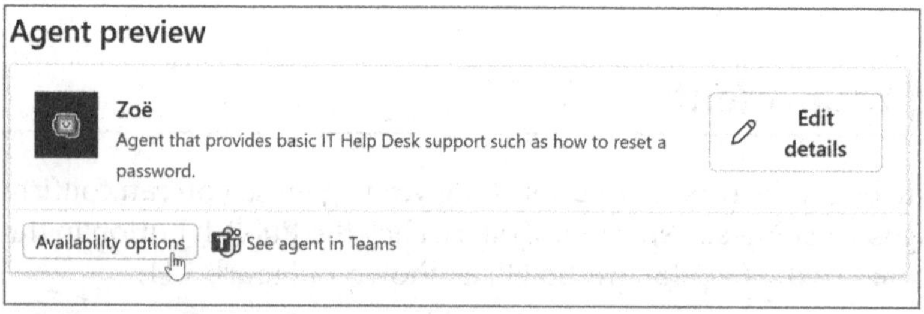

Agent preview

🔲 **Zoë**
Agent that provides basic IT Help Desk support such as how to reset a
password.   ✎ Edit details

[Availability options]   📧 See agent in Teams

Figure 3.13: Teams availability options

Clicking the Availability Options should bring up a new window, as shown in Figure 3.14. This window includes several choices for making your agent available to others through Microsoft Teams.

The first option is to get a link to your agent that you can share with others in your organization. First, you'll need to click the Manage Sharing link, and then search for a user or a group to share with. You'll then want to decide the level of permissions to grant. Your two options are Editor, so that they would have access to make modifications to your agent, or Viewer, which would only provide them with the ability to interact with your agent. You can choose to have Copilot Studio send an email by checking the Send an Email Invitation to New Users checkbox, as shown in Figure 3.15.

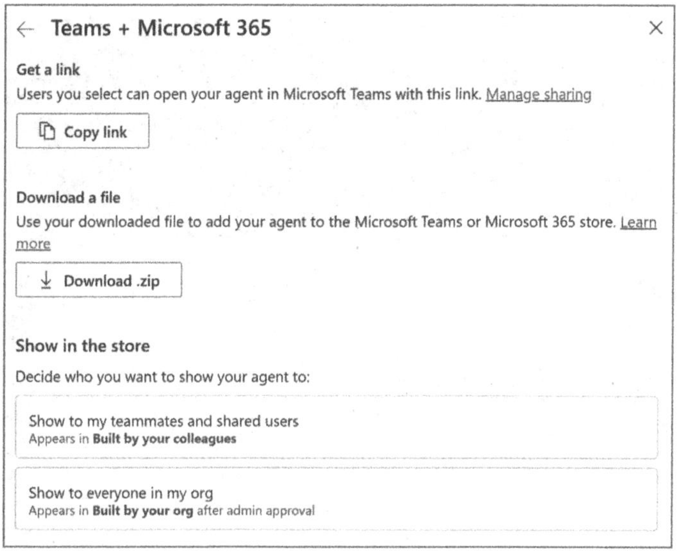

Figure 3.14: Teams sharing options

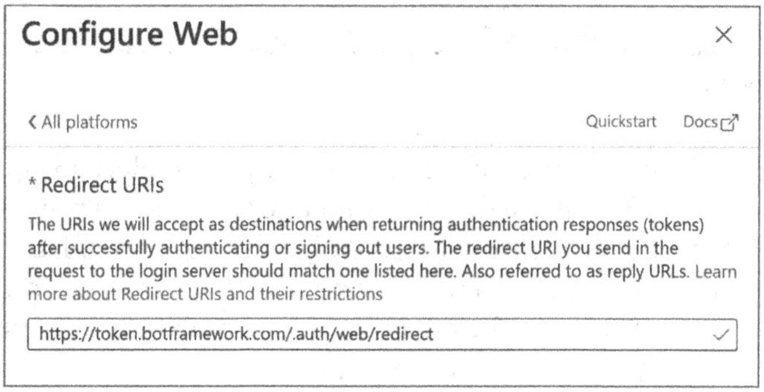

Figure 3.15: Editor vs. viewer permissions

> **NOTE** The user you choose will need to have access to the environment that your agent is stored in, and this is meant more for collaboration or agent co-authoring than publishing for your end user to consume.

Another option is to click the Download .zip link and then share that file with your colleague. They would then need to open their Microsoft Teams client and click the Apps link in the left-rail navigation. Then, they will need to click the Manage Your Apps link in the left navigation, and then click the Upload an App link in the top navigation. This will bring up a dialog box, as shown in Figure 3.16, where you can navigate your file system for the agent .zip file you just downloaded.

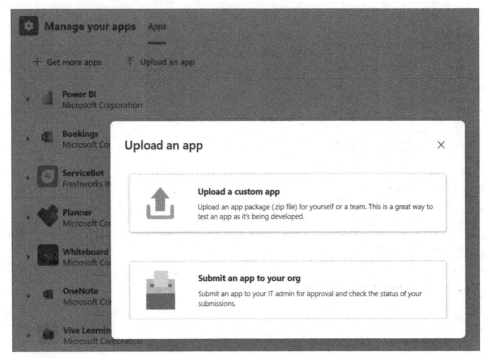

Figure 3.16: Uploading an app menu

Yet another option is to publish to Microsoft Teams, but only for a select group of users. If you click Show to My Teammates and Shared Users, as shown previously in Figure 3.14, you can start the process for making your agent available in Teams, but only to users that you've shared your agent with. However, you should note that even if you try to share with an Everyone Except External Users group, it will not show up for everyone in your organization.

A fourth option, which is the one we'll use, is Show to Everyone in My Org. This will make your agent available in the Teams app store so that everyone in your organization can add it to their Microsoft Teams client. Alternatively, this would also allow your Microsoft Teams Administrator to push this agent down to all clients. You might run into this scenario with all-employee-focused agents such as Human Resources, IT Services, Policies & Procedures, etc.

To get started, click the Show to Everyone in My Org button, which will bring up a new dialog, as shown in Figure 3.17. Notice that it generates a new

App ID. This App ID is a unique identifier for your application if you need to configure Teams Authentication with SSO. Remember, this is an optional step that is only required if you are using Azure AD v1 or an identify provider that does not support native SSO with Microsoft Teams.

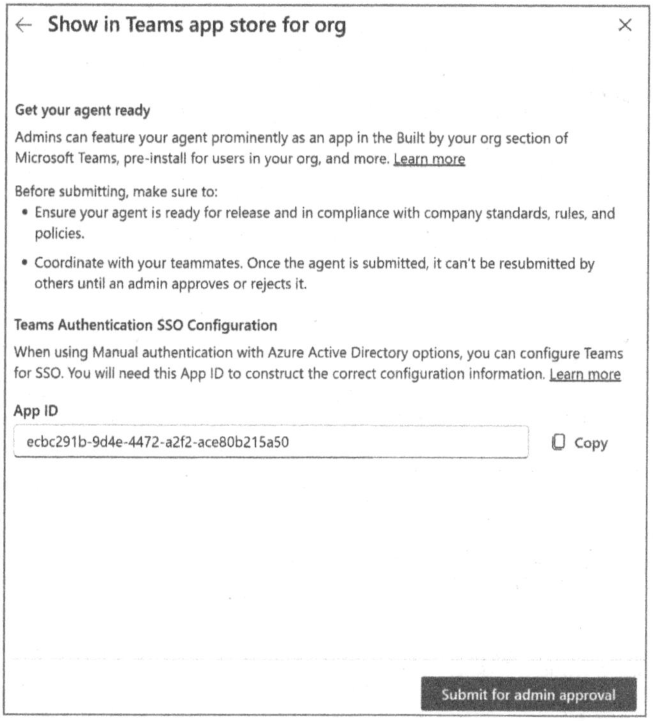

Figure 3.17: Submitting an agent for admin approval

Click the Submit for Admin Approval button to receive a notification confirming your intent of "Giving everyone access to this agent," as shown in Figure 3.18. This second reminder is a helpful nudge to ensure that you have thought through the use cases for your agent and that it definitely makes sense for all users to have access to it. If you needed to limit access—for example, if you were building a Manager Only agent—you could limit the availability of this agent to an Azure Entra group set up for just managers.

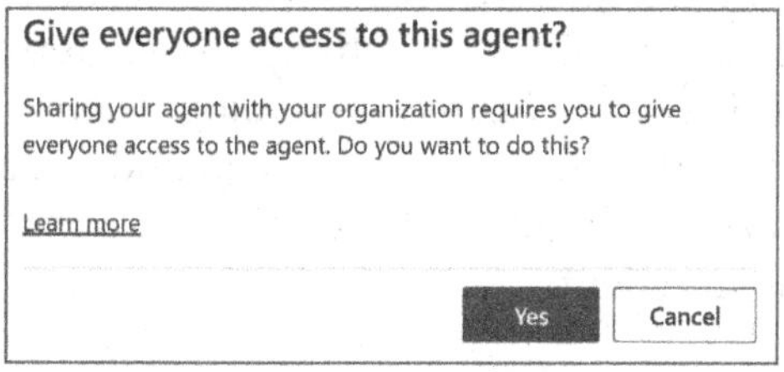

Figure 3.18: Giving everyone access

84 Chapter 3 ■ Publishing Your Copilot Agent

Click the Yes button, and you should see a confirmation similar to Figure 3.19, which informs you that your agent has been sent for approval to your Microsoft Teams administrator. Don't click Submit for Admin Approval again; otherwise, this will generate a new version of your agent.

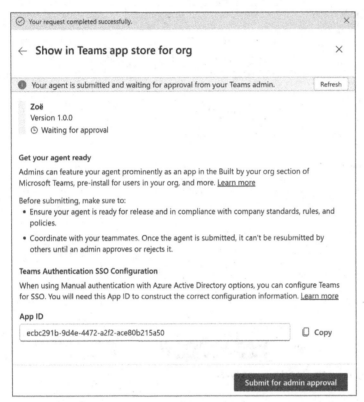

Figure 3.19: Submission confirmation

Next, if you are working in a production environment, you may need to engage someone from your Microsoft 365 Support Team to assist. Their role—or at least the permissions required—is Teams Administrator. You or your Microsoft Teams admin will need to navigate to the following URL: admin.teams.microsoft.com/policies/manage-apps, which should denote that one submitted application is pending approval. Your environment may denote more pending applications for review by an admin, as this is the same workflow for getting custom apps and first-party applications added to the Microsoft Teams app catalog. There is a search functionality that you can use to find your agent. When you find your agent, it will be listed as Blocked, as shown in Figure 3.20, which means that users cannot add it to their Microsoft Teams client.

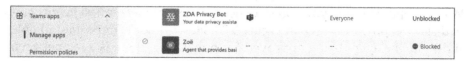

Figure 3.20: A blocked agent

If you click the app, you should see a screen, as shown in Figure 3.21, that allows your Microsoft Teams admin to either publish or reject the submission. Once the application has been approved, you will be able to further adjust the permissions should you decide that you would like to restrict who can access it. For example, rather than allowing everyone to have access, your Teams Administrator could restrict access to a specific group. Additionally, they can block the application from being used in the event that they find something harmful or malicious within the logic.

Figure 3.21: Publishing the Zoë app

Upon clicking the Publish button, you will see a confirmation dialog box, as shown in Figure 3.22. This is, once again, having you confirm that everyone with access to your Teams app store will have the ability to add this agent to their Microsoft Teams client. Click the Publish button to proceed.

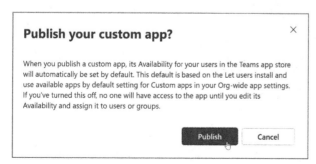

Figure 3.22: Confirming the publishing

Within Copilot Studio, you will see a notification of your request being completed successfully, as shown in Figure 3.23. However, it is important to note that despite the agent being approved for publishing, there is a lag between the approval and when the agent will become available. This may change over time, but it can take a few hours for the agent to appear in M365 Copilot. The publishing to Microsoft Teams, however, tends to be available within a few minutes of publishing.

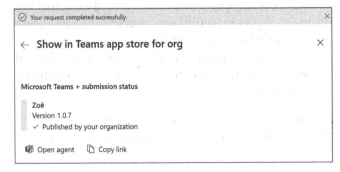

Figure 3.23: Confirming the publishing

Testing Your Agent in Microsoft Teams and M365 Copilot

What's left to do now is to test your agent to ensure that it's working outside of Copilot Studio. First, we will confirm that it works within Microsoft Teams. To do this, from within your Microsoft Teams client, click the Apps button on the left-side rail. Under the section titled Built for Your Org, you should now see your Zoë agent, as shown in Figure 3.24.

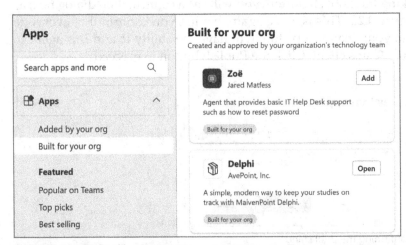

Figure 3.24: Finding the Zoë agent

You can click the Add button to add this agent to your Microsoft Teams application. You will see a dialog window, as shown in Figure 3.25, that displays the description text you provided, along with an outline of the features, version, author, etc. There is also the option to copy a direct link to this application if you want to share it with coworkers directly and get their feedback on your agent.

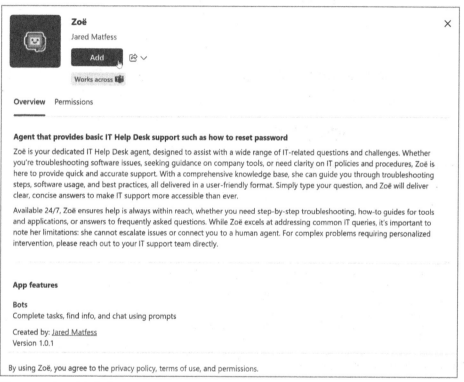

Figure 3.25: Adding the Zoë agent

Click the Add button from within this dialog, and you should receive a confirmation notification, as shown in Figure 3.26, informing you that your agent has been added successfully.

You can then click the Open button to be taken directly into a conversation with your agent. The Microsoft Teams experience is slightly different from what you may have observed in Copilot Studio, as, by default, agents deployed to Teams wait for the user to engage before sending a message. Therefore, you will want to ask your question or send a "Hi" to initiate the Greeting system topic. Alternatively, you could also just ask your question, as shown in Figure 3.27, and then receive the response back from Zoë based on information found in the defined knowledge source.

Figure 3.26: Adding the Zoë agent

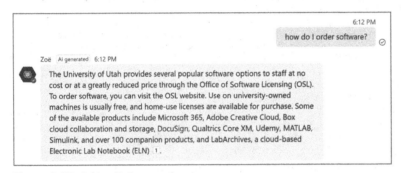

Figure 3.27: Asking Zoë a question

Now, let's confirm that our Zoë agent is working in Microsoft 365 Copilot. Note: to do so will require that you have a Microsoft 365 Copilot license assigned to the account that you are using to access the Copilot chat experience. Navigate to m365.cloud.microsoft, and then confirm that your chat experience is set to Work. You should then see a section called Agents in a right-hand navigation, as shown in Figure 3.28.

There are two ways for you to engage with your agent. You can click Zoë from the list of agents, or, alternatively, you can click the Chat with an Agent button in the lower-right corner of the chat window, as shown in Figure 3.29. This will bring up a dialog box that allows you to select from the agents you have access to.

If you click Zoë, it will then set the chat window to @mention that agent as part of your prompt, as shown in Figure 3.30. You can then type your question, such as "How do I reset my password," and then hit Enter. Your agent will then retrieve instructions for how to perform a password reset, as shown in Figure 3.30.

Chapter 3 ■ Publishing Your Copilot Agent 89

Figure 3.28: Agents in Copilot chat

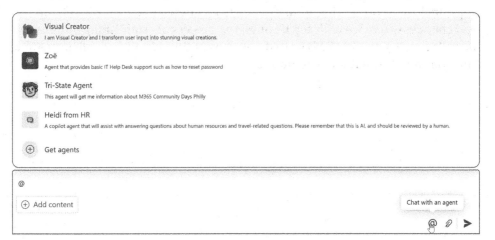

Figure 3.29: Chatting with an agent

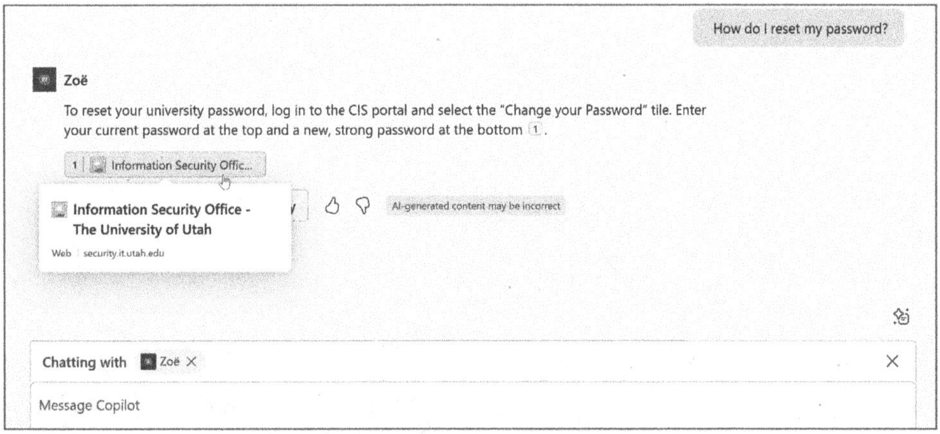

Figure 3.30: @mentioning the Zoë agent

Congratulations! You now have an agent that is accessible both through Microsoft Teams and M365 Copilot.

Conclusion

This chapter walked through the entire process of publishing your agent to Microsoft Teams and Microsoft 365 Copilot. We stepped through the various publishing options, including sharing with other makers who might need to coauthor your agent with you. We also covered making your agent available to your entire organization through the Teams App publishing process. This covered potentially working with your Microsoft Teams administrator to approve your publishing request. While that might have felt like a lot of effort, the governance required for most organizations would have included more steps, including promoting your agent across environments. This sets up the next chapter, where we will step through the process of establishing application lifecycle management (ALM) so that you can continue to add new features and functions and test without disrupting your users.

CHAPTER

4

Microsoft 365 Copilot Declarative Agents

As Microsoft progresses toward realizing its vision as the "Copilot Company," the marketing around copilots can be a bit confusing. In the previous chapter, we stepped through the process of using natural language to start building a Copilot agent. As mentioned, custom copilots are meant to be deployed for use cases where the user does not have a Microsoft 365 Copilot license. They can be developed for external parties like customers, partners, or employees who perhaps do not have work that keeps them stationed at a desk. There is a spectrum of Copilot agents, which vary in complexity and capabilities depending on your needs.

This chapter will discuss declarative copilot agents for Microsoft 365 Copilot, previously called copilot plugins. First, we will explain what a declarative agent is and the configuration files that make it work. Next, we'll walk through the steps for configuring a declarative copilot agent for knowledge retrieval using Agent Builder. And finally, we will summarize the differences between declarative agents and agents developed with the full Copilot Studio experience.

The Spectrum of Copilot Agents

The pace at which innovation is happening in this space makes defining categories difficult. By the time you are reading this book, there may even be new types of agents that have emerged, and the lines will continue to blur as the

91

92   **Chapter 4 ■ Microsoft 365 Copilot Declarative Agents**

technology matures. The kind of agent you decide to build will be driven by the business problem you are trying to solve, which will also have an impact on your overall solution in terms of tooling and technology. The three categories of agents, or rather the specific capabilities that they may have, are

- **Retrieval:** These agents can retrieve information from defined data sources. Their responses will be grounded in this data, meaning they will leverage the retrieval-augmented generation (RAG) pattern we discussed earlier. Their main purpose is to reason, summarize, and answer user questions using these defined data sources.

- **Task:** These agents can perform simple tasks on the user's behalf, such as completing repetitive tasks and automating certain activities using workflow technology.

- **Autonomous:** These agents can operate semi-independently, meaning that a user does not need to direct them to act. They can be planned dynamically based on conditions, such as a scheduled event or an invoked action, by defining an event such as receiving an email or a certain period of time after another action. These agents can also invoke and orchestrate other agents, in addition to being able to escalate tasks to a human when needed.

As mentioned, task, retrieval, and autonomous agents should not be considered rigidly distinct solution types. Instead, they encompass a spectrum of capabilities that your agent can perform. In real-world implementations, you should expect to see task agents that can also perform retrieval functions, showcasing the fluidity and interconnectivity of these roles.

M365 Copilot Agents

You may be asking yourself, "Why would I be building an agent for Microsoft 365 Copilot? Isn't Microsoft 365 Copilot meant to be an 'all-knowing' assistant?" The answer is yes and no. Remember, the way that M365 Copilot works is that it performs a graph-based search to further ground your prompt with additional data about you. The challenge with that approach is that there are certain activities or topics where you want to have a more structured and repeatable approach. For example, imagine you are asking Microsoft 365 Copilot to provide detailed information on your company's medical benefits. If you have a copy of a prior year's benefits in your OneDrive, it might reference that file instead of the most recent one hosted on your HR department's intranet site. You would want a technical solution that would ground the AI's response to a specific SharePoint site or set of documents instead of a wide-open search of everything you can access. These predefined technical functions can be developed by extending Microsoft 365 Copilot as an agent.

Declarative Copilot Agents

Microsoft uses the term *agents* to describe the ability to customize Microsoft 365 Copilot to help you deliver specific business needs. This allows you to start centralizing the delivery of business capabilities through a single UI entry point of Microsoft 365 Copilot. In a world where conversation is becoming the new UI, Copilot is the entry point for this seismic technological capability shift. There are two categories of agents from an extensibility perspective: agents you develop with Copilot Studio, as we covered in Chapter 2, and declarative agents, which can be created either through code or configuration.

When you create a declarative agent, you assemble the instructions, actions, and knowledge this AI assistant will use as a guide. Declarative agents run on the same AI orchestrator, foundation LLMs, and Responsible AI framework that power Microsoft 365 Copilot. We'll cover the AI orchestrator in more detail soon, but for now, think of it as a go-between for your agents and the core Microsoft AI infrastructure. Let's first break down the core elements included in a declarative Copilot agent as part of its configuration bundle, also known as the *agent app package*.

The Agent App Package

If you have ever developed a Microsoft Teams application, the term *app package* might be familiar, as declarative agents leverage a lot of the same publishing infrastructure. However, if not, an app package typically refers to a bundled file or set of files necessary to install and run an application on a specific platform. In this instance, you will be defining an app package for your declarative Copilot agent that will be hosted within the core infrastructure of Microsoft 365 Copilot. Within the app package, you will have the following components: the app manifest, app icons, declarative agent manifest, and the plugin manifest.

App Manifest

The app manifest helps configure and manage the agent's settings, capabilities, and permissions. It ensures that all necessary details about the agent are defined and structured in a standardized way. It is a text file included in your agent app package that describes how your app is configured, including its capabilities, required resources, and other parameters as you define them, including:

- **Metadata:** Unique identifiers, the version of this application, and the name.
- **Developer information:** Any information about the app developer you would like to include, such as name and perhaps contact information like an email address.

94 Chapter 4 ▪ Microsoft 365 Copilot Declarative Agents

- **Descriptions:** A detailed application description, including its purpose and other helpful information for someone to refer to if you were unavailable.

- **Icons:** URLs to the app's icons.

- **Capabilities:** Features like tabs, bots, and messaging extensions.

- **Permissions:** Required permissions for the app.

- **Web application info:** Entra ID Registered Application ID.

- **Valid domains:** Domains the app can interact with, for example, "yourcompany.com."

> **NOTE** Don't feel overwhelmed by all of these parameters. Copilot Studio streamlines the process of creating app manifests by automating many of the configurations and setups required.

App Icons

Perhaps one of the more straightforward elements of the agent app package is the *App Icons* configuration. This is where you can define your agent's design from a user experience perspective. If you recall the example in Chapter 2 of our Zoë agent, you can set a default icon that will be displayed as part of the chat interface and a border color to go around it. The intent is to make these agents appear as digital colleagues who can assist you with your daily work.

Declarative Agents Manifest

Similar to the app manifest, the declarative agent manifest is another configuration file accompanying your declarative agent. While the app manifest focuses more on the parameters needed to publish your agent, the declarative agent manifest defines what your agent can do. The declarative agent manifest describes the agent's behavior and its ability to understand and respond to user inputs. A declarative agent manifest file includes the following parameters:

- **Bot ID and name:** Unique identifier and name of the agent.

- **Starter prompts:** Initial instructions or greetings to guide user interactions. For example, "Where can I find benefits information?", "How many holidays do we get?", or "How do I submit a Help Desk ticket?"

- **Intents:** Defined purposes or goals behind user inputs. When configuring an intent, you need to define a name and trigger phrase:

- **Intent name:** A label that identifies the purpose of the user's input (e.g., "Greet," "Help," "Book Appointment").

    - **Trigger phrase:** Examples of what users might say to express that intent. These phrases help the AI recognize when the intent is being invoked (e.g., "hello," "hi," "I need assistance").

- **Actions:** The specific actions the agent should take when the intent is recognized (e.g., respond with a greeting, provide help information, start a booking process).

- **Capabilities:** Features and services the agent can provide. For example, you may include the ability for your agent to create images using Microsoft Designer.

- **Permissions:** Access levels required by the agent to function effectively.

Plugin Manifest

While not required for all declarative agents, this final configuration of the plugin manifest is needed when the agent requires integrations with external services or APIs. For example, suppose your agent needs to retrieve or send data to external systems (like a CRM, ERP, or any third-party service). In that case, a plugin manifest is essential to define these interactions. Here is an example of a JSON file that your agent might need to interact with a third-party application for a budget use case:

```
{
  "schema_version": "v1.1",
  "name": "Budget_Plugin",
  "description": "A plugin that interacts with REST APIs to manage
budgets.",
  "version": "1.0.0",
  "permissions": [
    "identity",
    "message.read",
    "team.readbasic"
  ],
  "capabilities": [
    "budget.query",
    "budget.create",
    "budget.update"
  ],
  "namespace": "com.yourcompanyname.myplugin",
  "localization": {
    "name": "MyPlugin",
    "description": "A plugin that interacts with REST APIs to manage
budgets."
```

```
    },
    "api": {
      "openapi": "https://yourcompanyname.com/openapi.json"
    }
  }
```

Configuration Options

While this book focuses on Copilot Studio, you should be aware that you can leverage the software tooling of your choice to build your declarative Copilot agent, as shown in Table 4.1.

Table 4.1: Tools to build declarative Copilot agents

TOOLING OPTION	DESCRIPTION
Teams Toolkit	The Microsoft Teams Toolkit is a set of tools and features designed to simplify the development of custom applications for Microsoft Teams. It integrates with Visual Studio Code and Visual Studio, providing developers with templates, automated registration, configuration, and debugging capabilities.
Copilot Studio	With Copilot Studio, you can either leverage the built-in Copilot to assist you with building your app package through natural language or use self-paced configuration within the UI.
Copilot Studio Agent Builder	This is a lightweight, natural language- and configuration-based approach to creating declarative Copilot agents from within the M365 Copilot interface. Behind the scenes, it uses Copilot Studio; however, the configuration is all performed through M365 Copilot.
SharePoint	Similar to the Copilot Studio Agent Builder experience, you can also define declarative agents directly from SharePoint. An everyday use case would be if you wanted to configure a declarative agent that only returns responses from a single SharePoint site, which you could configure directly within a SharePoint Document Library.

The AI Orchestrator

In the context of GenAI and specifically Microsoft 365 Copilot, an orchestrator is a component that manages and coordinates various AI tools and systems to work together effectively. Think of it as an orchestra conductor, ensuring each musician (or AI tool and service) plays harmoniously to create beautiful music. In Microsoft 365 Copilot, the orchestrator selects and runs the appropriate skills from various plugins to fulfill the user's requests.

As shown in Figure 4.1, the orchestrator sits between the customizations you are building and the core AI infrastructure, such as the backend LLMs that

Microsoft manages to help elegantly pull your solution together. For example, suppose you ask Copilot to summarize a meeting. In that case, the orchestrator will choose the right plugin to perform this task and ensure the response is accurate and relevant, leveraging both Microsoft-managed LLM models and the Responsible AI infrastructure delivered as part of the M365 Copilot service.

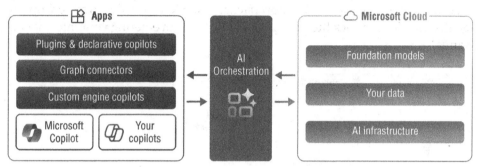

Figure 4.1: AI orchestration in M365 Copilot

Creating a Declarative M365 Copilot Agent with the Copilot Studio Agent Builder

So, let's put all this new learning to work by building a straightforward, retrieval-based M365 Copilot declarative agent to support answering questions regarding employee benefits-related information from within M365 Copilot. To begin, first navigate to m365.cloud.microsoft/chat/ to access the Copilot BizChat interface. Make sure that the Work/Web toggle is set to Work. Next, click the Create an Agent button in the Agents section in the right-hand corner of the BizChat interface, as shown in Figure 4.2, to launch the Agent Builder experience.

Figure 4.2: Create an Agent

> **NOTE** If you do not see the Create an Agent button, confirm that you are logged in with the Entra ID account that has an M365 Copilot license assigned to it.

Configuring Your Agent

This will open a new dialog window, as shown in Figure 4.3, with the Copilot Studio icon in the upper-left corner. Similar to what we saw in Chapter 2, you can describe the type of functionality that you are looking for, and Copilot will start to build your agent's functionality for you. For the purposes of applying what we just learned about the app package needed for a declarative Copilot agent, go ahead and click the Configure toggle to begin entering your information manually.

Figure 4.3: My Copilot Agent

After toggling the Agent Builder to Configure, you should see a screen similar to Figure 4.4, where you can enter information about your agent. There is also a drop-down option called Template, which allows you to pick from Microsoft-provided agent templates. These can be used as a starting point to develop your own Copilot agent.

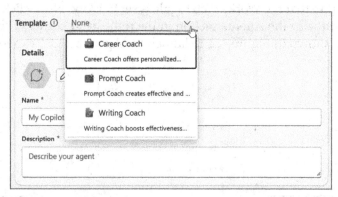

Figure 4.4: Configuring your agent

Let's start from scratch to help you understand the various options for creating this agent. Let's provide it a name, for example, **"Heidi from HR,"** and a description of **"A copilot agent that will assist with answering questions** about human resources and travel-related questions." If you scroll down a little bit further, you'll see a section for Instructions, which once again is where you direct the behavior of the copilot, including its tasks and how it completes them. Additionally, you can change the agent icon and background color by clicking the pencil icon next to the blue pentagon image with the conversation bubble, as shown in Figure 4.4. This will open a new dialog box where you can select either Change Icon or Change Background Color.

The icon must be in PNG format and cannot exceed 1 MB in file size. The Change Background Color option will bring up a color section tool, or you can enter either the Hex or Red Green Blue (RGB) values for the color. This additional personalization capability allows you to brand the agent with your organization's approved colors and make it more "human-like." While this is purely an optional step, you should consider personalization as a means to make your agent appear more accessible to your users.

Setting Instructions

A great tip for learning how to draft comprehensive instructions for your agent is to use Copilot for help. Just go to `copilot.microsoft.com` and ask it to help create instructions using natural language, and it will assist.

Per the tip, I sent this prompt to Copilot:

Can you please help me develop instructions to set for a copilot agent who will be returning HR and travel information? I am very concerned with AI returning bad or wrong information. Please create instructions that I can load into Copilot Studio. Please be as concise as possible and remove unnecessary language.

Copilot provided me with the following instructions, which are a fantastic starting point that can be further customized:

Responsible AI Guidelines for HR and Travel Copilot

Accuracy and Reliability

- Always cross-check information with reliable and up-to-date sources.
- Reference official company policies and verified databases to ensure accuracy.

Clarification and Transparency

- Ask for clarification if a user's request is ambiguous or incomplete.
- Provide clear context for shared information, including its relevance and source.

Updates and Notifications

- Regularly update the knowledge base with the latest HR and travel policies.
- Notify users about recent policy or guideline changes.

Ethical Boundaries

- Clearly state the limitations of the system's knowledge and capabilities.
- Direct users to human experts for detailed or sensitive inquiries.

Data Sensitivity and Privacy

- Handle sensitive information carefully and maintain confidentiality.
- Remind users not to share personal or sensitive details in chat.

Example Guidance

- **Prompt:** "What is our current leave policy?"
- **Response:** "Our leave policy allows 20 days of paid leave annually. Refer to the HR policy document [link] for details."
- **Prompt:** "Are there travel restrictions for our conference?"
- **Response:** "No current restrictions, but ensure you have a valid visa and review health advisories [link]."

NOTE The instructions should help guide Copilot toward an accurate response, but please remember to advise your users to review the output for accuracy.

Once you have modified the output provided by Copilot or have drafted your own set of instructions, paste that into the Instructions text box, as shown in Figure 4.5.

Figure 4.5: Agent Instructions

Configuring Knowledge

Rather than pointing to an Internet website as in Chapter 2, let's work with some internal content hosted on a SharePoint site. For this example, I have created a SharePoint Site called "HR" and have uploaded two files that we will use for our agent's knowledge source. The first will be an employee benefits document, and the second will be a "travel & expense" policy document. You can specify up to 20 knowledge sources, including SharePoint sites, folders, files, or Microsoft Graph connectors.

> **NOTE** You can find the *c04-Employee-Benefits-Overview.docx* file at www.wiley .com/go/copilotstudioqs. This chapter also uses the *c04-Travel-Expense-Policy. docx* file, which is also included in the ZIP file that can be downloaded for this book.

You'll notice within the Knowledge panel in Figure 4.6 that you can browse for files or folders across SharePoint Sites you can access. Additionally, a toggle allows you to enable or disable web content. When web content is enabled, the agent can use publicly available Internet information as a response. If an Internet source is included in that response, citations will be included and labeled with an icon to represent web content use. When web content is disabled, your agent will leverage the data it has been trained on and any knowledge sources you configure as part of the configuration.

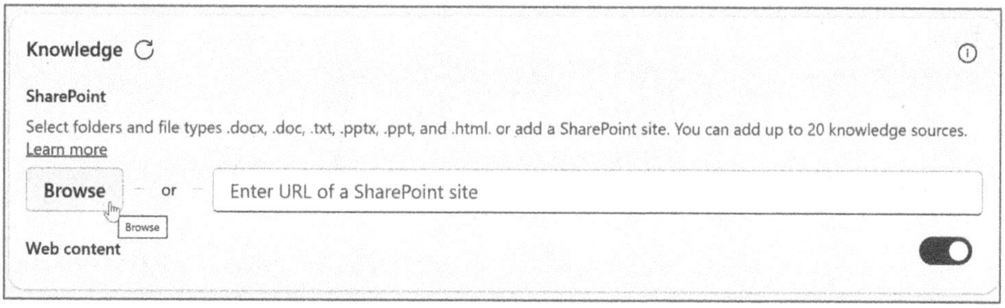

Figure 4.6: Configuring knowledge

By clicking the Browse button, you will open a dialog box, as shown in Figure 4.7, that allows you to browse the various Microsoft Teams you are either a member of or an owner of, as well as any SharePoint sites you can access. In larger environments, you might want to leverage the search functionality in the top-right corner of the dialog box to help locate the resource you are looking for. Another trick is if you modify a document and then click the Browse button, it should prioritize that resource in the Quick Access menu, as shown in Figure 4.7.

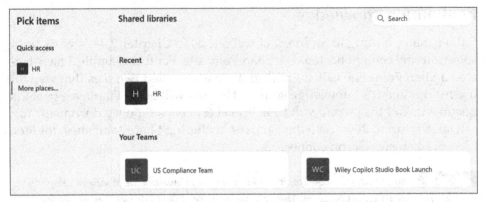

Figure 4.7: Browsing Teams and SharePoint sites

From here, you can click Site or Team where your files are stored, and then you can navigate the document libraries in that site collection. Note that you can select either a folder or individual documents. When you select files, as shown in Figure 4.8, the UI will reflect the number of files you have selected. Once you are done selecting files to be used for knowledge, click the Select button in the lower-right corner of the dialog box.

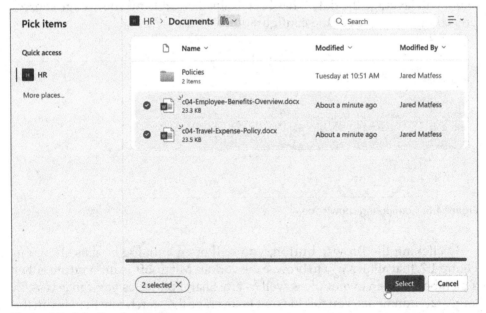

Figure 4.8: Selecting documents

Agent Builder supports document formats including Word, Excel, PowerPoint, PDF, text files, HTML, CSV, XML, OpenDocument, EPUB, Rich Text Format,

Apple iWork, JSON, YAML, and LaTeX. However, there are also certain file limits, as shown in Table 4.2.

Table 4.2: File size limitations

FILE TYPE	SIZE LIMIT
.docx	512 MB
.doc	150 MB
.pdf	512 MB
.txt	150 MB
.pptx	512 MB
.ppt	150 MB
.html	150 MB

Actions and Capabilities

Clicking Select, as shown in Figure 4.8, will take you back to the Agent Builder experience, where you can continue to scroll down past the Knowledge sources. Next, you'll notice two additional configuration options, as shown in Figure 4.9, which are "Actions." By the time you are reading this book, Microsoft will hopefully make this capability available to maintain similar functionality as the full Copilot Studio authoring experience. Actions, as we discussed in Chapter 2, are predefined tasks your agent can perform, like fetching data or triggering workflows. Below "Actions" is "Capabilities," another area that is likely to continue evolving as Microsoft continues to make investments. The example capability that you can see in Figure 4.9 at the time of writing is limited to Image Generator, which allows this agent to help create visual aids (like images and art) in response to user prompts.

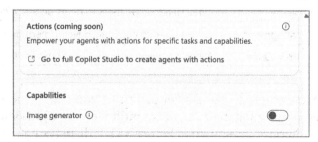

Figure 4.9: Actions and capabilities

Starter Prompts

Finally, below capabilities is a section called Starter Prompts, as shown in Figure 4.10. Starter prompts allow you to provide a visual cue to your users about how they might engage with your agent and the types of capabilities that it may have. The Title field will appear above the prompt, which is the message. While there isn't a limit to how many starter prompts you can create, from a user experience perspective, you do not want to create a scenario where users are scrolling through too many starter prompts to get to the message area. So, you will want to prioritize which prompts have the highest likelihood of being utilized and deprioritize any edge cases or what you believe would be less popular use cases.

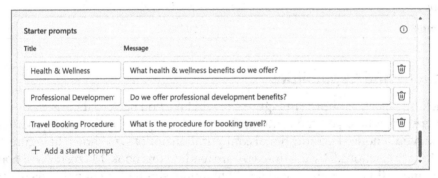

Figure 4.10: Starter prompts

Based on our HR Benefits and Travel Policy, the content here includes example prompts that help the user understand the types of questions they can ask and that likely have solutions, as shown in Table 4.3.

Table 4.3: Example starter prompts

TITLE	MESSAGE
Health & Wellness	What health & wellness benefits do we offer?
Professional Development	Do we offer professional development benefits?
Travel Booking Procedures	What is the procedure for booking travel?

Once you have entered your starter prompts, you should notice that your agent has been coming together as you've built it on the right-hand side of the Agent Builder interface. As shown in Figure 4.11, it displays your agent's name, the description you provided, and your starter prompts. When you click one of your starter prompts, you'll notice that it populates the message text in the chat window.

Figure 4.11: Selecting a starter prompt

Before clicking the Create button in the upper-right corner, confirm that everything is working as expected. Pick one of your starter prompts and click the Send Message button to submit it to the agent. You should see a response similar to what is displayed in Figure 4.12, including an answer and the document used to develop the response. You can continue conversing and asking more specific questions if you would like to understand how it works further.

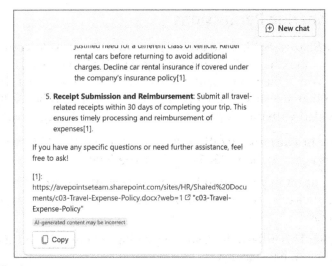

Figure 4.12: Testing your agent

Creating Your Agent

Now that you have tested your agent, go ahead and click the Create button in the upper-right corner. Note that the auto-save feature may cause the Create button

106 Chapter 4 ▪ Microsoft 365 Copilot Declarative Agents

to be disabled. If you make a small change to your agent, it should enable the Create button again. After a few seconds, you should receive a success message that your agent has been created, as shown in Figure 4.13.

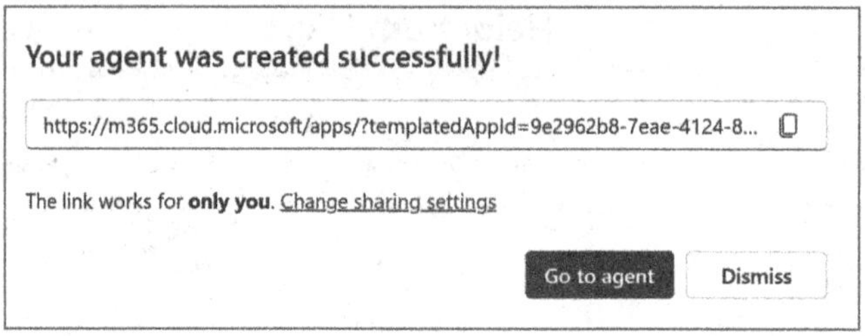

> **Your agent was created successfully!**
>
> https://m365.cloud.microsoft/apps/?templatedAppId=9e2962b8-7eae-4124-8... ⧉
>
> The link works for **only you.** <u>Change sharing settings</u>
>
> Go to agent   Dismiss

Figure 4.13: Agent created successfully

There are a couple of points to note: upon initial creation, this agent is only available to you. It is not available for others to access until you modify the share settings and provide them with the URL.

> **NOTE** If you receive a Responsible AI error message during the creation phase, you should check the Instructions section of your configuration for incompleteness or special characters that may be causing it to halt.

Adjusting Sharing Permissions

Click Change Sharing Settings to provide others with access to your new agent. When you click the Change Sharing Settings link, it also copies the URL to your clipboard for you to then share with others. Next, you'll see what should hopefully be a familiar sharing experience that you've seen in other M365 services. You are provided with three options for who to share this agent with:

- **Anyone in your organization:** Anyone that has this URL will be able to add this agent to their M365 Copilot experience.

- **Specify users in your organization via security groups:** This opens up a people-picker experience that is filtered to return only groups within your tenant.

- **Only you:** This is the default sharing setting, where only you, as the author of this agent, have access.

The sharing dialog box also provides a helpful reminder, as shown in Figure 4.14, that "People in your organization might not have to access some SharePoint files or folders." This is a useful reminder that you should always double-check the knowledge sources for your agent to ensure that your target user base has access to the files, folders, etc., accessed through your agent. Since this is a declarative copilot agent, there is no additional capability to leverage a superuser or impersonation functionality to access the backend files. This is a positive from a security perspective, as it cannot serve as a loophole to surface content that people shouldn't have access to, but it is another consideration for planning your solution.

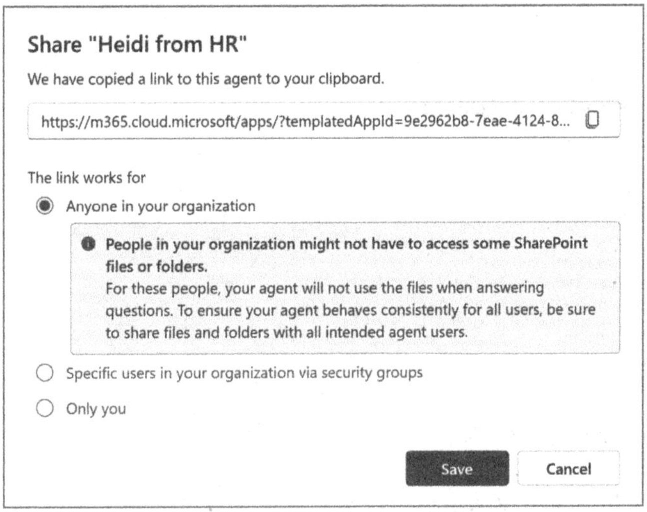

Figure 4.14: Agent sharing permissions

Either adjust the permissions for your agent if you intend to share it with others, or click the Cancel button to return to the previous screen, as shown in Figure 4.14. Instead of going to the agent, click the Dismiss button. You'll be back in the Agent Builder experience, with a few options:

- You can continue configuring or adjusting your agent, and then click the Update button at the upper-right corner to rebuild.
- You can click the ellipses in the upper-right corner and click the Delete button to discard your agent.
- You can select Download .zip file, which exports the agent package and downloads it to your computer, as shown in Figure 4.15.

Let's go ahead and download your agent to your computer so that we can review how the pieces come together. Extract all the content from your ZIP file, and you should see four files, as shown in Figure 4.16. The two files you should look at are the application manifest, which is the file called *manifest.json,* and the declarative manifest, which is the file called *declarativeAgent_0.json.* Next, we will review the contents of these files so you can start to understand how the pieces come together to host your agent.

108 Chapter 4 ■ Microsoft 365 Copilot Declarative Agents

Figure 4.15: Downloading the ZIP file

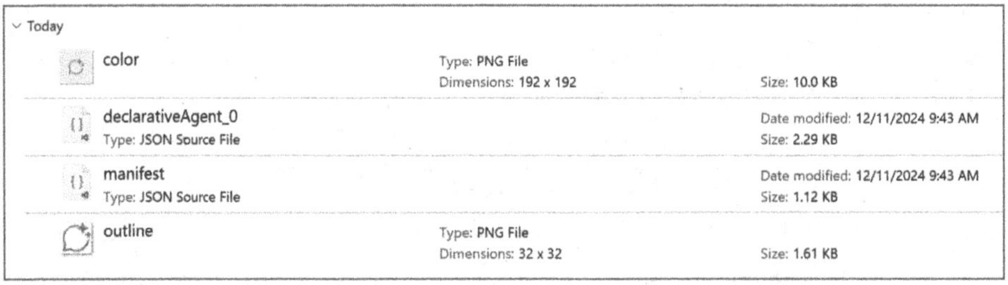

Figure 4.16: Extracting the ZIP file

Application Manifest: Manifest.json

Depending on how your workstation is configured, opening the *manifest.json* file may vary. For instance, it could automatically open in your web browser, especially if your system defaults to viewing .json files that way. Alternatively, it might open in an integrated development environment (IDE), such as Visual Studio or Visual Studio Code, if those are installed on your machine. If your machine does not have a default application registered to open .json files, you can always rely on a basic text editor such as Notepad on Windows or TextEdit on a Mac to render the contents.

Now, let's take a closer look at the structure of this file so you can see the configurations you made in Agent Builder and how those were translated to this JSON file. As you scroll through, you will notice the name and description of your agent. In this case, we named our agent "Heidi from HR," with a description of "A copilot agent that will assist with answering questions about human resources and travel-related questions." As you continue reviewing the file, another key parameter to pay attention to is `declarativeAgents`. This parameter specifies the *declarativeAgent_0.json* file, which is included in our ZIP file, and establishes a link between the application and the declarative agent manifest. This connection ensures that the application knows where to find the logic and configurations defined in the declarative agent file.

Another important parameter is `validDomains`. Here, you'll see it populated with URLs like `botframework.com` and `copilotstudio.microsoft.com`. These entries are important because they indicate the domains where the application's resources are hosted and accessed. By including these URLs, you explicitly define which domains are allowed to serve or interact with the application; in this case, they are Microsoft-managed domains where your agent will be running.

```
{
  "$schema": "https://developer.microsoft.com/en-us/json-schemas/teams/
vDevPreview/MicrosoftTeams.schema.json",
  "manifestVersion": "1.19",
  "copilotAgents": {
    "declarativeAgents": [
      {
          "id": "9f7e8381-c319-4b76-9117-b11b25ebcf89",
          "file": "declarativeAgent_0.json"
      }
    ]
  },
  "version": "1.0.0",
  "id": "4a95222a-6d5c-4226-b3c5-d360dd622820",
  "developer": {
    "name": "Jared Matfess",
    "websiteUrl": "https://go.microsoft.com/fwlink/?linkid=2138949",
    "privacyUrl": "https://go.microsoft.com/fwlink/?linkid=2138865",
    "termsOfUseUrl": "https://go.microsoft.com/fwlink/?linkid=2138950"
  },
  "name": {
    "short": "Heidi from HR",
    "full": "Heidi from HR"
  },
  "description": {
    "short": "Built using Microsoft Copilot Studio",
    "full": "A copilot agent that will assist with answering questions
about human resources and travel-related questions."
  },
  "icons": {
    "outline": "outline.png",
    "color": "color.png"
  },
  "accentColor": "#E0F6FC",
  "permissions": [
    "identity",
    "messageTeamMembers"
  ],
  "validDomains": [
    "*.botframework.com",
    "*.*.botframework.com",
    "copilotstudio.microsoft.com",
```

Chapter 4 ▪ Microsoft 365 Copilot Declarative Agents

```
      "copilotstudio.preview.microsoft.com"
  ],
  "webApplicationInfo": {
    "id": "00000000-0000-0000-0000-000000000000",
    "resource": "https://copilotstudio.microsoft.com"
  }
}
```

The DeclarativeAgent_0.json File

Now that you've seen some of the high points for the application manifest file,
let's look at the *declarative_agent0.json* file. When you open the *declarativeAgent_0.
json* file, you'll notice that this is where much of the agent's core functionality
is defined, as shown here:

```
{
  "id": "9f7e8381-c319-4b76-9117-b11b25ebcf89",
  "actions": [],
  "conversation_starters": [
    {
      "text": "What health \u0026 wellness benefits do we offer?",
      "title": "Health \u0026 Wellness "
    },
    {
      "text": "Do we offer professional development benefits?",
      "title": "Professional Development"
    },
    {
      "text": "What is the procedure for booking travel?",
      "title": "Travel Booking Procedures "
    }
  ],
  "name": "Heidi from HR ",
  "description": "A copilot agent that will assist with answering
questions about human resources and travel-related questions.",
  "instructions": "Responsible AI Guidelines for HR and Travel Copilot\
nAccuracy and Reliability\nAlways cross-check information with reliable
and up-to-date sources.\nReference official company policies and
verified databases to ensure accuracy.\nClarification and Transparency\
nAsk for clarification if a user\u0027s request is ambiguous or
incomplete.\nProvide clear context for shared information, including its
relevance and source.\nUpdates and Notifications\nRegularly update the
knowledge base with the latest HR and travel policies.\nNotify users
about recent policy or guideline changes.\nEthical Boundaries\nClearly
state the limitations of the system\u0027s knowledge and capabilities.
\nDirect users to human experts for detailed or sensitive inquiries.
\nData Sensitivity and Privacy\nHandle sensitive information carefully
and maintain confidentiality.\nRemind users not to share personal or
```

Chapter 4 ■ Microsoft 365 Copilot Declarative Agents 111

```
sensitive details in chat.\nExample Guidance\nPrompt: \u0022What is our
current leave policy?\u0022\nResponse: \u0022Our leave policy allows
20 days of paid leave annually. Refer to the HR policy document [link]
for details.\u0022\nPrompt: \u0022Are there travel restrictions for our
conference?\u0022\nResponse: \u0022No current restrictions, but ensure
you have a valid visa and review health advisories [link].\u0022",
  "capabilities": [
    {
      "name": "WebSearch"
    },
    {
      "name": "OneDriveAndSharePoint",
      "items_by_sharepoint_ids": [
        {
          "site_id": "7caf08ec-f8ea-4ac8-a848-eb3533b8d66d",
          "web_id": "a04c16b2-f8a2-4e70-bc70-4f55f9e26938",
          "list_id": "d4fe9d85-f66b-4dd8-b08a-599681ae380a",
          "unique_id": "2f370da8-10c4-4ff7-b578-3e4a7c46f7f2"
        },
        {
          "site_id": "7caf08ec-f8ea-4ac8-a848-eb3533b8d66d",
          "web_id": "a04c16b2-f8a2-4e70-bc70-4f55f9e26938",
          "list_id": "d4fe9d85-f66b-4dd8-b08a-599681ae380a",
          "unique_id": "f9aa30dc-a2fe-4b99-9df0-e1c50bc4e14d"
        }
      ],
      "items_by_url": []
    }
  ]
}
```

The JSON structure outlines the essential parameters that govern how the agent behaves and interacts with users. As you examine the file, one of the first things you'll encounter is the `conversation_starters` parameter. This was referred to as "starter prompts" within the Agent Builder experience, which defines the initial prompts or suggestions that guide the user's interaction with the agent. The `text` parameter within the file is the actual prompt, whereas the `title` parameter is the heading that appears above the text, as we saw earlier in Figure 4.11.

Further down, you'll find the `instructions` parameter. This is where we set the instructions for how to handle user prompts and explicitly define your agent's behavior. Another interesting parameter is `web_search`. You'll notice that this parameter doesn't have a value assigned. This absence indicates that the agent is not configured to perform web searches or fetch information from the Internet. In this case, since we are handling HR-related questions, we consciously decided not to allow the Internet to serve as a knowledge source for our agent.

Chapter 4 ▪ Microsoft 365 Copilot Declarative Agents

Finally, look at the `OneDriveAndSharePoint` parameter. Here, you'll see Globally Unique Identifiers (GUIDs) for the files you've designated as knowledge sources. For those of you who have worked with SharePoint over the years, you'll probably be familiar with the internal names of site, web, and list. Essentially, in this configuration, you are specifying the SharePoint Site Collection, the Site, the List, and the final parameter, `unique_id`, which represents the individual documents that we selected for our knowledge sources.

Code Versus Configuration

You might be asking yourself if these files can be edited or even created manually. The answer is yes, you can. However, as you've likely noticed, a significant amount of the heavy lifting is already done for us through the Agent Builder configuration. Agent Builder is designed to streamline the process, reducing the chances of errors and saving you time. For example, configurations that can be tedious and error-prone, such as tracking down the GUIDs for Sites, Lists, files, etc., are automatically handled during the configuration process. By removing these potential configuration errors, Agent Builder lets you focus more on higher-value tasks, such as building out your agent's functionality, rather than on lower-value runtime configuration. However, this also should help shed light on how your full-code developers might build the same functionality using the Teams Toolkit, as mentioned earlier.

Test Driving Your Agent

Now that we have explored what makes your agent work from a configuration perspective, go ahead and try it. Go to `m365.cloud.microsoft/chat`, toggle to the Work setting, and you should see your agent on the right-hand side, as shown in Figure 4.17. You have the option to pin this agent by clicking the pushpin icon so that it will appear above the horizontal ruler. This will help you prioritize agents and make them easier to find when you become inundated with multiple agents for all sorts of tasks. If you click the three-dot button, the only option available is to uninstall the agent, which will delete it from the Cosmos DB in your tenant and remove it from the right rail.

Click the Heidi from HR text to toggle to the agent view. From here, you can choose to select one of the starter prompts or craft your own to confirm everything is working as configured. Try the starter prompt, **"What health & wellness benefits do we offer?"** and you should see a response similar to what is shown in Figure 4.18, along with the referenced file from where it grounded its response.

Chapter 4 ■ Microsoft 365 Copilot Declarative Agents 113

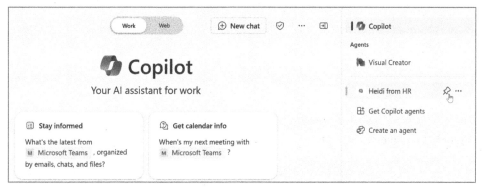

Figure 4.17: The Heidi from HR agent

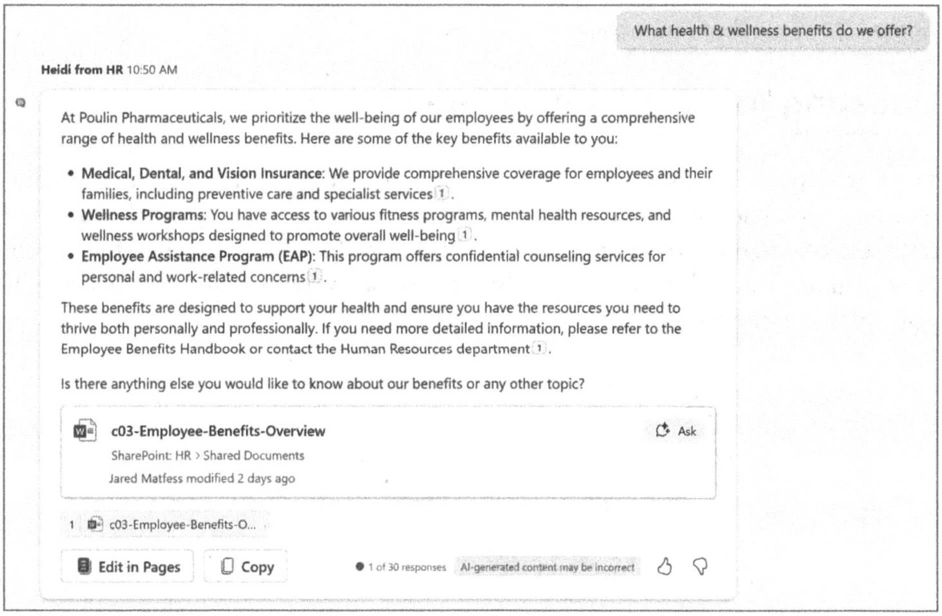

Figure 4.18: Benefits

You might have noticed an icon within the panel featuring the source document with a conversation icon and the word "Ask." This allows you to further interact with the document using GenAI to gain additional insights. Clicking the Ask button will produce a list of suggested prompts, as shown in Figure 4.19.

If you click List Key Points, you'll notice that it pre-populates the chat window with the prompt, "Give me a bulleted list of a key points from," as shown in Figure 4.20. When you send your prompt, Copilot then includes a reference to the Employee Benefits document originally returned. Rather than searching across all knowledge sources, which, in this example, would just be two documents, the bullet points will be based on the one document included in the prompt.

Figure 4.19: Suggested prompts

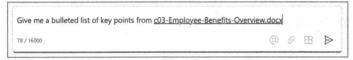

Figure 4.20: Grounding your prompt

Updating Your Declarative Agent

There may be times after you've deployed your agent when you need to make modifications, such as adding additional instructions or changing the knowledge data sources. To edit an existing agent, you'll need to once again click the Create New Agent button, but this time, click the drop-down menu to select one of your existing agents, as shown in Figure 4.21.

Figure 4.21: Selecting an existing agent

This will bring up the Agent Builder configuration screen with the current parameters. You can then choose to make any necessary adjustments, such as changing the name, description, icon, starter prompts, etc. Once completed, you can click the Update button, as shown in Figure 4.22, to publish your changes. Then, just like before, you can choose to adjust the sharing permissions or access your agent from the Copilot chat experience.

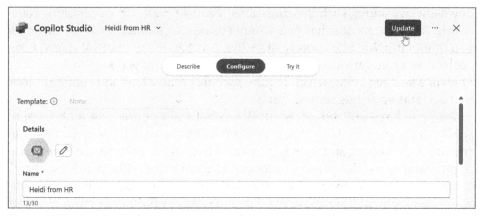

Figure 4.22: Updating your agent

Copilot Studio Agent Builder Limitations

As Uncle Ben famously said in *Spider-Man*, "With great power comes great responsibility." Similarly, with configuration-based approaches, we might say that with great simplicity comes some limitations. While the Agent Builder experience in Copilot Studio is incredibly powerful, there are some limitations compared to building agents using the full Copilot Studio at `copilotstudio .microsoft.com`. While these limitations are subject to change over time, it is important to know that Agent Builder might not always have feature parity. Therefore, you might want to check Microsoft's official documentation before building your solution to ensure you're aware of any potential limitations.

> **NOTE** Microsoft's official Agent Builder documentation can be found at `learn .microsoft.com/en-us/microsoft-365-copilot/extensibility/ copilot-studio-agent-builder`.

Data Storage

One of the fundamental differences between declarative agents developed using Agent Builder and Copilot Studio agents is that they are stored in different places. When you create a declarative agent using Agent Builder, the configuration files are stored in a Cosmos DB instance within your Microsoft 365 tenant. Copilot agents developed using Copilot Studio are stored within an environment in your Power Platform Dataverse. The hosting location of your agents impacts downstream features, such as permissions, sharing options, and publishing capabilities. This also means that you cannot support Customer Lockbox, meaning you cannot provide Microsoft with secure direct access to your solutions. Also, declarative agents are incompatible with customer-managed keys in Azure Key Vault or Managed HSM, which require specific permissions and configurations that declarative agents cannot handle.

You may have noticed a few subtleties between publishing with Copilot Studio and Agent Builder. When you publish your agent, it's almost akin to creating a document and managing access to groups. I can foresee this paradigm changing as enterprise customers find themselves with "mission-critical" declarative agents managed by individual users and not through a gated software development lifecycle (SDLC) process. Agent Builder is more of a user productivity capability than an enterprise solution, which means you will need to develop internal governance to help guide users on how to manage these powerful but limited solutions.

Application Lifecycle Management

We will dig into true application lifecycle management later, but for now, it is important to know that it is challenging to create any application lifecycle management (ALM) process with declarative copilots. At a high level, ALM is about ensuring that you have separate instances of your technical solutions to ensure that you are not "developing in production." This means that if a user finds an issue with your technical solution, you are not making changes to a solution while users are also interacting with it. With solutions developed using Copilot Studio, you can establish ALM processes and move solutions through Power Platform environments. However, that same concept does not exist with declarative agents.

User Experience

The last limitation you should be aware of is that declarative agents don't support topics, as we covered in Chapter 2. Declarative agents are meant to be single-task focused, executing predefined tasks or actions. They do not offer the same flexibility or complexity as multi-topic solutions. This means declarative agents are great for executing specific commands, such as our example, which can provide users with information on benefits or policies. They start to fall when you need to insert logic or multi-conversational workflows to complete tasks. Essentially, they work best in scenarios where the interaction is straightforward and doesn't require the nuanced adaptability that topics bring to full Copilot experiences.

When to Use Declarative Agents

As Microsoft continues to invest in agents, you should anticipate the gap in feature parity between declarative agents and Copilot Studio agents to grow smaller. However, at the time of writing, there is a significant difference between the two types of agents. When weighing your options, you should consider the following parameters, as outlined in Table 4.4.

Table 4.4: Comparison of declarative agents vs Copilot Studio agents

CONSIDERATION	DECLARATIVE AGENT	COPILOT STUDIO AGENT
Agent complexity	Simple application logic, such as basic retrieval or simple task completion.	More complex application logic, including advanced error handling and multiple conversation dialogues.
User interaction	Limited dialogue needed to complete tasks. Estimate 2–3 prompts per activity.	More in-depth conversations, multiple topics, and extended dialogue needed to complete tasks.
Maintenance	Limited maintenance required to support the use case.	Full application lifecycle management required to support the agent, including gated reviews of functionality.
Scalability	The agent is relatively contained with limited functionality.	Will need to scale to support multiple personas or departments and potentially will need to connect to several systems.

As you can see from the table, declarative agents work best for simple tasks that don't require extensive context or ongoing dialogue with your users. The level of complexity is much more streamlined, and therefore, you would anticipate very little configuration to build. Copilot Studio agents are meant for more complex tasks, such as tasks with multi-step processing or the need to personalize based on your users. While these guidelines are not meant to be set in stone, they should hopefully serve as a guide for informing where you start. Another consideration is that if you are on the fence about which solution makes the most sense, you could consider starting with a declarative agent to first prove out your idea or use case, and then transition to a full Copilot Studio agent if needed to satisfy your use case.

Conclusion

In this chapter, we explored the different categories of agents that you might develop. We then did a deep dive into the foundational elements of declarative agents for Microsoft 365 Copilot, focusing on their technical structure and understanding how manifest files define their capabilities. Through a hands-on walkthrough, we demonstrated how to build an HR "Benefits & Travel" policy agent leveraging content stored in a SharePoint Library. We also covered some of the differences between declarative agents and agents developed using the full Copilot Studio experiences. In the next chapter, we will walk through application lifecycle management for your agents to ensure that you have a repeatable process for developing and publishing agents in your organization.

CHAPTER 5

Planning ALM for Your Copilot Agents

The role of IT in many organizations is a careful balance between enabler and gatekeeper. On the enabler side, IT plays a key role in helping to introduce new technologies, automate business processes, and provide the business with access to data to make important decisions. IT's core responsibilities include safeguarding enterprise systems against cyber threats, ensuring data privacy, and complying with regulations (e.g., GDPR, HIPAA, PCI-DSS). Without context, the people within a business may sometimes view the IT team as making it difficult to get their work done, when in reality, the IT team is actually trying to help protect the business.

In the same vein, balancing business enablement with protecting the business from itself is an important concept of enabling application lifecycle management (ALM). As we discussed earlier, Copilot Studio targets makers who do not always have formal education or experience with IT. With the examples in Chapters 3 and 4, agents were deployed directly into a production-like environment. The goal in this chapter is to help establish ALM so that you can deploy agents and have a safe path to make updates or changes without impacting users as they continue to interact with your agent. We'll start by helping you understand the ALM framework that will enable this safe development and deployment process. We'll then cover the need for an environment strategy to put this idea into practice, followed by the technical details needed to bring your vision to life.

119

The ALM Framework

Before jumping into any of the technical details around ALM, it's helpful to step through the scenario that we are hoping to achieve. The best way to think of this is to walk through a likely business scenario and observe how you might improve that process using technology. To start, imagine that your Human Resources (HR) group has asked you to build an agent to help answer benefits-related questions. This is quite similar to the use case covered in Chapter 4. However, based on the availability of members from HR, they've asked for you to be relatively flexible with the requirements and that they would like to learn from employee interactions to help drive functionality. In other words, they would like you to take an iterative-based approach to introducing new functionality and have monthly releases of those new capabilities.

Building the initial functionality is not a problem. Still, your mind wanders and questions how you would continue adding new features and functions while users interact with your agent. What if you accidentally introduce a breaking change or notice that the agent is returning incorrect answers when you add a new knowledge source? The last thing you want to do is create a new feature and then have it generate support tickets or, even worse, upset your users or make them feel turned off by the technology. You know that your IT developers have a process for making changes to other applications, and you wonder if you can apply their best practices to building custom agents. The good news is that you can, and it starts with adopting ALM for your development process.

If you aren't familiar with ALM, the simplest definition is that it is an IT framework that encompasses the end-to-end processes involved in the development, deployment, and maintenance of software applications. It integrates requirements gathering, software development, testing, and continuous delivery to streamline the entire application lifecycle. We will cover each of these core stages of ALM next:

- Requirements gathering
- Design
- Development
- Testing
- Deployment
- Maintenance and retirement

Requirements Gathering

Technology is implemented to solve business problems, and to understand business problems, you need to engage with your stakeholders. Your business stakeholders will influence what you build and how you do so.

ALM starts with requirements gathering. This phase is where you will identify and agree upon the scope of your agent, including authoritative knowledge sources, tone, and any boundaries you might need to set to ensure a positive user experience. Requirements gathering will also help define the timeline, which ultimately could impact which features are prioritized and included in the initial release and which features might not be included or may be introduced later.

If you are doing Agile-based development, you may find yourself repeating the requirements gathering phase for each of your sprints, whereas, in Waterfall, it might be a single exercise culminated by the approval of a document or deliverable. The requirements gathering phase sets up the subsequent design phase and your whole project.

> **NOTE** Project management methodologies such as Waterfall and Agile are beyond the scope of this book. But at a high level, with Waterfall project management, you do not begin development until you have defined all the requirements, resulting in a long timeline between requirements and working code. Agile project management is more iterative, where you show progress and possibly make changes at regular intervals rather than at the end of the project.

Design

In the design stage of ALM, you take the requirements and begin mapping them out to determine how you will build your solution. This is where you start making architectural decisions, such as potential integrations with third-party applications, handling authentication and authorization, and any regulatory or security considerations that might impact your solution. In the design phase, you should also start thinking about how to develop your solution and what a release cycle might be.

The project management approach will also be impacted based on whether you follow a Waterfall process, where all requirements are fully defined before starting development, or if you will follow an Agile methodology, where you will release value iteratively. An important decision when designing agents is understanding which channels you might publish to meet your users where they are—whether it be Microsoft Teams, a custom app, a website, Facebook, Slack, or something else. Additionally, as noted in Chapter 4, you should also consider the complexity, user interaction, maintenance, and scalability of your agent, which will also help with determining if you should build a declarative agent or will require a full Copilot Studio agent.

Development

In the development stage of ALM, you start to bring your design to life through a combination of configuration and potential full-code development, depending on your business use case or any integrations with third-party applications. This stage is one of the core concepts we will cover in more detail later in this chapter, as it will drive your environment structure, managed versus unmanaged solutions, and potential reusable components.

Additional high-value activities during the development phase that do not involve writing code or performing configuration include reviewing your approach with others, confirmation that your solution aligns with best practices, and any governance or compliance checks warranted based on your organization or industry. You should also start documenting your solution following your organization's solution documentation requirements. This enables you to capture any complicated configuration while it is still fresh in your mind and is easier to complete.

> **NOTE** Don't worry if some of these phrases, such as "environment structure" and "managed versus unmanaged," are unfamiliar; they will be covered in greater detail later in this chapter.

Testing

The testing phase within ALM is where the rubber hits the proverbial road, as they say. This is when you invite your users to test your agent to confirm that it meets both their written and sometimes unwritten requirements. Before entering testing, you'll want to ensure that you have a defined process for capturing user feedback and prioritizing the input into any enhancement requests that should be made to your agent. Helping your business champion understand the need to balance "must haves" versus "nice to haves" when it comes to user testing will help provide a path out of the testing phase. Additionally, your environment strategy will enable your users to test without impacting them as you make additional changes to your agent based on their feedback. This phase should last until you receive a sign-off from your business stakeholders or users testing your agent.

Deployment

After receiving sign-off, you should be ready to make your agent available to a broader user base. We stepped through the process of publishing your agent to Microsoft Teams in Chapter 4, which was a straightforward one-environment process. However, for production environments, you will likely have a multi-environment architecture requiring additional setup and configuration. Additionally, as you promote your agent into production, you will also want to ensure that safeguards are in place to prevent someone from making a change in production and bypassing your entire deployment process. We'll step more into deploying your solution across environments later in this chapter.

Maintenance and Retirement

Depending on the lifecycle of your agent, you may find yourselves adding new features and functionality over time. This might be through approved maintenance or deployment windows as defined by your organization or as instructed by your business champions. Some organizations have formal change control boards that may require you to submit detailed information about your changes to help evaluate the impact of your change before deployment. This is meant to protect users from an unplanned breaking change and ensure that the development team adheres to your organization's best practices and requirements.

An additional consideration for how you approach maintenance will also likely be driven by the project management methodology adopted by your organization. For companies that typically run IT projects using the Waterfall methodology, maintenance activities may be run as mini-projects, where requirements are formally documented, and there are multiple stages of review and approval before any new functionality is deployed to production—outside of any sort of bug fixes that come up. However, if your company typically runs IT projects using an Agile methodology, you may also see new features and functions delivered more frequently and with fewer approval gates.

Eventually, when your agent has outlived its need or is replaced by newer technology, you may also find yourself retiring the agent from production and exporting its configuration to a file for archival purposes. It is helpful to have this retirement plan defined in advance of that milestone so that you're executing against a playbook versus creating that playbook on the fly.

ALM Summary

While the intent of this book is to help get you up and running with Copilot Studio agents quickly, it is important to ensure that you do so in a way that helps treat agents like a true enterprise IT service. Therefore, it is important to plan early for how you will integrate this into your existing procedures for application lifecycle management. Or it will hopefully serve as a catalyst to converse with your IT team about creating an ALM framework for low-code solutions such as agents such as Power Apps, Power Automate flows, and others.

Power Platform Environments

Now that you understand the stages within a typical ALM framework, let's examine one of the foundational elements for putting this all together: Power

124 Chapter 5 ▪ Planning ALM for Your Copilot Agents

Platform environments. As we touched on earlier, environments are spaces within the Microsoft Power Platform where you can store, manage, and share your organization's business data, apps, chatbots, agents, and flows. Each environment acts as a container to separate apps with different roles, security requirements, or target audiences for those resources. Environments play a key role in ensuring that development activities can be separated from user testing and agent production usage. Therefore, it is important to have an environment strategy in place to enable makers to build technical solutions while also providing the necessary guardrails to ensure they do so in compliance with policies and governance.

Environment Strategy

While every organization operates slightly differently, Table 5.1 outlines a recommended starting point to establish your environment strategy to support agents as well as other Power Platform development activities.

Table 5.1: Recommended Power Platform environments

ENVIRONMENT	PURPOSE
Developer/ Sandbox	This is an environment that developers have full access to and are able to create new solutions and modify them with minimal overhead. Typically, each developer will have their own environment or be added to a shared Sandbox environment to enable experimentation of features and tooling without the worry of impacting any users or production workloads.
Integration (optional)	For some enterprise environments or when you may have multiple developers working on a project, Integration is a helpful environment to have as a separation between where developers are actively working and user acceptance testing (UAT), where you'll be inviting business users to test. This allows you to have a stable environment for developers to test their work and confirm any integrations with third-party applications.
User Acceptance Testing	This environment is crucial for stakeholders and end users to validate the changes and ensure they meet the requirements before going live. It's a critical step for catching any issues that might not have been identified in earlier testing phases.
Production	The final environment where the application is deployed for end users. This environment should be stable and thoroughly tested to minimize any disruptions.

Environment Costs

An additional consideration for your environment strategy is the costs associated with multiple environments. Your developer environments typically come with

Chapter 5 ■ Planning ALM for Your Copilot Agents   125

Power Apps Developer plans (which were free at the time this was written); however, the additional environments will incur both Microsoft-related costs for the Dataverse storage and user licenses, in addition to IT administrative costs to govern those environments.

NOTE Additional information about Power Apps licensing can be found at `microsoft.com/en-us/power-platform/products/power-apps/pricing`.

Managed Environments

Power Platform has certainly lowered the bar to entry when it comes to who can create advanced technical solutions using configuration instead of code. With that impressive capability has come the need to provide IT administrators with greater controls to help ensure that their makers can focus on building value while also complying with the organization's governance and security requirements. Microsoft has invested in creating additional governance capabilities designed to help IT administrators manage Power Platform at scale with more control, visibility, and less effort. Included in this capability are the features outlined in Table 5.2.

Table 5.2: Managed environments premium features

FEATURE	DESCRIPTION
Environment Groups	Allow you to define a logical container to organize and manage multiple Power Platform environments as a cohesive unit. This helps streamline governance, apply policies consistently, and get consolidated insights across all environments within the group.
Limit Sharing	Helps administrators control how widely canvas apps can be shared within an organization. This feature allows you to set rules and restrictions on app sharing, ensuring that sensitive or critical apps are accessible only to the right users.
Weekly Usage Insights	Provides a snapshot of app and user activity within Power Platform on a weekly basis. These insights help administrators monitor how apps are being used, identify trends, and make informed decisions about resource allocation, user training, and app development.
Data Policies	Help safeguard your organization's data by controlling how data can be shared across different environments and connections. With data policies, you can define which connectors can be used and how data is accessed, ensuring that sensitive information remains protected and compliant with organizational standards.

Continues

Chapter 5 ▪ Planning ALM for Your Copilot Agents

Table 5.2 (*continued*)

FEATURE	DESCRIPTION
Pipelines in Power Platform	Provide application lifecycle management (ALM) automation to streamline the development, testing, and deployment of your Power Platform solutions. This feature enables you to create and manage pipelines that define stages such as development, testing, and production. With pipelines, you can automate the process of moving your solutions through these stages, ensuring that your applications are built, tested, and deployed consistently and efficiently.
Maker Welcome Content	Allows administrators to provide customized welcome messages and resources for new makers when they first sign in to Power Apps or Copilot Studio. This feature replaces the default first-time help experience with tailored content that can include guidance, training resources, company policies, and links to internal sites or wikis.
IP Firewall & IP Cookie Binding	The IP Firewall in Power Platform Managed Environments restricts user access to Microsoft Dataverse from only allowed IP locations, enhancing data protection by mitigating insider threats. IP Cookie Binding adds another layer of security by comparing the current IP address with the one stored in the session cookie, preventing session hijacking through cookie replay attacks. Both features work together to safeguard your organizational data.
Customer Managed Key (CMK)	Allows organizations to manage their own encryption keys for data stored in Microsoft Dataverse. By default, Microsoft manages the encryption keys, but with CMK, you can create and manage your own keys, providing greater control over your data security.
Customer Lockbox	Provides an interface for customers to review and approve (or reject) data access requests from Microsoft personnel. This is particularly useful in scenarios where a Microsoft engineer needs to access customer data, such as in response to a support ticket or to troubleshoot an issue.
Extended Backup	Allows administrators to extend the backup retention period from the default 7 days to up to 28 days.
Export Data to Application Insights	Allows you to monitor and analyze telemetry data from your environments. This integration helps you diagnose and troubleshoot issues by providing insights into performance, diagnostics, and usage patterns.
Catalog in Power Platform	Allows developers and makers to crowd-source and find templates and components within their organization easily.
Default Environment Routing	Ensures makers will land in their personal developer environment instead of the default environment, promoting better organization and security.

Managed Environments Considerations

Deciding whether to invest in managed environments will come down to the potential value your organization may realize from these expanded capabilities. Additionally, you may choose to balance whether you can realize similar benefits by leveraging third-party products at a different price point, building similar solutions either using full-code or low-code. Every organization handles business case development differently; therefore, it will be important to understand how business cases are evaluated by your leadership team prior to pulling yours together. You'll also want to engage with your point of contact for Microsoft licensing to help understand what the cost might be for managed environments. An important note to consider is that Managed Environments is a premium add-on offering, and users connecting to the managed environment must have this additional license.

> **NOTE** Managed environment licensing is a complicated topic and can be further reviewed at `learn.microsoft.com/en-us/power-platform/admin/managed-environment-licensing`.

Solutions

Now that you have a handle on environments and the various considerations for your environment strategy, let's take that understanding to the next level with solutions. Solutions are used to package and deploy applications or individual components between different environments. When you apply this to the environment strategy that we talked about earlier, solutions serve as the "what" you will be moving between your developer sandbox and your integration environment. There are two types of solutions:

- **Unmanaged solutions** are targeted at developer sandbox environments or any environment where you will be actively editing the files and components frequently.

- **Managed solutions** are used when you are deploying your solutions to a non-developer environment, such as integration, user acceptance testing, and production. This is for scenarios where you don't want the source files modified.

Within these solution files themselves are what's referred to as *solution components*. These are resources that make up your solution, including apps, site maps, tables, processes, web resources, etc. Essentially, these are the culmination of the various dependencies needed to run your application—or, in this instance, your agent. The solution file is the packaging of these resources in a way that allows you to cleanly deploy your solution across environments.

128 Chapter 5 ■ Planning ALM for Your Copilot Agents

Let's start by creating our first solution from the Zoë agent that we published in Chapter 3. Navigate back to the Agents menu from `copilotstudio.microsoft.com`, and then click your Zoë agent. From within your agent, click the three ellipses, as shown in Figure 5.1, and then select the Export Agent option from the drop-down menu.

Figure 5.1: The Export Agent option

From there, you will be redirected to a screen, as shown in Figure 5.2, which displays the solutions within the Power Platform environment where your agent is hosted. Here is where you can create a new solution or import an existing one that's either custom-developed or hosted on the Microsoft AppSource website. You can also publish all your pending changes (customizations) to the metadata of your entities and components live, view all the solution activity in your environment, and set the preferred solution for your environment.

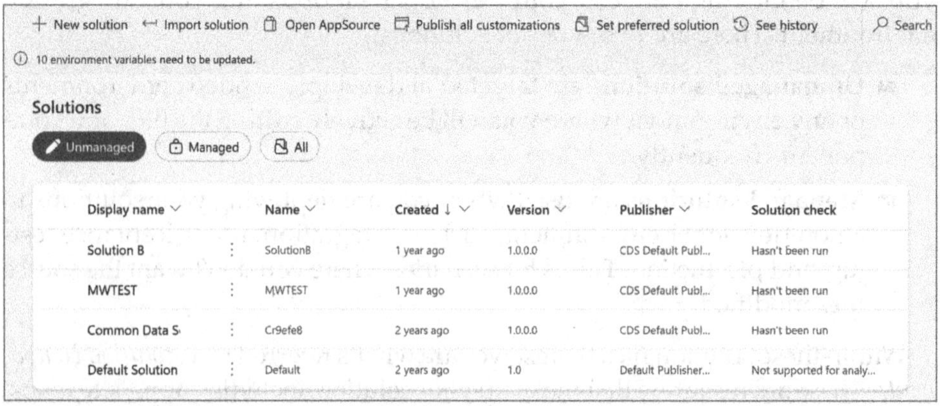

Figure 5.2: Copilot Studio solutions overview

In Power Platform, setting a preferred solution allows makers to specify which solution will support their edits and customizations. By default, all components are stored in the Common Data Services Default Solution (sometimes referred to as the Default solution), so this would be how you set a different solution as your default for making customizations.

Creating a Solution

Let's walk through creating the first solution of our Zoë agent so that we can deploy it to another environment. Start by clicking the +New Solution button in the upper-left corner navigation, as shown in Figure 5.2. This will bring up the New Solution dialog box, as shown in Figure 5.3. Here, you can fill in the Display Name and Name for your solution. Note that you can't use spaces or special characters other than underscores in the Name field.

Figure 5.3: The New Solution dialog box

Next, click the New Publisher link to open the New Publisher dialog box, as shown in Figure 5.4. Most organizations will want to put the individual developer's name, the team, the department, or the organization name, etc., depending on your organization's governance policies. Here, you can include both a display name and the name for the developer. Remember that you cannot have spaces or special characters in the Name field, as this is the unique identifier for

130   Chapter 5 ▪ Planning ALM for Your Copilot Agents

your publisher. You'll also notice that it creates both a prefix and choice value prefix. The prefix consists of characters that will prepend your solutions, and the choice value prefix is used when you add options to choices and provides an indicator of which solution was used to add the option. This is used to help avoid naming conflicts, especially when multiple solutions are in use within the same environment.

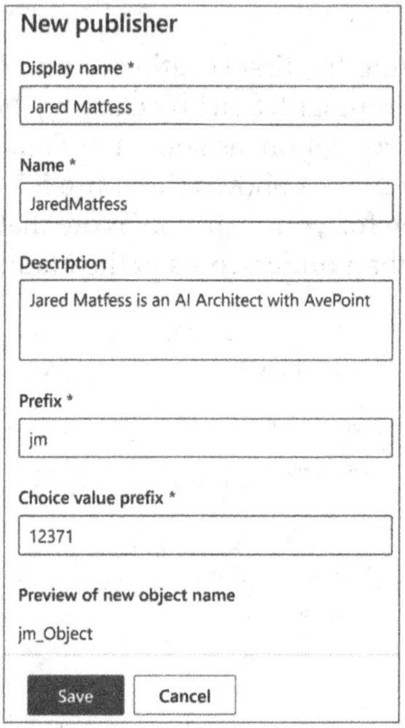

New publisher

Display name *

Jared Matfess

Name *

JaredMatfess

Description

Jared Matfess is an AI Architect with AvePoint

Prefix *

jm

Choice value prefix *

12371

Preview of new object name

jm_Object

Save   Cancel

Figure 5.4: Creating a new publisher

Next, click the Save button to create your publisher, and then click Save again on the New Solution screen to save your solution.

Your solution has now been created; however, you have not added anything to the solution package yet. You will be redirected to the Solutions Overview screen for this new Zoe_Agent solution package that you just created. Notice that from this screen, you have the option to create new artifacts, including agents, connections, Power Apps canvas apps, etc. This would initiate the subsequent wizards or dialog boxes to start the process of creating those objects and associating them with this new solution.

Next, click the Add Existing button, as shown in Figure 5.5, to add an agent to the existing solution.

This will take you to a screen that has filtered the list of objects in this Power Platform environment to just agents. If your environment has a lot of agents, you can leverage the "search agents" functionality. However, if there are just a few, you can scroll through the list and then click the checkbox next to the agent or agents that you want to include in your solution, as shown in Figure 5.6.

Figure 5.5: Select Add Agent

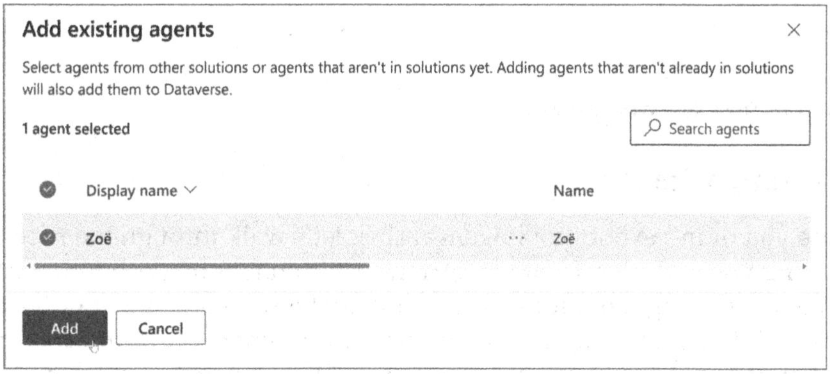

Figure 5.6: Confirm Adding Your Agent

Clicking the Add button will import your agent, including all of the dependencies, into your new solution. You'll then be redirected to the agent overview screen, as shown in Figure 5.7. Notice that it lists all of the various objects that make up your agent, including the topics and connection references to the files stored in SharePoint that serve as the agent's knowledge source.

If you look at the left-hand panel, as shown in Figure 5.8, you can see a numerical breakdown of the various objects included in your solution. You can also click each of these items to filter your view to those specific object types. For now, click the Back to Solutions button to go back to the solutions overview screen.

	Display name ↑ ∨	Name ∨	Type ∨	Managed ∨	Customized ∨	Last Modif... ∨
	[Copilot] IT Help Desk ...	[Copilot] IT Help ...	Topic	No	Yes	2 months ago
	Conversation Start	Conversation Start	Topic	No	Yes	2 months ago
	Conversational boosti...	Conversational b...	Topic	No	Yes	2 months ago
	cr0d7_itHelpDeskAssis...	cr0d7_itHelpDes...	Connection Refe...	No	Yes	2 months ago
	cr0d7_itHelpDeskAssis...	cr0d7_itHelpDes...	Connection Refe...	No	Yes	1 month ago

Figure 5.7: Zoe_Agent solutions overview

Figure 5.8: The solution breakdown

Exporting a Solution

In case you didn't export your agent earlier, let's walk through the process of exporting your solution from the current environment to a solution package and then importing the solution into a different environment. Exporting your agent and then importing it into another environment will mimic a typical development process in your organization. Once a developer's code is in a state where they want to receive feedback from users, they typically promote that functionality to a higher-level environment, such as integration or user acceptance testing, to enable business users to test while the developers continue to build new functionality.

To get started, first find the Zoe_Agent solution within the list of solutions and click the checkbox next to it. Then, click the three vertical ellipses before selecting Export Solution from the displayed popup menu, as shown in Figure 5.9.

This will display a new window, as shown in Figure 5.10, that prompts you to first publish any changes that were made to the solution you are publishing. In this instance, we haven't touched any of the objects included in the solution package since first creating the solution, so this step is not necessary. However, in other scenarios where you first create your solution package and then make modifications, you will want to publish those changes before exporting the solution to ensure that the most recent versions are included in your export.

Figure 5.9: The Export Solution option

You will also notice that the publishing window has an informational message about pipelines: "Deploying with a pipeline allows you to quickly copy a solution, and all objects associated with it, into a new environment." Pipelines were briefly mentioned earlier as a feature that is included as part of the Managed Environments license. Since this tenant isn't using pipelines, simply click the Next button, as shown in Figure 5.10, to advance in the export process.

This will bring you to the Export This Solution dialog box, as shown in Figure 5.11. The first choice you'll have is to assign a number to the version of this solution. This is helpful for managing and tracking changes so that you can document what new features and functions are being included as part of your release. Copilot Studio will automatically provide you with the next increment in the numbering sequence—in this case, it is suggesting 1.0.0.1 as the version number; however, you can choose to override this with your own numbering sequence.

Next, it will offer two different export options: either to export it as a Managed solution or Unmanaged. As a reminder, when promoting your solution across environments (e.g., from developer sandbox to integration), you will want to set the solution as Managed to prevent others from making changes to the underlying files within the solution in a downstream environment. The reason behind this is you want to have a repeatable development process to help keep your changes organized and sequenced. If changes are being made in both your developer sandbox and the integration environment, it will be very difficult to reconcile those changes across multiple instances of your solution. Therefore, to help control the chaos, it is best to set your solutions to Managed when you intend on deploying them to additional environments.

Figure 5.10: The Before You Export dialog box

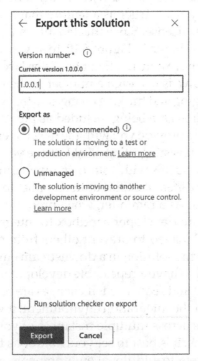

Figure 5.11: The Export This Solution dialog box

Last, you will notice a checkbox next to a label called Run Solution Checker on Export. Within the Power Platform, there is a functionality called the Solution Checker that will inspect your solution and provide recommendations for anything that may prove to be problematic in your solution that might negatively affect your performance, reliability, etc.

Click the Export button. You will need to wait a little bit for Copilot Studio to package your solution and make it available. Once Copilot Studio has finished exporting, you should see a message: "Solution 'Zoe_Agent' Exported Successfully," with a Download button, as shown in Figure 5.12.

Figure 5.12: Downloading your solution

Click the Download button, and your browser will download the managed solution ZIP to your local computer, as shown in Figure 5.13. Note that this will look slightly different if you are on a Windows-based OS versus a Mac OS. As we reviewed in Chapter 4, the contents of this ZIP file include the *manifest.json* and *declarativeAgent_0.json* files, as well as other supporting resources that make up your solution.

Figure 5.13: The downloaded solution

Importing a Solution

Next, we are going to import our solution to another Power Platform environment. Start by navigating to `copilotstudio.microsoft.com` and then clicking the environment navigation menu in the upper-right corner. From there, you can select an environment from the list of environments, as shown in Figure 5.14. Your environment list will vary based on what your account has access to and the Power Platform environments that exist in your tenant.

> **NOTE** This book does not cover creating or managing Power Platform environments, but you can always reference Microsoft's official documentation at `learn.microsoft.com/en-us/power-platform/admin/create-environment`.

136 Chapter 5 ■ Planning ALM for Your Copilot Agents

Figure 5.14: Selecting an environment

Once you have selected an environment, click the three ellipses on the left side of the Copilot Studio navigation, as shown in Figure 5.15, and select the Solutions navigation item.

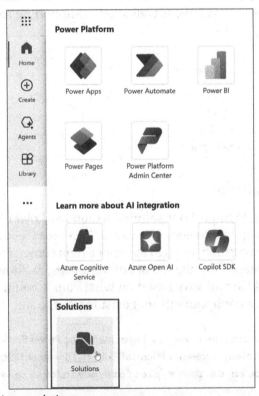

Figure 5.15: Navigating to solutions

From here, click the Import solution button, and then click the Browse button, as shown in Figure 5.16, to browse your local computer for the solution you just exported from your other environment. Once you select the solution .zip file, click the Next button to begin importing the solution.

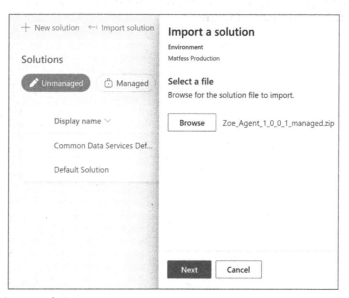

Figure 5.16: Import solution

The import process will first confirm the solution that is being imported, as shown in Figure 5.17, including the name of the solution, the type, the publisher, and the version. Notice that it also includes a parameter called Patch, which is set to No. Patching is a process where you can make slight updates to an existing solution without having to completely remove and replace it. For example, if you were adding a small bit of a new functionality or perhaps fixing a typo in a topic, these would be some examples of small changes that might not warrant having to completely remove the previously deployed version of your solution and replace it with a new one. Since this is our first time deploying the solution, there's no need for the patch flag to be set. So, from here, you can click the Next button to continue the import process.

The next step to importing your solution is re-establishing connections used as part of your solution. Remember, as part of the escalation process for our Zoë agent, we had created an action that would allow the agent to send an email to a defined email address. We leveraged the Copilot author's credential to perform that action; therefore, we need to re-establish that connection to Microsoft Exchange Online to enable the agent to work properly in this other environment. For real-world scenarios, you might also have situations where the downstream connections are made with developer accounts, and then as you publish your agent to production, you may need to leverage a different account (e.g., a service account) to perform these actions. This ensures that your agent will continue to function should the author of the agent's account get terminated. This is quite common when development is performed by consultants or third parties on behalf of an organization. Click the Import button once you have re-established the connection to Exchange Online.

Figure 5.17: Import confirmation

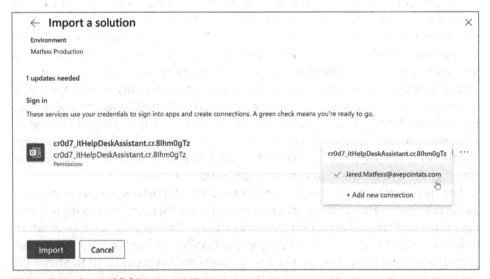

Figure 5.18: Re-establishing connections

Chapter 5 ▪ Planning ALM for Your Copilot Agents 139

After a little bit of time, you should see a notification message that your solution has been imported successfully. If you click the Managed icon, as shown in Figure 5.19, you should now see that the Zoe_Agent solution has been deployed to your other environment.

Figure 5.19: A successful import

From here, navigate back to the Copilot Studio homepage and then click the Agents navigation link in the left-hand rail. You should see a list of agents, as shown in Figure 5.20. Notice that your Zoë agent will be in the list of agents and show that it has never been published. This process only imports the solution to your Power Platform environment. You would still need to follow the publishing process, as covered in Chapter 3, to make your agent available to others, for example, from within Microsoft Teams.

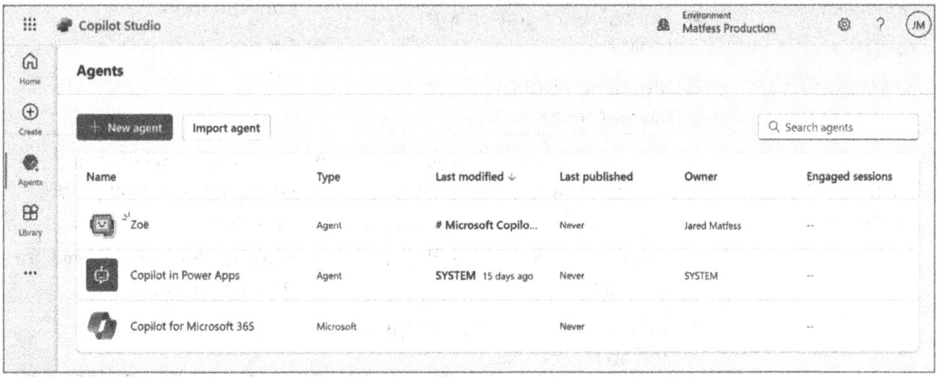

Figure 5.20: The unpublished Zoë agent

CI/CD Pipelines

Now that you have an understanding of what it takes to move a solution between environments, you are probably thinking to yourself, "That's a rather tedious process if I must export and import my solution multiple times a day, week, etc." You might be starting to see the need for investing in an orchestration layer that can facilitate the process for promoting solutions across environments using automation.

When you talk about performing professional development, the term continuous integration and continuous deployment (CI/CD) is often mixed with pipelines. At a high level, CI/CD pipelines is a technical approach for building a software deployment process through automation to promote changes from development all the way to production. While they are not mandatory for agent development, I believe—and hopefully, you can agree—that automating processes is a way to drive greater efficiencies.

Table 5.3 outlines the three main options for creating Power Platform deployment pipelines.

Table 5.3: Pipeline deployment options

OPTION	FEATURES	CONSIDERATIONS
Power Platform Managed Environments Pipelines	■ Integrated within Power Platform ■ Targeted at citizen developers ■ Easy to set up and manage	■ Requires additional licensing costs ■ Limited advanced customization
Azure DevOps Pipelines	■ Advanced CI/CD capabilities ■ Extensive integration with other tooling ■ Meant to support large team development	■ Requires more setup and configuration ■ Steeper learning curve for usage
Power Platform Command-Line Interface (CLI)	■ Command-line interface for managing solutions and pipelines ■ Flexibility in scripting; can be integrated with other tools, such as Azure DevOps ■ Suitable for both pro developers and advanced users	■ Requires knowledge of command-line tools and scripting ■ Steeper learning curve for those new to CLI

> **NOTE** There are also other third-party products, such as AvePoint EnPower, CircleCI, and JIRA, to name a few, that support the creation of Power Platform pipelines. Each comes with its own unique features and cost.

Conclusion

In this chapter, we walked through how to manage the entire lifecycle of copilot agents. We started by covering the typical ALM framework, which involves gathering requirements, designing, developing, testing, deploying, and maintaining. Each step is essential for ensuring that agents are built and deployed safely and efficiently. We also highlighted the value of having a clear environment strategy, as well as the technical details needed to implement ALM effectively. Then, we walked through how to create a solution, export it, and then import it into another Power Platform environment. This process shows how to move your solution through different environments in a real-world deployment scenario. Finally, we covered how to potentially automate the deployment process using pipelines. In the next chapter, we will dive into autonomous agents, which represent the next evolution of solutions you can create with Copilot Studio.

CHAPTER 6

Deep Dive into Agent Templates

Chapter 2 explored foundational concepts within Copilot Studio, including the topics functionality. Building on this knowledge, we are now ready to delve into more advanced configurations. This chapter will guide you through the intricacies of designing a multi-topic agent.

Our example: an agent that can serve residents of a community by answering questions across a range of topics. The agent will engage with a human when it can't support a particular set of questions from the user. We will begin by selecting one of the agent templates that Microsoft provides to serve as a starting point for this type of effort. This will serve as a great starting point for our agent, as well as serve the purpose of showcasing what's possible through configuration. The example will also show what a potential fully functioning agent could look like.

We will then customize the agent by removing some of the starter configuration and layering in our own use case. A deep dive into topics will be used as a way to help organize and streamline our agent's conversation flow.

Topics and planning your conversation flow will not only set the stage for the use case we cover here, but also help you better understand the value proposition for autonomous agents, which will be covered in Chapter 8. Finally, this chapter will conclude with closing thoughts on how you can further extend this agent with other functionality and line-of-business applications.

143

Prerequisites

Before beginning the creation of our new agents, it is important to quickly cover the topic of data loss prevention (DLP) policies. DLP policies are meant to help prevent the accidental loss of business data through solutions developed using the Power Platform. The way it works is: Power Platform connectors to third-party systems are categorized as either:

- **Business connectors:** Systems that are managed by your organization, such as Salesforce, SAP, and the Microsoft services, including Exchange Online, SharePoint, OneDrive, etc.
- **Non-business connectors:** Systems that are not managed by your organization but are perhaps used by your organization. For example, oftentimes certain social media services such as X or Bluesky are categorized as non-business for your marketing or communications teams.
- **Blocked connectors:** These systems are not permitted by your IT organization and cannot be used in flows, agents, or apps.

The way it works is that, by default, Power Platform is configured to ensure that you do not mix business connectors with non-business connectors within the same application, flow, or agent. This is to ensure that you do not create scenarios where data is being exfiltrated from your network accidentally by your users. An example is that, without blocking or categorizing connections as non-business, a user could create a Power Automate flow that copies files from their OneDrive for Business to their personal OneDrive. Now, there may be additional monitoring tools in place to detect that activity, but Microsoft also provides tools directly within Power Platform to limit this from happening.

It's important for you to be aware of DLP policies, even if you are not an admin, because as a maker, you could be impacted by them. For example, some of the agent templates provided by Microsoft include connections to third-party systems. If you attempt to publish one of these agents, you will notice obscure error messages indicating that you are unable to publish your agent, but it will not always tell you why. Alternatively, as you are in the process of authoring your solution, you may find error messages when attempting to create connections. Sometimes these errors are very clear that you are encountering an issue with DLP; other times, there is little indication of what is happening.

If you do happen to run into a strange error when attempting to add or use a connector, you should ask your Power Platform administrator which DLP policies are in place. It is important to note that DLP policies are set at the environment level; therefore, you could also find strange behavior when moving your agent between Power Platform environments. So, it's important for you to be aware of any DLP policies in both your developer sandbox environment as well as any user acceptance testing (UAT) or production environments. Now that you have an understanding of DLP policies and how they could potentially impact building out certain functionality with your agents, let's go ahead and start building a new agent from one of Microsoft's starter templates.

Selecting Our Agent Template

Go ahead and open your web browser, navigate to Copilot Studio at `copilot studio.microsoft.com`, and then select the + Create button on the left-hand rail navigation. This will present you with several options for starting, as shown in Figure 6.1. You can either choose to create an agent from scratch or describe to Copilot the functionality you are looking for by clicking the New Agent button. Or you can install one of the managed agents, which are prebuilt autonomous agents that Microsoft allows you to add and then further customize in your environment to meet your specific use case. Finally, you have the option to select from one of Microsoft's scenario-based agent templates, which include predefined settings, conversation flows, and integration options tailored to particular use cases.

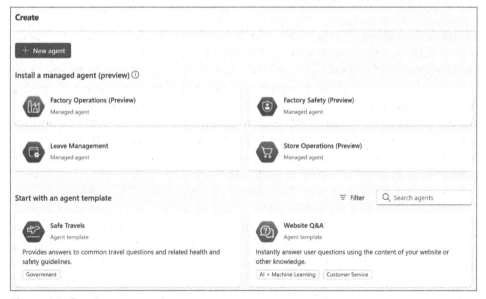

Figure 6.1: Creating agent options

For our example, select the Citizen Services agent template as a starting point. Go ahead and type in **citizen** into the search box above Start with an Agent Template, as shown in Figure 6.2. You can then select the Citizen Services agent template to begin creating your new agent.

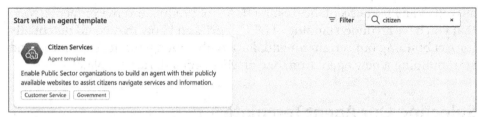

Figure 6.2: The Citizen Services agent template

> **NOTE** Agent templates are currently available in English and will require additional configuration to meet the language requirements for your use case.

Next, rename your agent to **GovBuddy** or something similar, so that it will not inherit the default Citizen Services agent name. You can leave everything else as-is for now, as we will first explore the initial configuration provided with the template and then further personalize it for our use case. Click the Create button in the upper-right corner, and once your agent has been provisioned, you will be redirected to the agent configuration screen.

Citizen Services Template

With Microsoft being headquartered in Redmond, it should come as no surprise that the Citizen Services template has been preconfigured for that city. You should set a description for your agent in case others want to understand the purpose or use case it supports. There is no direct GenAI tie-in with a description; this is more of a good practice to get into the habit of doing. Typically, this is helpful for the teams that are responsible for managing Power Platform, so that they know how various apps, flows, and agents are being used within the tenant. There are also inputs for instructions and orchestration, which we will dive into more in Chapter 8. You can note the following text in the agent description:

"*Enable Public Sector organizations to build an agent with their publicly available websites to assist their citizens navigate government services and information through Q&A. For demonstration purposes this agent uses the City of Redmond's public website as knowledge source and traffic alerts API. Disclaimer: 'Commercial use of text, city logos, photos, and other graphics is prohibited without the express written permission of the City of Redmond.' Please see* `https://www.redmond.gov/384/Social-Media-Policy#copyright` *for details.*"

Knowledge Sources

At a high level, this agent is preconfigured to support answering questions from two government websites, as shown in Figure 6.3. One is the root website, and the second is two levels deep within the hierarchy:

- `https://www.redmond.gov`
- `https://www.redmond.gov/9/I-Want-To`

You may be asking yourself, why would this agent have two knowledge sources for the same top-level website? A common reason is that you want to ensure the accuracy of the responses your agent provides. Remember, we are not training our agent based on the data, but rather leveraging the retrieval-augmented generation (RAG) pattern to match the intended user intent with information within Bing's search index. Having a knowledge source that is two levels down allows the agent to access more specific and relevant information based on the user's inquiry. Based on the user's query, you can configure your agent to provide answers from the best source of knowledge.

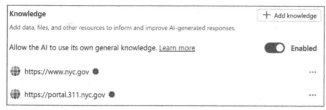

Figure 6.3: Preconfigured knowledge sources

Topics

Next, click Topics in the top navigation to review the list of custom topics that are included with this custom agent template. Notice there are the pre-built topics that you typically see, such as Goodbye, Greeting, Start Over, and Thank You, but there are also additional ones that were built specifically for this template, as shown in Figure 6.4. These include the following:

- Apply for a Service
- Data Collection
- Road Closures

Name	Trigger	Description	Editing	Last modified	Errors	Enabled
Apply for a service	Phrases	This topic g...		Jared Matfess 49...		On
Data collection	On redi...	This topic c...		Jared Matfess 49...		On
Goodbye	Phrases	This topic tr...		Jared Matfess 49...		On
Greeting	Phrases	This topic is...		Jared Matfess 49...		On
Road Closures	Phrases	This topic g...		Jared Matfess 49...		On
Start Over	Phrases	This topic g...		Jared Matfess 49...		On
Thank you	Phrases	This topic tr...		Jared Matfess 49...		On

Figure 6.4: Custom topics

Apply for a Service Topic

Go ahead and click the Apply for a Service topic so that we can further review how it is configured. The first thing you will see in the authoring canvas is the Trigger node, as shown in Figure 6.5, which includes all the text-based phrases that will invoke this topic. You typically want to provide your agent with 5–10 trigger phrases to help guide your agent on when to invoke this topic within the conversation flow.

Figure 6.5: Apply for a Service trigger phrases

Continue to scroll down on the page and you will see a Go to Another Topic node, as shown in Figure 6.6, with the title of Redirect. This node is configured to call the Data Collection topic. When you have topics calling other topics, this is referred to as *topic linking* or *topic chaining*. This technique is used to create a seamless and logical flow within conversations, ensuring that your agent can navigate complex dialogues and provide coherent responses. It also allows for flexibility to help you scale your agent to support multiple use cases. By linking topics, you can reuse existing conversation paths and responses, saving time and effort in creating new content for similar scenarios.

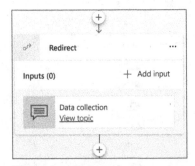

Figure 6.6: Redirect node

Data Collection Topic and Adaptive Cards

Click the View Topic link in the Redirect node to open the Data Collection topic. As you can see in Figure 6.7, the trigger for this topic is the On Redirect action. This means that the Data Collection topic is called only when redirected to by another topic and is not triggered automatically through phrases, unlike the Apply for a Service topic.

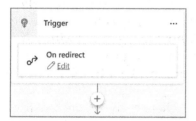

Figure 6.7: Data Collection trigger phrases

Scrolling further down, you will see a node titled Adaptive Card, as shown in Figure 6.8. This Adaptive Card has three questions and a Submit button.

Figure 6.8: Tell us about your needs

Adaptive Cards are a powerful way to create interactive and visually appealing content for many applications within the Microsoft ecosystem, including Microsoft Teams, Outlook, Microsoft 365 Copilot, SharePoint, Power Automate, etc. They allow makers to design rich, card-like user interfaces that can be dynamically updated with data to satisfy multiple use cases, including collecting data. Adaptive Cards are defined using JavaScript Object Notation (JSON). JSON serves as the data format that structures the content, layout, and behavior of an Adaptive Card.

> **NOTE** Microsoft maintains an interactive designer experience where you can design your Adaptive Card using a web-based designer that will create the necessary JSON at `adaptivecards.io/designer`.

If you click the form within the node, the Adaptive Card Node Properties panel will be displayed, as shown in Figure 6.9. Here you can see all of the inputs defined, along with the presentation for how they appear within the card. You'll note the use of ColumnSets and Columns to format the input fields within the card. You can also copy the JSON from the Adaptive Card node and paste that into the Card Payload Editor on `adaptivecards.io/designer` to further customize the look and feel of the card. Then, once you are satisfied with the changes, you can copy and paste that into the Adaptive Card node, as shown in Figure 6.9.

Figure 6.9: The Adaptive Card Node Properties panel

Adaptive Cards have a couple of key principles that make them appealing to both makers and developers alike. These are:

- **Multi-platform support:** They are designed to work across multiple platforms and devices, ensuring a consistent user experience regardless of where they are displayed.
- **Open standards:** They are not tied to a specific programming language, library, framework, or platform, which means you do not have to worry about any sort of vendor lock-in scenarios.

- **Configuration-based:** They are created declaratively through JavaScript Object Notation (JSON) format, which means that they are declarative and relatively easy to learn and understand.
- **Performant:** Since they are lightweight, they render very quickly across the multiple supported platforms.

You can click the "expand" button in the Adaptive Cards property panel to either view or edit the JSON configuration, as shown in Figure 6.10. You will notice that there's a schema definition in the first line that points to adaptivecards.io/schemas/adaptive-card.json. A JSON schema ensures that data adheres to a specific structure and set of rules. This is kind of like those validation checks for when you enter in an email address or telephone number, to ensure that it meets a specific format. By defining a schema, you can ensure interoperability between different systems and applications.

```
</> Edit JSON ∨
{
  "$schema": "http://adaptivecards.io/schemas/adaptive-card.json",
  "type": "AdaptiveCard",
  "version": "1.0",
  "body": [
    {
      "type": "ColumnSet",
      "columns": [
        {
          "type": "Column",
          "width": 2,
          "items": [
            {
              "type": "TextBlock",
              "text": "Tell us about your needs",
```

Figure 6.10: Expanded JSON

If you close the expanded properties and the normal properties windows, you'll return to the Copilot Studio authoring canvas. You can then scroll down to see a link called Outputs below the Submit button in the Adaptive Card. Click Outputs to expand the drop-down list within the node. You should see the outputs, as shown in Figure 6.11.

Figure 6.11: Node outputs

152 Chapter 6 ▪ Deep Dive into Agent Templates

In this scenario, the outputs are variable assignments for each input displayed in the form. For instance, when you examine the Adaptive Card JSON, you'll find that the Type of Assistance question is identified by the ID `serviceType`. In the Outputs section of the node, a variable named `serviceType` is created as a string, and it is assigned the value provided by the Adaptive Card:

```
{
    "type": "Input.Text",
    "id": "serviceType",
    "label": "Type of Assistance",
    "isRequired": true,
    "regex": "^[a-zA-Z0-9,'.-\\s]+$",
    "errorMessage": "Please enter your service type using alphanumeric
characters and the following symbols ',.-"
},
```

Looking closer at the JSON for the Type of Assistance input, you will notice that there is built-in data validation as part of the definition. There is a parameter `isRequired`, which is set to `true`, meaning the user must provide an input for it to be valid. There is also a regular expression called `regex`, which is used to ensure only alphanumeric characters and a few symbol characters are allowed as a valid input. Finally, there is also a parameter called `errorMessage` that will be invoked and displayed to the user when the values of the `serviceType` input fail. The two situations where this message would be displayed are if the user does not input any text into the field, or if they include characters outside of a single quote, comma, period, or dash.

> **NOTE** If you are not familiar, a *regular expression* is a sequence of characters that defines a search pattern. They are typically used for string-matching within texts.

Scroll down in the canvas to the next node titled Set Variable Value. You'll see two sections for this node: a Set Variable, which is initializing a variable called `dataCollected`, of type `string`, and then a To Value section, which includes a formula. If you click the > arrow button next to the To Value input, as shown in Figure 6.12, you will be able to view and edit the formula.

This particular formula is used to format and display the values of variables in a text block. Here's a breakdown of what it does:

- `Service Type: {Topic.serviceType}`: Inserts the value of the `service Type` variable.

- `{Char(13)}{Char(10)}`: Adds a carriage return (Char 13) and a line feed (Char 10), effectively creating a new line.

- `Purpose: {Topic.servicePurpose}`: Inserts the value of the `service Purpose` variable.

- `{Char(13)}{Char(10)}`: Adds another new line.
- `Resident: {Topic.currentResident}`: Inserts the value of the `current Resident` variable.
- `{Char(13)}{Char(10)}`: Adds a final new line.

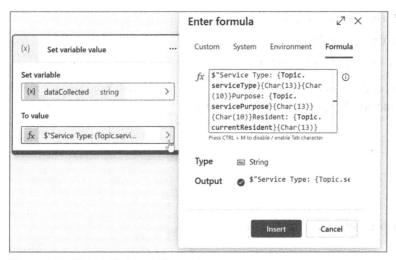

Figure 6.12: The Set Variable Value node

Finally, below the Set Variable Value node is a node called Message, which is of type Send a Message. In other words, this node is having the agent respond back to the user with text. If you click the node, it will expand, as shown in Figure 6.13. The message that will be sent back to the user is a combination of "This is a placeholder with sample for submitting data to an API with the following data:" and then the formatted `dataCollected` variable that was defined in the previous step, with its own formatting.

Figure 6.13: The Message node

If you want to confirm what the output of the message looks like, you can run a test of the agent by clicking the Test icon in the upper-right corner of the Copilot Studio UI. Your agent will invoke the Conversation Start System topic and greet you with "Hello, I'm BigAppleBuddy, a virtual assistant. I can help you navigate government services and information. Just so you are aware, I sometimes use AI to answer your questions." You can then type in **How do I apply** as the trigger to invoke the Data Collection topic. Next, you can provide the following values to the three questions:

- **Type of assistance:** I need help
- **Reason:** Because I do
- **Are you a current resident?:** Yes

Then, when you press the Submit button, your agent will respond with the following formatted text, as shown in Figure 6.14.

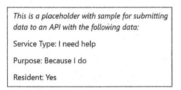

Figure 6.14: The returned message to the user

Road Closures Topic

If you navigate back to your agent configuration page, you can click the Topics link in the top navigation to review your system and custom topics. Refer back to Chapter 2 if you would like a refresher on the various system topics that are created as part of any new agent creation. Let's go ahead and open the Road Closures custom topic. As you can see in Figure 6.15, this topic can be triggered by a user's input just like the Apply for a Service topic.

Figure 6.15: Road Closures trigger phrases

If you test the agent with one of the trigger phrases, such as "Are there any road closures," as shown in Figure 6.16, you will see that it displays a list of streets where there are road closures, as known in the ArcGIS API. For the sake of brevity, since this is a rather complex topic, know that it is making HTTP requests to an API hosted on gis.redmond.gov, and then looping through the results and providing an output back to the user.

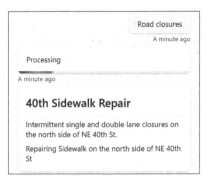

Figure 6.16: Displaying road closures

Two requests are needed for this specific use case due to how the backend data is structured. Other use cases may have multiple data requests; it is highly dependent on how the data in the system you access is organized. For this example, one table manages all planned closures due to construction; the second table holds unplanned closures due to events such as traffic accidents.

The requests look almost the same, but one uses "layerId": 1, and the other uses "layerId": 0. In ArcGIS, each layer corresponds to a different dataset in the same service. A change in "layerId" means the service is providing more than one data layer through the same endpoint. Checking both layers ensures we cover planned work and unexpected events.

Conversational Boosting Topic

If you navigate back to the Topics page of your agent configuration, this time, click the System icon underneath the + Add a Topic button, and then select the Conversational Boosting topic. This will open that topic, as shown in Figure 6.17. The Conversation Boosting logic is triggered when the agent does not know the intent of the user or otherwise isn't quite sure what information the user is looking for.

The next step in your conversation flow is the Create Generative Answers node, and it passes the Activity.Text variable as an input, which is the text content of a user message or interaction within a conversation. What happens next includes the following:

- **Check knowledge sources:** The agent references knowledge sources you've configured, such as documents, FAQs, websites, or databases, to retrieve relevant information.

156 Chapter 6 ■ Deep Dive into Agent Templates

- **Contextual understanding:** The agent analyzes the user's input—in this case, the Activity.Text variable—and the context of the conversation to understand the user's intent and determine the most appropriate knowledge source to consult.

- **Answer generation:** Based on the retrieved information and the conversation context, the agent generates a contextually relevant response to the user's query.

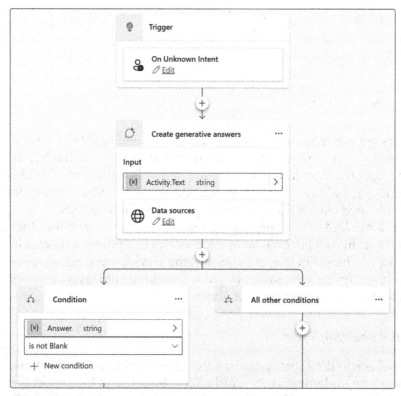

Figure 6.17: The Conversational Boosting topic

As an example, if you were to test your agent with the following question, *"How do I do business with the city of Redmond?"* you will see it invoke the Conversational Boosting topic based on an unknown user intent. It will then pass the Activity.Text variable to the Create Generative Answers node, and then return the information shown in Figure 6.18, including references to where it found the information.

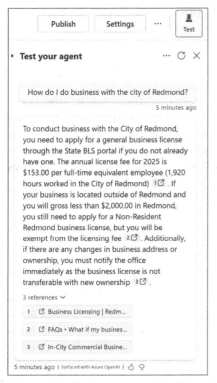

Figure 6.18: Testing conversational boosting

Summarizing Topics

Hopefully, you are starting to understand the importance of topics in managing a conversation flow, as well as helping separate out different types of functionality. The Apply for a Service topic invokes the Data Collection topic to capture information from the user, whereas the Road Closures topic queries an ArcGIS API to return road closure information. Finally, the Conversational Boosting API uses the power of GenAI to retrieve answers to constituent questions.

Building Our Agent from the Citizen Services Template

Let's make a few modifications to show how quickly you can build a functioning agent from the existing template provided by Microsoft. For this use case, let's assume that we are building the agent to support residents of New York City.

First, click the Overview link in the top navigation to begin making modifications. Instead of GovBuddy, let's call it something more relevant to New York

City, such as BigAppleBuddy. Click the Edit button in the Details section, type in **BigAppleBuddy**, and then click the Save button.

Updating Knowledge Sources

Next, navigate down to the Knowledge Sources section and click the three ellipses next to the https://www.redmond.gov knowledge source, and then click the Delete button, as shown in Figure 6.19. A pop-up window will appear to confirm that "Deleting a knowledge source is permanent and cannot be undone." Click the Delete button to confirm, and the data source will be removed from your agent. Complete the same steps for the https://www.redmond.gov/9/I-Want-To knowledge source.

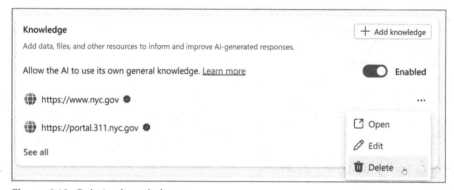

Figure 6.19: Deleting knowledge sources

Now, complete the following steps to add your new data source:

1. Click the Add Knowledge button.
2. Select Public Websites in the pop-up window.
3. Enter **https://www.nyc.gov** in the Public Website link field.
4. Click the Add button in the upper-right corner.
5. Enter **https://portal.311.nyc.gov** in the Public Website link field.
6. Click the Add button in the upper-right corner.
7. Check the Confirm checkboxes under the Owner column, as shown in Figure 6.20.
8. Click the Add button in the lower-right corner to finish adding your new knowledge sources.

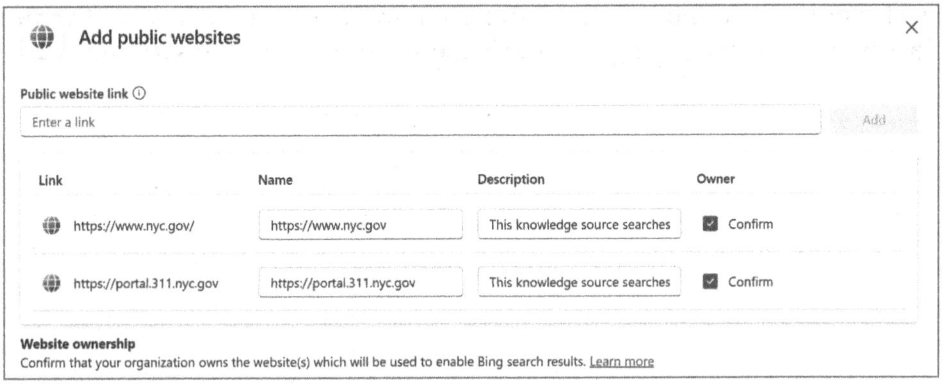

![Add public websites dialog showing two websites: https://www.nyc.gov/ and https://portal.311.nyc.gov with confirm checkboxes]

Figure 6.20: Confirming website ownership

Updating Topics

Next, we will update the topics for our agent. Click the Topics navigation link in the top menu, and then click the System navigation link to filter to the system topics. Click the Conversation Start topic to edit the initial message you will receive when engaging with the agent. From within the Message node, click the text underneath Message Variations, as shown in Figure 6.21, to edit the initial message that your agent sends when triggered.

Figure 6.21: Message variations

To help better personalize our agent, we can update this text to help inform the user about what this agent is capable of. To do so, delete all of the text after the first paragraph: *"Hello, I'm Bot.Name, a virtual assistant. I can help you navigate government services and information. Just so you are aware, I sometimes use AI to answer your questions."* Click the canvas, which will then enable the Save button in the upper-right corner. Click the Save button to save your changes to the Conversation Start topic.

Next, click the trash can icon near the Quick Replies section of the Message node, as shown in Figure 6.22. Then click the X button next to each of the preloaded quick replies in the Message node. We will cover Quick Replies in the next chapter, so for now, let's remove them from our agent. Finally, click the Save button in the upper-right corner of the authoring canvas to save your topic.

Figure 6.22: Quick replies

Now, click the Topics navigation link to go back to your list of topics. Find the Road Closures topic and toggle it to disabled, as shown in Figure 6.23. We won't be using this topic at this time, but we will disable it rather than delete it, should we decide to add this functionality to a future version of the agent.

Name	Trigger	Description	Editing	Last modified	Errors	Enabled
Apply for a service	Phrases	This topic g...		Jared Matfess 8 h...		On
Data collection	On redir...	This topic c...		Jared Matfess 8 h...		On
Goodbye	Phrases	This topic tr...		Jared Matfess 8 h...		On
Greeting	Phrases	This topic is...		Jared Matfess 8 h...		On
Road Closures	Phrases	This topic g...		Jared Matfess 2 s...		Off
Start Over	Phrases	This topic g...		Jared Matfess 8 h...		On
Thank you	Phrases	This topic tr...		Jared Matfess 8 h...		On

Figure 6.23: Disabling the Road Closures topic

Next, click the Data Collection topic to open that topic and begin editing it in the authoring canvas. What we would like to do is have the user provide an email address so that this agent can record who it was that was engaging with them and provide a summary of the correspondence. To do that, we will need to make a few changes to the Adaptive Card node. Now, there's a couple of ways that we can tackle this request, but since this is a book on Copilot Studio, let's show how Copilot can assist with this task.

NOTE If you run into any issues with Copilot not producing reliable results, you can find the *C06-AdaptiveCard.json* file to complete the next few steps at www.wiley.com/go/copilotstudioqs.

First, click the Copilot link in the editing toolbar, as shown in Figure 6.24. This will open an Edit with Copilot panel on the right side of the authoring canvas.

Figure 6.24: The Copilot link in the editing toolbar

Type in **Remove the text "Note: This is a sample form and it will not be saving or submitting any information" from the Adaptive Card**, and then click the Update button, as shown in Figure 6.25. Add a new field to the Adaptive Card called Email, update the JSON schema, and create a new output.

Figure 6.25: Updating formulas with Copilot

After a few seconds, you should receive a confirmation that says, "The topic has been updated with AI. Before saving this update, make sure that all the content is appropriate and accurate." You should also notice that the disclaimer text is no longer present in the Adaptive Card node.

Next, type the following text into the Copilot chat window: **Update the "Are you a current resident?" question in the Adaptive node from being a text input to being a select menu with the choices of yes and no with no value initially selected, and make it a required field.** Click the Update button, and once again you should receive a positive confirmation that the topic has been updated with AI. You should also see the changes reflected in your Adaptive Card, as shown in Figure 6.26.

Finally, let's go ahead and use Copilot to assist with creating a new field called Email and have that added to your form. Once again, type in the Copilot chat window, **Add a new field called email**, and then click the Update button.

Chapter 6 ■ Deep Dive into Agent Templates

Depending on when you try this, it may work successfully, or it might throw an error message, as shown in Figure 6.27.

Figure 6.26: Updating the field type with Copilot

Figure 6.27: The JSON string for the Adaptive Card is invalid

If an error message is thrown, then copy the JSON schema from within the Adaptive Card Node Properties panel, as shown in Figure 6.28. You can do this by pressing Ctrl+A on Windows.

We are going to use the Copilot web experience, not to be confused with the Copilot we were just using in Copilot Studio, to fix the JSON schema. To proceed, open a new tab in your web browser, navigate to copilot.microsoft .com, in the prompt menu type **Can you please fix this JSON schema**, and then paste the JSON schema within a pair of double quotes, and press Enter.

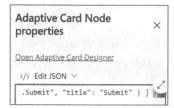

Figure 6.28: Copying the JSON schema

Click the Copy button in the upper-right corner of the Copilot response, as shown in Figure 6.29. This will copy the updated JSON schema to your clipboard.

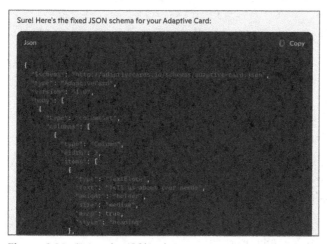

Figure 6.29: Fixing the JSON schema

Now open the tab where you were working in Copilot Studio, and in the Adaptive Card Node Properties panel, replace the contents under Edit JSON with the contents of your clipboard. This should fix the JSON schema error and render the Email field, as shown in Figure 6.30. Notice that it ensures that the Email field is required, which is ideal from a business process perspective. I recommend that you click the Save button at this time. Close the Adaptive Card Node Properties menu.

To help improve our agent's user experience, we should send an email to the email address provided by the user. We should recap the information they provided so that they will know that someone that manages the agent will be in touch to help them out. To do this, we will need to add a new Action node to our canvas to initiate the email.

Click the + Add a Node button directly underneath the Set Variable Value node. Click the Add an Action choice, and then toggle from Basic Actions to Connector. You can then either scroll through the list of available actions, as shown in Figure 6.31, or type **send an email office 365 v2** in the search menu

164 Chapter 6 ■ Deep Dive into Agent Templates

to find the correct action. Click Send an Email (V2) from the list of available actions. Copilot Studio will prompt you with the following warning message: "Users with edit access to this agent can reuse your connection in other topics of this agent. You can set up agent access in Security settings later." Then, click Submit to add this new action to your canvas.

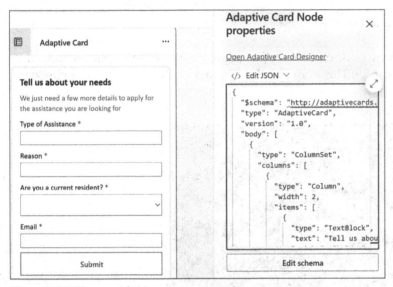

Figure 6.30: The email field rendering correctly

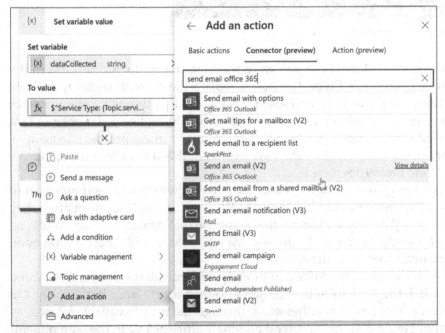

Figure 6.31: Selecting an email (V2)

Next, we'll need to ensure that the action is set to use Copilot authentication instead of user authentication. Click the ellipses in the right-hand corner of this new node. From the Connector Action Properties, select Copilot Author Authentication in the drop-down menu, as shown in Figure 6.32. Then click the X button to minimize the properties panel.

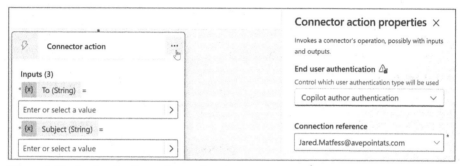

Figure 6.32: Setting Copilot author authentication

Now, we will configure the inputs for this node. Start by clicking the > arrow next to Enter or Select a Value for the To field. Select the `email` variable, as shown in Figure 6.33.

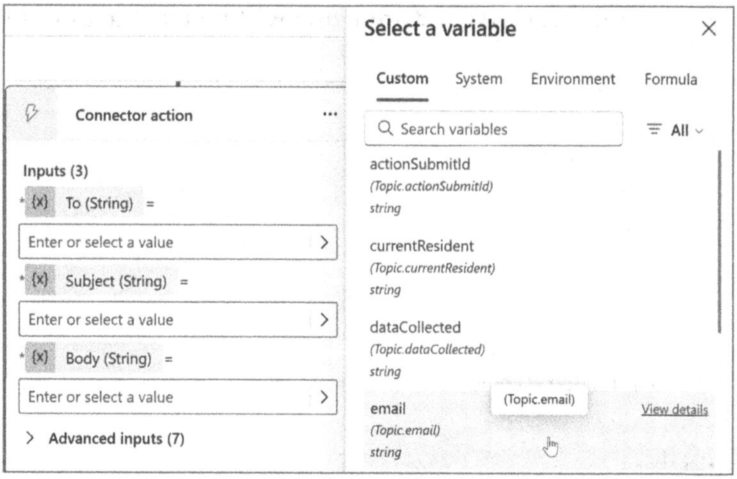

Figure 6.33: Selecting the email topic variable

For the Subject field, enter the following text: **City of New York: Service Request Received**.

Click the > button in the third input field under Body, and then click Formula in the pop-up menu. Enter the following formula: **"The city of New York has received the following service request and will be with your shortly:" & Topic.dataCollected**. Then, click the Insert button, as shown in Figure 6.34.

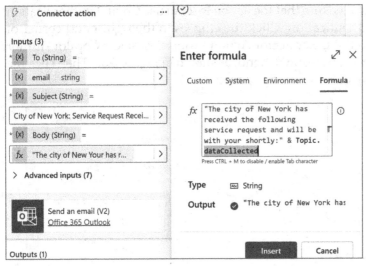

Figure 6.34: The email body formula

Finally, let's put one last finishing touch on our agent by updating the message that will be presented back to the user after they have submitted information to the Adaptive Card form. Click the body of the Message node and enter the following text, as shown in Figure 6.35: **Thank you, the City of New York has received the following service request and someone will be reaching out to your shortly:**.

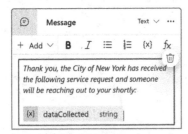

Figure 6.35: Updating the confirmation message

Testing Your Agent

There potentially is more that could be done to further improve the user experience, but for now, let's go ahead and test our agent to make sure all of our changes have been recorded. Click the Test button in the upper-right corner of the Copilot Studio user interface. Type in **"How do I apply?"** and hit Enter. Fill out the Adaptive Card, as shown in Figure 6.36, to **Apply for a business license**, with the reason of **Establishing a new business**, select Yes to confirm you are a resident, and then enter your email address. Finally, click the Submit button to post your form.

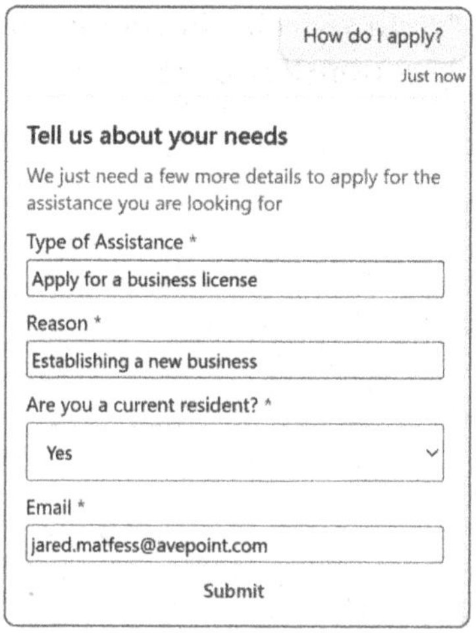

Figure 6.36: Applying for a business license

This will present the confirmation message, as shown in Figure 6.37, to let you know that your request was received.

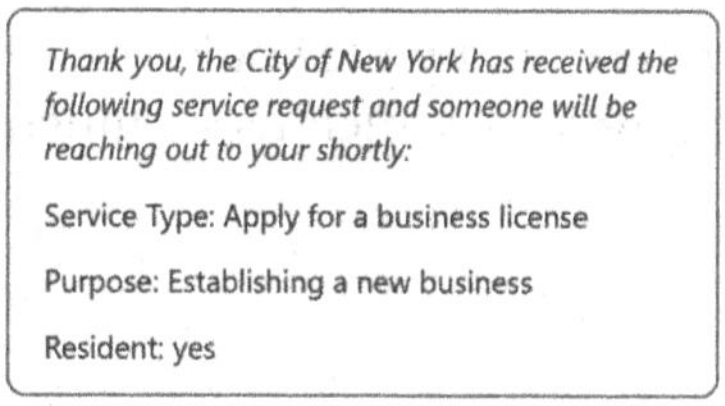

Thank you, the City of New York has received the following service request and someone will be reaching out to your shortly:

Service Type: Apply for a business license

Purpose: Establishing a new business

Resident: yes

Figure 6.37: The confirmation message

When you check your email, you might notice that the formatting doesn't look quite right, as shown in Figure 6.38.

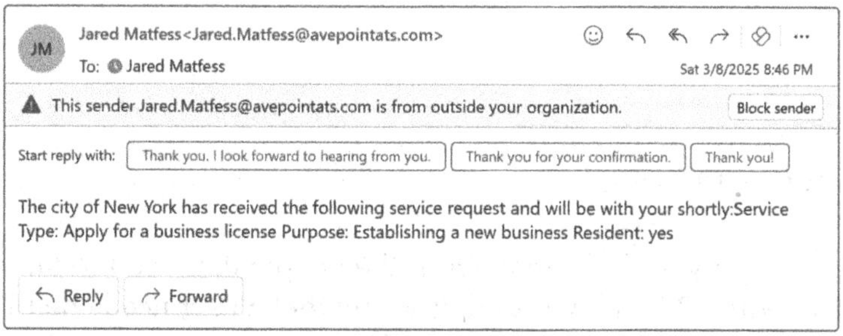

Figure 6.38: The email confirmation

What we will need to do is navigate back to the Data Collection topic and adjust the Set Variable Value node. Click the > button next to the variable assignment. Enter the following text into the formula, as shown in Figure 6.39, and then click Insert: "<p>Service Type: " &Topic.serviceType&"
Service Purpose: " & Topic.servicePurpose & "
Resident: " & Topic.currentResident.

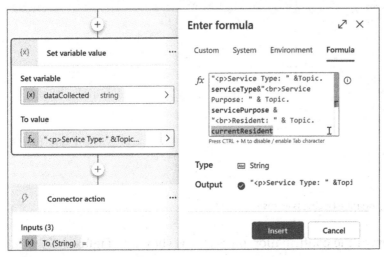

Figure 6.39: The updated formula

Run a test again of your agent with the same values, and you should see an email formatted similarly to what appears in Figure 6.40, which looks much more presentable.

Figure 6.40: The updated email formatting

Now, you may be asking yourself, what about the people that need to take action on this service request? How would they know that a user needs help? Well, a really quick change that we can make would be to add a shared mailbox to the CC field of the message. To do that, navigate back to the Data Collection topic, and expand the Advanced Inputs for the Send Email connector action. Add a shared mailbox in your environment (or your own email address for testing), as a formula between double quotes, as shown in Figure 6.41. Click the Insert button, and then save your topic. Now you can test one more time to ensure that your shared mailbox is CC'd on the confirmation email that is returned back to your constituent.

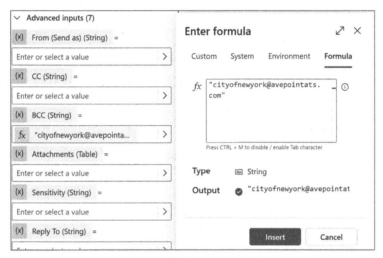

Figure 6.41: Mapping advanced inputs

Conclusion

In this chapter, we explored how topics can help drive a conversational flow, be chained together, and leverage the GenAI capability in Copilot Studio. We started by creating a new agent from the Citizen Services template and went through its initial setup.

Next, we adapted the agent for a "City of New York" scenario so it can answer questions using two public websites as its main knowledge source. To make the experience more interactive, we used Adaptive Cards to collect user information. We then added a connector action to automatically send a confirmation email back to the user, copying a shared mailbox to verify that the service request was received.

This combination of topics and connector actions lays a solid foundation for building more complex, dynamic conversational experiences in Copilot Studio. We'll be revisiting this use case again in the next chapter to further optimize our agent to serve its user base.

CHAPTER

7

Real-World Use Cases and Inspiration

Agents fit into the IT portfolio as a flexible automation and augmentation layer, bridging the gap between traditional business applications and workflow automation. By "augmentation layer," I mean that agents don't necessarily replace existing IT tools or applications. For many use cases, agents will work alongside enterprise systems, bridging the gaps between platforms, automating repetitive tasks, and providing AI-driven decision support. We have already worked through a couple of use cases as a means to help familiarize you with the technology and to show you how to configure agents.

In this chapter, we are going to switch gears a little bit from how to build agents to which use cases might make sense to build an agent for. We will look at examples that are both industry- and function-specific. My intent is to provide real-world examples of how agents can deliver real business value. I hope to spark your creativity so that when you are analyzing your own organization and the potential opportunities, you'll be able to drive productivity and deliver real business value.

Agents in the Contact Center

Contact centers or customer call centers can be some of the more challenging environments to work in. Your productivity is monitored and tracked across multiple dashboards; customers are usually calling with complicated scenarios

171

172 Chapter 7 ■ Real-World Use Cases and Inspiration

that require great attention to detail; there's a host of policies and procedures that you need to be familiar with; and overall, contact centers are high-pressure environments where every minute matters. Additionally, contact centers have some of the highest turnover rates due to the high-pressure environment.

Whenever you think about roles or functions that have a high degree of turnover, you need to think about how you bring someone on board to your organization and get them up to speed with the policies, procedures, and technology needed to make them successful and productive. In addition to the roles and responsibilities, there is also a cultural element to how an organization delivers customer service. Over time, we will see many customer service software packages include AI assistant features to help address some of these gaps. In the meantime, there is a real opportunity to experiment with agents to assist with onboarding a new employee to a customer. Let's go ahead and target one specific area where a new employee may benefit from an agent assisting them with their work: navigating a set of policies and procedures.

The Scenario

Policies and procedure documents tend to be very long, detailed, technical, and differ from company to company. When you consider people who work in contact centers, you need to assume there is a mix of folks who have worked previously in similar roles with different policies and procedures, while others may be brand new to the role.

Usually, when someone is referring to policies and procedures, it's in the context of what a customer is trying to do. For example, if a customer is inquiring about performing a return or exchange of a good that they purchased, the contact center representative may need to look up the policy given the customer's scenario. A return may have very different guidelines than an exchange. And certainly, when you are supporting a customer looking to perform either of these transactions, it is important to be accurate as well as resolve the issue in a timely manner.

When you consider how a new customer service representative may handle a customer inquiry that they do not know the answer to, they will likely either ask for time to review the policy documentation or ask a colleague. Some individuals may be uncomfortable asking a supervisor or colleague, as this may reflect a lack of retention from onboarding training or just an overall gap in knowledge. These individuals may choose instead to try to sift through lengthy documentation while the customer waits for next steps on their path to resolution. Others may feel very comfortable asking for help, perhaps even too comfortable sometimes. However, if you take a step back, either scenario lends itself to being a potentially good application for an agent.

Since policy and procedure documentation is typically viewed as proprietary, we will instead use data that is both confusing and openly available: the

Microsoft 365 Licensing Guide. Imagine that you are supporting a contact center that answers questions about which products are included in each of Microsoft's various SKUs. So, we will use the Microsoft 365 Enterprise Licensing Guide as our knowledge source.

> **NOTE** You can download the sample file called *Chapter 7.zip* from the downloadable file on the Wiley site at www.wiley.com/go/copilotstudioqs.

Technical Setup

So, let's create a new knowledge-based agent called "Contact Center Charlie." Open your browser and navigate to copilotstudio.microsoft.com. Make sure you are in your developer sandbox environment in the upper-right corner, and then click the Agents link in the left-hand navigation. Next, click the + New agent button, and then click Skip to Configure to exit creating your agent using natural language. Name your agent **Contact Center Charlie**, and then enter the following description for your agent: "**This agent will assist contact center representatives navigate policy and procedures documentation to help deliver greater customer service. It will allow the user to ask questions in natural language and receive an answer that includes where the agent found the answer within the documentation.**"

Go ahead and create the agent, and then we will continue with the configuration. Next, we are going to set agent instructions. In the Instructions section, enter the following text:

Instructions:

* **Please only return responses based on the information found in the knowledge source.**

* **Do not attempt to answer the question on your own.**

* **If you are unsure or if the question is not clear, please prompt the user to ask the question differently.**

* **If you find more than one answer, please present both options to the user so that they may decide which one best meets their needs.**

Confirm that your agent configuration looks similar to what is shown in Figure 7.1, and then click the Create button in the upper-right corner.

Next, let's configure the knowledge source that the agent will reference when answering questions. Scroll down to the Knowledge section of the agent configuration. Locate the toggle labeled "Allow the AI to use its own general knowledge," as shown in Figure 7.2. It's currently set to enabled, which means that the agent could potentially respond with information beyond its knowledge. You do not want your agent to respond with information that is not considered official, so

Chapter 7 ▪ Real-World Use Cases and Inspiration

go ahead and toggle that to disabled. A dialog box will appear confirming that "When disabled, your agent will not use the default AI knowledge and only reference the sources listed under Knowledge." Click the Continue button.

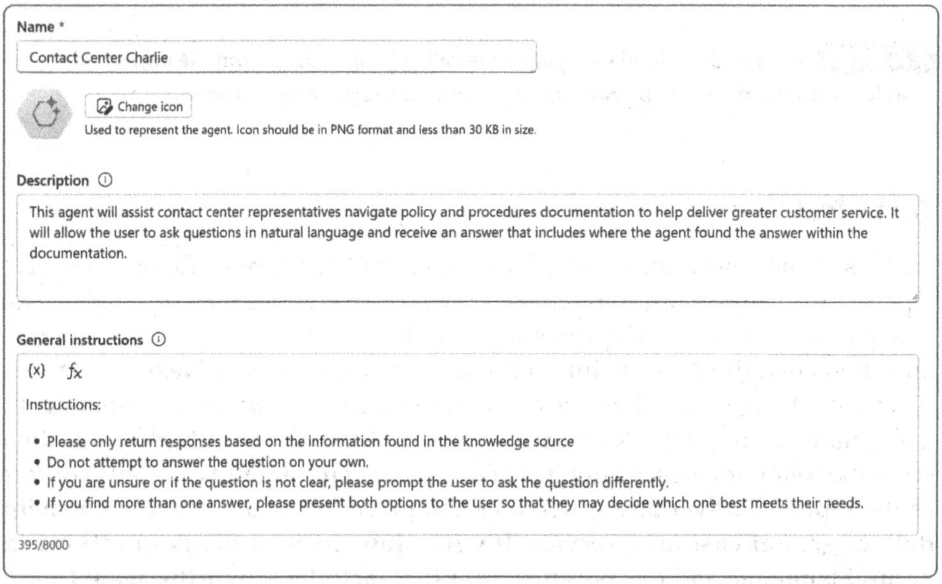

Name *

Contact Center Charlie

🔄 Change icon
Used to represent the agent. Icon should be in PNG format and less than 30 KB in size.

Description ⓘ

This agent will assist contact center representatives navigate policy and procedures documentation to help deliver greater customer service. It will allow the user to ask questions in natural language and receive an answer that includes where the agent found the answer within the documentation.

General instructions ⓘ

(x) ƒx

Instructions:

- Please only return responses based on the information found in the knowledge source
- Do not attempt to answer the question on your own.
- If you are unsure or if the question is not clear, please prompt the user to ask the question differently.
- If you find more than one answer, please present both options to the user so that they may decide which one best meets their needs.

395/8000

Figure 7.1: The Contact Center Charlie agent's initial configuration

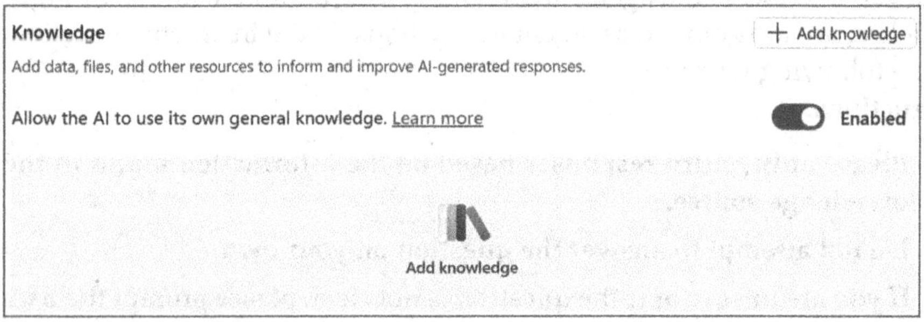

Knowledge   ➕ Add knowledge

Add data, files, and other resources to inform and improve AI-generated responses.

Allow the AI to use its own general knowledge. Learn more   🔵 Enabled

Add knowledge

Figure 7.2: Configuring the knowledge source

Next, click the Add Knowledge button and notice there's a section to upload files. Either drag the Microsoft Licensing Guide PDF to the dialog box or click the Click to Browse link, as shown in Figure 7.3, to upload the file to Dataverse.

Next, you'll need to provide a name and description for the file. Feel free to leave the name as-is, but for the description, include the following text: **This file contains a comprehensive list of all Microsoft 365 products and their corresponding SKUs. It includes detailed information on the features and services included in each SKU, allowing for easy comparison and verification of product offerings across different plans and bundles.** Once you've updated the text, click the Add button to upload the file to Dataverse.

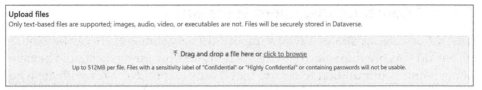

Figure 7.3: Uploading files to Dataverse

> **NOTE** To upload files to Dataverse as a knowledge source, you'll need available storage in your environment. For more details on Dataverse licensing costs, refer to `docs.microsoft.com/en-us/power-platform/admin/pricing-billing-skus`.

Testing the Contact Center Agent

Now that you have set up your knowledge source, you can test your agent from within Copilot Studio. Click the Test button in the upper-right corner to open the conversation window. The following are a couple of questions that you can pose to your agent based on the data:

- What's the difference between E3 & E5 licenses?
- What licensing is available for Frontline Workers?
- What's the difference between F1 & F3 licenses?

As you'll notice in Figure 7.4, each time your agent answers a question, it references the file where it found the information. If you want, you could pull in additional licensing guides for the other major Microsoft offerings, such as Dynamics 365, Azure, etc., and expand your agent's knowledge.

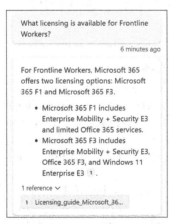

Figure 7.4: Testing Contact Center Charlie

Contact Center Charlie Agent Summary

This use case demonstrates just how impactful a very simple agent can be. Notice, all we did was provide some light instructions for how the agent should behave, some minor configuration to ensure that it only responded back with answers found in the knowledge source, and then we configured the knowledge source. Now you have an agent that can easily answer questions about one of the most complicated topics in the IT world, Microsoft licensing bundles.

Agents in the Public Sector

Public sector employees are often met with the challenges of a never-ending volume of work, complicated collective bargaining agreements, a wide variety of people to serve, and chronic underfunding and underinvestment. While employees are often met with very challenging scenarios, their ingenuity at building out processes to help better serve their constituents can be rather impressive. As we touched on in Chapter 6, shared mailboxes are used quite frequently as a work intake mechanism, as we developed with our BigAppleBuddy agent. Typically, these mailboxes are managed by multiple individuals, with folks taking turns based on scheduling, capacity, etc.

One of the challenges with using a shared mailbox setup is that it is hard to stay organized in terms of who is working on which request. Usually, you would attempt some sort of first in, first out (FIFO) method, but there is no built-in assignment to emails. Additionally, there isn't an easy way to track the volume of requests coming in for repeatable patterns or to understand the current workload of members managing the mailbox. For this example, let's extend the BigAppleBuddy agent from Chapter 6 with some additional functionality to help our public sector employees structure their work a bit better.

Technical Setup

Before we start working in Copilot Studio, it would be helpful to have a shared mailbox created in Exchange Online that has been delegated either to your Entra ID or to an Entra ID that you have access to. Delegated access to a shared mailbox means that you have access to send emails on behalf of that mailbox. If you're in a scenario where this isn't possible due to your organization's requirements, that's okay—you can use your own account, and I will call out the slight modifications needed when applicable.

Second, to organize these constituent requests, it would be helpful to have a SharePoint list to track them. Some organizations have workflow management tools like ServiceNow, Zendesk, Jira, etc., but in lieu of an enterprise workflow management system, we can rely on good old SharePoint to help manage our work. You will need a SharePoint site, and then within that site a custom list called Requests. In case it has been a little bit since the last time you've had to make a SharePoint list, click the gear icon within your SharePoint site, and then select the Add an App link, as shown in Figure 7.5. Then, click the Custom List app from the list of available apps either in the Noteworthy section or below in the list of Apps You Can Add. Next, name your app **Requests**, and then click the Create button.

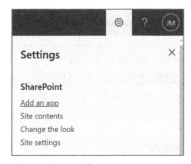

Figure 7.5: Adding an app

You should be redirected to the site contents view of your SharePoint site, and see a new List called Requests, as shown in Figure 7.6. Click the Requests list so that a few columns can be added to your custom list.

Name	Type	Items	Modified
Documents	Document library	0	2/24/2025 10:29 PM
Form Templates	Document library	0	3/10/2025 5:20 AM
Site Assets	Document library	4	3/10/2025 5:19 AM
Style Library	Document library	0	2/24/2025 10:29 PM
Requests	List	0	3/10/2025 5:36 AM
Site Pages	Page library	2	3/10/2025 5:19 AM

Figure 7.6: Site contents

What we are going to do is create a column for each of the fields in our SharePoint list to match the data that we collect from the Adaptive Card in the Data Collection topic. We will create five custom columns, as noted in Table 7.1.

Chapter 7 ■ Real-World Use Cases and Inspiration

Table 7.1: Custom Columns

NAME	TYPE	DETAILS
ServiceType	Text	This captures the type of request that the person is looking for help with.
ServiceReason	Text	This is the reason for the service request.
CurrentResident	Text	This notes if the person submitting the request is a resident of New York City.
Email	Text	This is the email address of the person submitting the request.
Status	Choice	This is for internal tracking of the request with the following options: New, Assigned, and Completed.
Assignee	Person	This internal column is used to track who worked on the request.

To create these columns, perform the following steps:

1. Click the Add Column link, as shown in Figure 7.7.
2. Select the type of column you want to create.
3. Click the Next button.
4. Type the name of the column.
5. Click the Save button to create the column.

Repeat these steps to create all five columns.

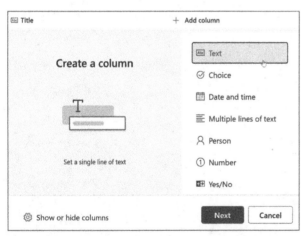

Figure 7.7: Adding columns

Now that you have created the columns, navigate back to Copilot Studio and open your BigAppleBuddy agent. What we're going to do is have the agent create an item in the SharePoint list that we just created.

Chapter 7 ■ Real-World Use Cases and Inspiration 179

> **NOTE** If you didn't create the BigAppleBuddy agent in Chapter 6, you can create a new agent and select from the Citizen Services agent template to pick up from here to follow along.

To get started, first click the Actions link in the top navigation, and then click the + Add an Action button. Click the + New Action drop-down menu, as shown in Figure 7.8, and then select New Power Automate Flow from the list of choices. This will launch you into Power Automate.

Figure 7.8: Selecting the New Power Automate Flow

Click the Run a Flow from Copilot text in the upper-left corner and type the text **BigApple Create Service Request** to rename your Power Automate flow. I prefer the classic Power Automate designer, so I will toggle off New Designer in the upper-right corner. We are going to add the outputs from the Adaptive Card as inputs to this flow to help create the list items in SharePoint. Click + Add an Input from the Skills node at the top of the canvas, select the Text type of input, and then enter **ServiceType**. Repeat these same steps to create the ServicePurpose, Resident, and Email inputs, as shown in Figure 7.9.

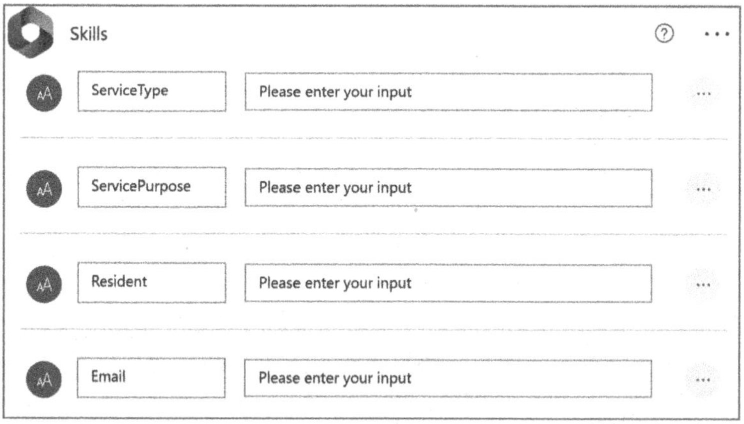

Figure 7.9: Creating the inputs

180 **Chapter 7 ▪ Real-World Use Cases and Inspiration**

Next, click the + Add Action button below the Skills node, and then type in **SharePoint Create item** in the search menu. Select the SharePoint Create Item action to add that to the authoring canvas, as shown in Figure 7.10.

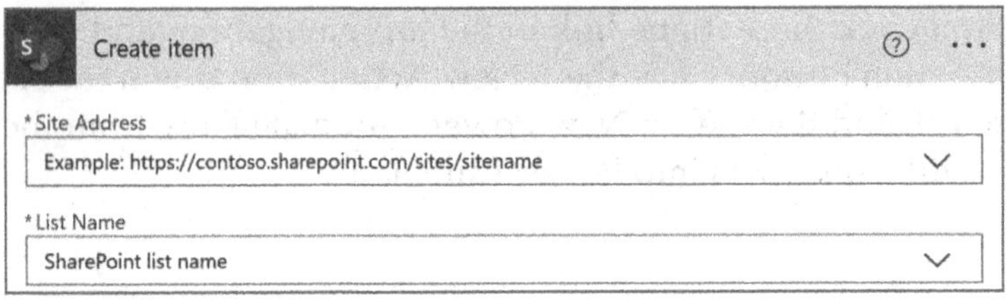

Figure 7.10: Creating an item action

From here, we will need to add the site address, which is the URL to the SharePoint site you created earlier. The List Name should be Requests if you are following along. Once you populate both the Site Address and List Name fields, the node should pull in the applicable fields associated with that list. You'll notice that the Title field is required, as shown in Figure 7.11. Sometimes people use that field to create a numbering system for referencing the tickets, so you can do something like Service Type - Email, as I have done, or you can choose your own convention. Then, map the rest of the fields to the inputs, as shown in Figure 7.11. Lastly, set the Status Value field to New since this is a new service request.

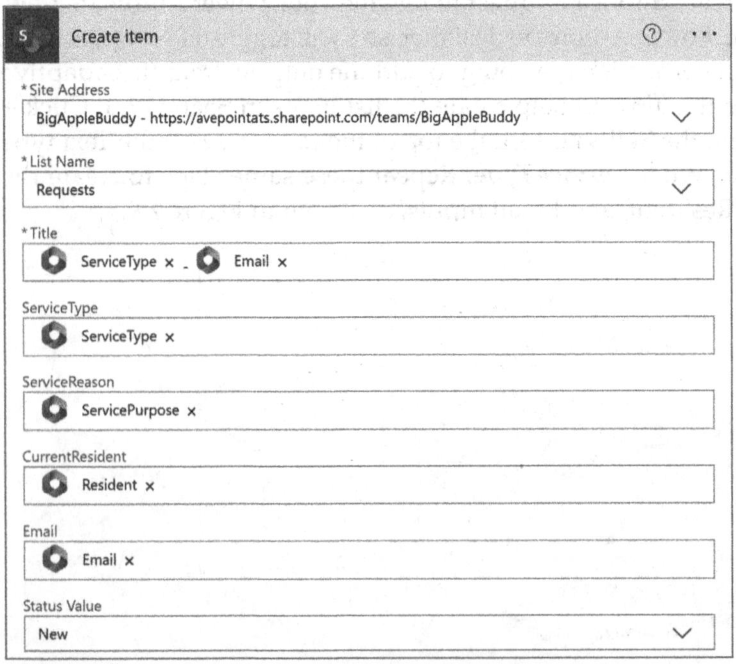

Figure 7.11: Configuring the Create Item action

Once you have confirmed that all the values have been set, click the Save button. Go back to Copilot Studio and navigate to Actions. Click + Add an Action, and then select the BigApple Create Service Request flow, as shown in Figure 7.12. Finally, click Add Action in the next window.

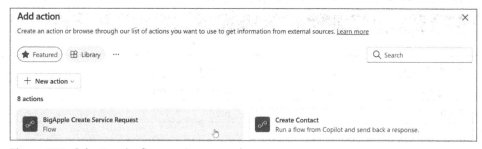

Figure 7.12: Selecting the flow you just created

You should now see your BigApple Create Service Request action in the list of available actions. Click the Topics link in the top navigation, and then open the Data Collection topic. Scroll down and just before the last node in the workflow, click the Add Node button. Then, click the arrow next to Add an Action from the pop-up menu and select your BigApple Create Service Request action, as shown in Figure 7.13.

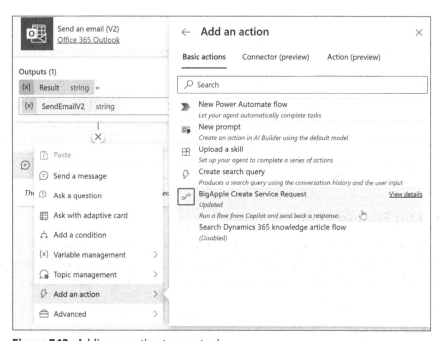

Figure 7.13: Adding an action to your topic

Now, the Action node that was just added to your canvas will need to be configured. We need to map the variables captured in the Adaptive Card to the input needed to run our Power Automate workflow, as documented in Table 7.2.

Table 7.2: Power automate inputs to topic variable mapping

POWER AUTOMATE INPUT	COPILOT STUDIO VARIABLE
ServiceType	serviceType
ServicePuprose	servicePurpose
Resident	currentResident
Email	mail

Once you have finished mapping the variables, your node should look like Figure 7.14. Click Save and exit Power Automate.

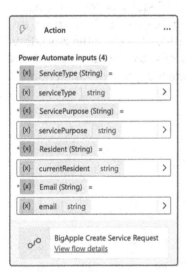

Figure 7.14: Configuring node inputs

Testing Our Shared Mailbox Agent

Navigate back to your agent and click the Test button in the upper-right corner to open the chat window. Remember that the Apply for a Service topic is what calls the Data Collection topic, so you can use one of the following trigger phrases:

- Apply for a license
- How do I apply?
- I would like to apply for
- etc.

You will be presented with the Adaptive Card to fill out just like before, and when you submit it, the agent will start processing your request. As it works through the process, however, it will throw the error message, as shown in Figure 7.15.

Figure 7.15: Adding an action to your topic

While it may appear that you can resolve this by clicking the Connect button, that won't solve the problem and is an example where sometimes error messages are a little misleading. The error message is correct that there is a user permissions error, but it's actually with the Power Automate flow we just created and not with the action or connections configured in Copilot Studio.

To resolve this, start by opening a new tab. Navigate back to `make.power automate.com` (Power Automate) and click My Flows in the left navigation. You should see your BigApple Create Service Request flow under the Cloud Flows section. Click it to open the flow.

Scroll down until you see a section on the right side called Run Only Users, as shown in Figure 7.16.

Figure 7.16: Run only users

Click the Edit button to open the Manage Run-only Permissions panel, and then click the SharePoint button. Next, select the Site from the drop-down menu and your Requests List from the List/Library menu, as shown in Figure 7.17. Then, click the Add button to enable users to run your flow against that list. Scroll down to the Connections Used section and notice that it's currently set to Provided by Run-only User. This means that the user would be prompted to provide their credentials, which is what's causing the flow to break. Set this to Use This Connection to use the connection you made to SharePoint, and then click the Save button.

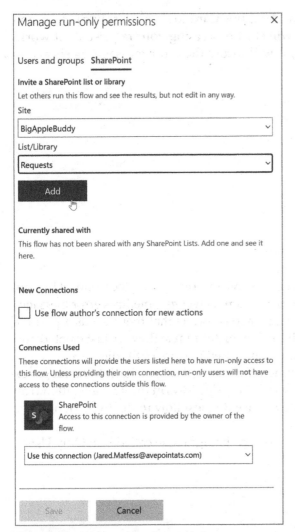

Figure 7.17: Manage run-only permissions

In Power Automate, run-only permissions allow users to execute a flow without having the ability to modify it. This is useful when you want to share a flow with others but don't want them to make any changes to it. You can also choose to have run-only users provide their own connections, which is what this flow initially had set. This means that when the flow runs, it uses the context of the user running the flow instead of the connection configured in the flow. This is useful for creating items or documents based on the user. However, for our scenario, these would be external users who would be initiating these requests, so they would not have access to the backend SharePoint "list."

With our flow's Run-Only Users setting updated, let's go back to Copilot Studio to once again test our flow. Click the circular arrow in the right-hand corner of the Testing menu to refresh the chat conversation. Then, use one of the same trigger phrases as before, such as Apply for a License. Fill out the Tell Us About Your Needs Adaptive Card that's presented to you, as shown in Figure 7.18. Be sure to put your own email address.

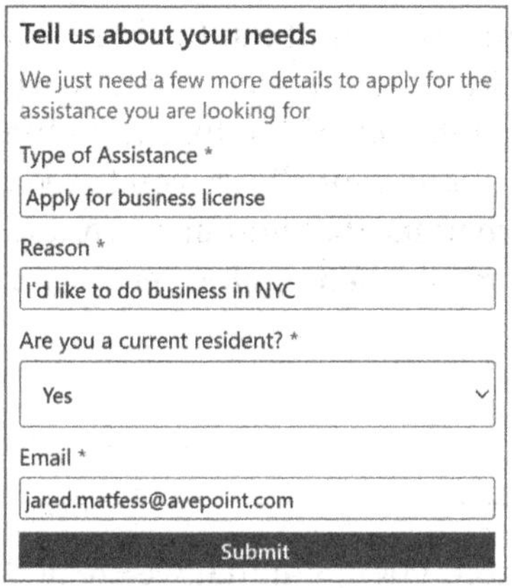

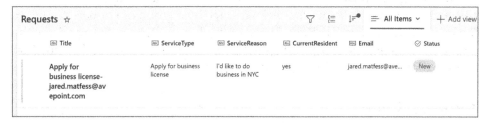

Figure 7.18: Tell us about your needs

Click the Submit button, and your agent will respond with the following message:

"Thank you, the City of New York has received the following service request and someone will be reaching out to your shortly:

Service Type: Apply for business license

Service Purpose: I'd like to do business in NYC

Resident: yes

"You should receive an email notification at the email address you provided in the Adaptive Card confirming your submission."

Next, navigate back to the SharePoint site you created and click Site Contents in the left-hand navigation. Click the Requests list in the Site Contents view, and you should see a new item in your list, as shown in Figure 7.19.

Figure 7.19: The new item is added to the SharePoint list

Summary of the Shared Mailbox Agent

In this example, we took our knowledge agent that was able to return information from a couple of websites and extended it to help facilitate a business process.

Chapter 7 ■ Real-World Use Cases and Inspiration

We've gone from having public sector workers needing to worry about the order in which emails come in to having them logged to a SharePoint list for assignment. This is a first step in creating structure for a slightly unstructured business process.

As you can imagine, this use case could continue to be built out further with automatic assignment to individuals based on current workload or to look up common resolutions from knowledge and automatically share that with the constituent. Also, maintaining the information in SharePoint allows you to look for patterns in the data. This would also inform changes that you may want to make either to the agent or to the knowledge sources to help make it easier for people to find the information they are looking for.

Agents in Human Resources

For the last use case, I want to revisit our Heidi from HR agent that we created in Chapter 4. This agent was a classic example of an agent focused on supporting a knowledge use case. We provided a set of instructions to try and keep the agent from deviating from responding back with anything besides resources it found in our HR sites. But life tends to be a bit more complicated, and not everything can be solved by reading a policy or procedure document. Also, when it comes to HR-related matters, there are certainly legalities and sensitivities that would be better suited for a human to address. As we talked about earlier, there are examples of agent-to-human handoff through certain contact center solutions—Dynamics 365 Customer Service, Salesforce Service Cloud, ServiceNow, LivePerson, Genesys, etc.

However, not all organizations have one of these solutions in place to support back-office support functions like Human Resources, Legal, Marketing, etc. In this scenario, let's make some modifications to our Heidi from HR agent to help support an agent-to-human handoff through Microsoft Teams. We will once again leverage the power of connectors in the Power Platform to handoff a user request to a Microsoft Teams channel managed by a group of Human Resources Business Professionals (HRBPs). These individuals will be able to address the employee's issues and not put the company in any sort of a liability position by potentially disclosing incorrect information.

Technical Setup

You can choose to either start with the previous Heidi from HR agent or a brand new agent; either is fine, as we will be focused on building the agent-to-human handoff functionality. You will also need to create a Microsoft Teams team called "HR Business Partners" or something similar. What our agent will do is collect the severity and nature of the request and then post that to a Microsoft

Teams team for an HR Business Partner to look into. Depending on the nature of the request, the HRBP with the correct subject-matter expertise can provide the response back to the individual. There isn't anything special needed for the Microsoft Teams team, but of course, if you were to create this agent in a production environment, you would definitely want to make sure that it is a private team with access restricted to just those who should have access.

We will build out the escalation to the HRB from within the Escalate topic next. Navigate to Topics from within your agent, click the System button, and then click the Escalate topic to begin editing it. Notice the list of trigger phrases preconfigured, as shown in Figure 7.20.

Figure 7.20: Escalation trigger phrases

These are worded for a customer service type of use case. Let's create a couple of trigger phrases that are more suitable for an HR use case. As someone who doesn't have a ton of HR experience, this is a great use case for pulling in Copilot to help. Open a new tab in your browser and navigate to `copilot.cloud.microsoft`. Try typing in the following prompt: **Can you please brainstorm 5-10 short trigger phrases that can be used for an HR agent that would make sense to hand off to a human? For example, "I need to speak with someone in HR"?**, and then press Enter. You should receive a list of potential trigger phrases, as shown in Figure 7.21. While this list may not be exhaustive, it's a great starting point.

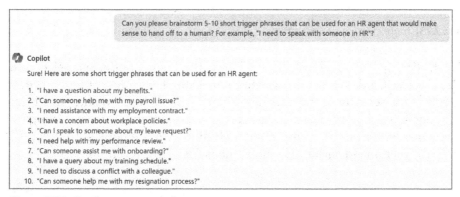

Figure 7.21: Copilot suggested phrases

Flip back to your open Copilot Studio tab and click the Edit button beneath On Talk to Representative, as shown in Figure 7.20. This will open an On Talk to Representative Properties panel window, where you will click the Phrases button, as shown in Figure 7.22.

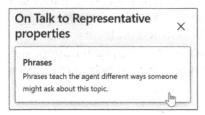

Figure 7.22: Editing the trigger phrases

There are a couple of options for loading in phrases to your topic. You can enter them in one at a time, clicking the "+" button for each phrase. There is an option to bulk copy and paste them in by line-separating each phrase, or, finally, you can upload them in a file. You'll notice that Copilot Studio provides you with a sample file to download, as shown in Figure 7.23, to help assist with bulk loading in phrases. Choose the approach you are most comfortable with, and then let's continue.

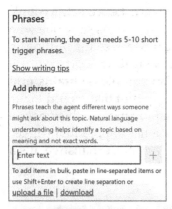

Figure 7.23: Trigger phrase loading options

Next, click the + Add a Node button below the Trigger node, and select Ask with Adaptive Card. What we're going to do is display an Adaptive Card that will collect the severity of the issue and then allow the user to enter in a brief description to send to the HR team. You can type the code presented in Listing 7.1 or copy the code from the sample file included with the book's downloads, which was mentioned earlier. The filename is *C07_HR_Agent.json*.

Chapter 7 ▪ Real-World Use Cases and Inspiration 189

Listing 7.1: The Adaptive Card text (C07_HR_Agent.json)

```
{
    "$schema": "http://adaptivecards.io/schemas/adaptive-card.json",
    "type": "AdaptiveCard",
    "version": "1.0",
    "body": [
      {
        "type": "ColumnSet",
        "columns": [
          {
            "type": "Column",
            "width": 2,
            "items": [
              {
                "type": "TextBlock",
                "text": "How can we help you?",
                "weight": "bolder",
                "size": "medium",
                "wrap": true,
                "style": "heading"
              },
              {
                "type": "TextBlock",
                "text": "We just need a few details to share with the
HRBP team",
                "isSubtle": true,
                "wrap": true
              },
              {
                "type": "Input.ChoiceSet",
                "id": "severity",
                "label": "How urgent is this issue?",
                "isRequired": true,
                "choices": [
                  {
                    "title": "Normal - 1-2 hours response",
                    "value": "normal"
                  },
                  {
                    "title": "Urgent - 1-2 hours response",
                    "value": "urgent"
                  }
                ],
                "errorMessage": "Invalid response. Please select Normal
or Urgent."
              },
              {
                "type": "Input.Text",
                "id": "description",
```

```
                "label": "Description",
                "isRequired": true,
                "isMultiline":true,
                "regex": "^[a-zA-Z0-9,'.-\\s]+$",
                "errorMessage": "Please enter your service type using
alphanumeric characters and the following symbols ',.-"
            }
          ]
        }
      ]
    }
  ],
  "actions": [
    {
      "type": "Action.Submit",
      "title": "Submit"
    }
  ]
}
```

Click the ellipses in the upper-right corner of the Adaptive Card node, and then click Properties to open the Adaptive Card Node Properties menu. You'll want to paste this JSON beneath the Edit JSON label, as shown in Figure 7.24.

Figure 7.24: Creating your Adaptive Card

Now, we're going to create two variables to pass to the Power Automate flow that will notify the HR team on Microsoft Teams about the submission. Click the Add Node button directly below the Adaptive Card node, then hover over Variable Management, and, finally, select Set a Variable Value. Click Select a Variable, and then click Create a New Variable from the pop-up window. This will create a variable called "Var1," as shown in Figure 7.25.

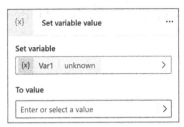

Figure 7.25: Configuring the Var1 variable

Click Var1, which will open a Variable properties panel. Rename the Var1 to Email, and then click the X button to minimize the panel. Next, click the Select Variable button on the input under To Value. Click System, as shown in Figure 7.26, type in **User.Email**, and then select that from the list of variables.

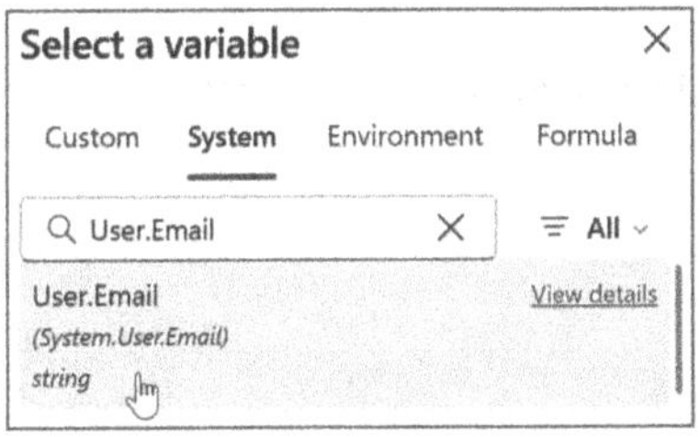

Figure 7.26: Configuring the Email variable

Repeat those same steps to create a second "DisplayName," and set the value to **User.DisplayName**, which can also be found under the System variables. Next, click the last node called "Message" to edit the text. Delete all the existing test and type in the following: **Your request has been sent to the HR Team, and you should be hearing from someone soon!** Click the Save button to save your progress.

Now, we are going to create the Power Automate flow that will receive this information and post it into Microsoft Teams. To get started, click the Actions button in the navigation, and then click +Add an Action. A pop-up window will appear to add an action. Click the + New Action from the drop-down menu and select New Power Automate Flow. In the Skills node, create four text inputs: Email, DisplayName, IssueSeverity, and IssueDescription. Next, click + Insert a New Step after the Skills node, and then click the Add an Action link. Type in **Microsoft Teams post card in a chat or channel** and select that action from the list.

Next, leave the Post As defaulted to Flow Bot, and then in the Post In drop-down menu, select Channel. From the Team drop-down menu, select your HR Business Partners team that you just created. Then click the Channel drop-down menu and select General or your channel of choice to have your agent post to

192   Chapter 7 ▪ Real-World Use Cases and Inspiration

that channel. Next, copy and paste the text from Listing 7.2 into the Adaptive Card field.

Listing 7.2: Adaptive Code text (C07_HR_PowerAutomate_Flow.json)

```
{
    "type": "AdaptiveCard",
    "body": [
        {
            "type": "TextBlock",
            "size": "Medium",
            "weight": "Bolder",
            "text": "New HR Request",
            "style": "heading",
            "color": "Dark"
        },
        {
            "type": "TextBlock",
            "text": "The following request has been submitted by:",
            "wrap": true
        },
        {
            "type": "TextBlock",
            "text": "",
            "wrap": true
        },
        {
            "type": "TextBlock",
            "text": "Issue Severity:",
            "wrap": true
        },
        {
            "type": "TextBlock",
            "text": "",
            "wrap": true
        },
        {
            "type": "TextBlock",
            "text": "Issue Description:",
            "wrap": true
        },
        {
            "type": "TextBlock",
            "text": "",
            "wrap": true
        },
        {
            "type": "TextBlock",
            "text": "Email address:",
            "wrap": true
        },
        {
```

```
                "type": "TextBlock",
                "text": "",
                "wrap": true
            }
        ],
        "$schema": "http://adaptivecards.io/schemas/adaptive-card.json",
        "version": "1.5"
}
```

If you look closely at the JSON, you'll notice there are four parameters called `text`, each with a value of `""`. What you'll be doing next is mapping the inputs from the first step in the flow into the double quotes to render those as values. For example, if you look at Figure 7.27, you will need to add the `DisplayName` input variable after the first `TextBlock` that displays "The following request has been submitted by."

```
{
  "type": "TextBlock",
  "text": "The following request has been submitted by:",
  "wrap": true
},
{
  "type": "TextBlock",
  "text": "   DisplayName ×  ",
  "wrap": true
},
```

Figure 7.27: Inserting the `DisplayName` variable

You'll repeat the pattern of adding the inputs between quotes for the remaining three empty double quotes. The order of inputs should be DisplayName, IssueSeverity, IssueDescription, and Email. Click the Run a Flow from Copilot text and rename the flow to Post a Message to HR, and then click the Save button. Click the back button to go back to Power Automate. Scroll down to the Run-Only Users section, click the Edit button, scroll down to the Connections Used section and change Provided by Run-only user to your connection to Microsoft Teams, as shown in Figure 7.28. Then click the Save button.

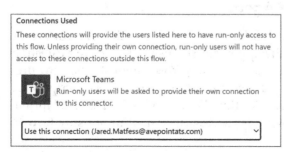

Figure 7.28: Configure Microsoft Teams connection

Navigate back to your agent, and then click the Actions link in the top navigation. Click + Add an Action, and this time select the Post a Message to HR flow you just created. Click Add Action in the open dialog box. Click the Topics link in the top navigation, click System, and then open the Escalate topic.

Scroll down to the bottom of your workflow, and right before the Message node, click the + Add Node button, and then hover over Add an Action, and then select the Post a Message to HR action you just created. This will add that node to the canvas, and our next step is to map the variables to the inputs for that action.

Once again, they should be relatively straightforward, but you should click the > arrow next to each input, and then select the Copilot Studio topic variable that matches the action input. So, for example, may the Email topic variable to the Email input. Once you're done selecting the variables, your node should look like Figure 7.29 without any error messages. Click the Save button to capture all of your changes, and then click the Go Back to Previous Page button in the upper-left corner of the Power Automate UI to exit out of your flow.

Figure 7.29: Mapping the input variables

Testing Your Heidi from HR Agent

Now we are ready to test all of our work to make sure everything is working as expected. Click the Test button in the upper-right corner, enter **I have a question about my benefits**, and then press the return key. Your agent should now present your Adaptive Card. Select the urgency, and then type a brief description of your issue, and then click the Submit button. For example, I selected a Normal urgency and provided the following issue description: "I'm not sure how to add my spouse to my benefits." Your agent will then return the following text: "Your request has been sent to the HR Team, and you should be hearing from someone soon!"

Now, open Microsoft Teams and navigate to the HR Team that you created. Assuming that everything is working as expected, you should see your submission posted as an Adaptive Card in the General channel for that Team, as shown in Figure 7.30. Notice that you have the full functionality of being able to like, reply, etc., just as if it were a message sent to Teams.

Figure 7.30: New HR Request in Teams

Summary of the Updated Heidi from HR Agent

In this example, we developed one of the most important aspects of working with AI: the capability to hand off a request to a user. This didn't require any special business process or workflow platforms; we were able to leverage services available as part of our Microsoft 365 subscription. Perhaps even more importantly, we were able to create these integrations and build this solution in less than an hour instead of over the course of several days or even weeks. And this solution is applicable beyond just HR; it can help support a relatively seamless handoff from agent to human across multiple use cases.

Conclusion

In this chapter, we covered a wide variety of examples of how you can introduce agents into your organization. We went through both industry and functional use cases and helped demonstrate the breadth of what this technology can do. Our agents grew beyond just knowledge use cases to support lightweight workflows to automate processes. In the next chapter, we will take our agent development skills one step further and explore the exciting capabilities of Microsoft's autonomous agents.

CHAPTER

8

Building an Autonomous Agent

Up until this point, we have mostly focused on building knowledge agents that serve in a question-and-response capability. However, the real potential opportunity for agents lies not in being able to answer questions but rather in their ability to complete tasks that you would otherwise have to do.

In this chapter, we will focus on building an autonomous agent, which is an agent that can operate independently, dynamically plan, orchestrate other agents, learn, and escalate. We'll step through the concepts of autonomous versus semi-autonomous when it comes to creating agents, before we then walk through creating an autonomous agent to help support a sales team with customer follow-up. We will configure the necessary triggers and actions to invoke the agent, followed by configuring actions that will help automate tasks that might otherwise be left to humans.

Let's start by digging into the term *autonomous agents* a bit more.

Autonomous vs. Semi-autonomous Agents

With all the excitement around GenAI, it can be challenging not to feed into the marketing hype and instead focus on what business problems we are looking to solve. There is a huge focus on *autonomous AI*, meaning that you are enabling AI to act independently from human oversight. However, given the current

197

maturity level of AI, this is most likely not ideal for most organizations. There is still the risk of AI producing hallucinations when returning responses to users.

Hallucinations refer to instances where an LLM generates content that is incorrect, despite appearing logical or plausible. This can happen when the LLM tries to fill in gaps in its training data with its own "imaginative" extrapolation. The challenge is that, despite being wrong, the LLM responds back with great confidence, which can be hard to detect when it's extrapolating versus correctly answering a question. Therefore, when planning your agent, it is important to think through some of the "what could go wrong" scenarios associated with handing AI the metaphorical wheel.

Considerations for Autonomous Agents

When considering the integration of AI into business processes, it is crucial to determine appropriate instances where human oversight is necessary to review AI-generated responses. Each business and use case varies, making it challenging to provide a definitive guideline. However, one should consider the potential consequences of an inexperienced employee performing a task incorrectly. Examples include providing customer quotes, managing sensitive HR matters, calculating severance packages, or handling complex financial transactions.

While technology advocates may highlight the efficiency and benefits AI offers, claiming it can complete tasks in seconds rather than minutes, its reliability and consistency remain uncertain. When developers create intricate platforms, they often invest considerable time in understanding and implementing business rules within the application logic. For instance, if a quote exceeds a certain threshold, managerial approval may be required before it is sent to a customer. Recognizing and documenting conditions that necessitate human verification of AI's work is an essential aspect of the development process.

When people talk about *responsible AI*, they often focus on the training data or perhaps on ensuring that AI doesn't release sensitive information accidentally, but you need to be the most diligent about something else. It is really the more benign examples—such as quoting a policy or procedure to a customer or providing pricing information—where you may want to consider implementing some level of checks and balances prior to information being provided by AI. Balancing which tasks are safe for AI versus where you might want to include a human to review AI's output prior to it being made available to your end customer is perhaps one of the most challenging aspects of developing agents.

How Microsoft's Autonomous Agents Work

Microsoft's initial release of its autonomous agents is quite interesting, as it is built upon many of the foundational elements that exist today within the Power Platform. For starters, invoking an agent up until this point has involved a user sending a text-based message to an agent to initiate a topic on the backend. However, when it comes to autonomous agents, the opportunity for invoking an agent is expanded significantly through the Power Platform. Microsoft has integrated Power Automate into Copilot Studio, which unlocks the ability to leverage triggers to invoke your agent to perform a series of tasks.

In the context of Power Automate, a trigger is an event that starts a workflow that you have defined. Think of a trigger like an "on switch" that kicks things into gear when a certain condition has been met. For the previous Zoë agent, the built-in trigger to invoke the agent is receiving a message from the user. Triggers in Power Automate, however, can be based on a variety of events, such as:

- **Time-based events:** For example, run a workflow every weekday at 8 a.m. from now until December.
- **Action-based events:** For instance, whenever a new email arrives in your inbox.
- **Changes in data:** For example, when a new item is added to a SharePoint list or a new file is uploaded to a defined OneDrive.

Once the trigger condition is met, the workflow will start executing the steps you have defined as part of your Power Automate flow. This helps provide some level of guardrails, in that the workflow will only be run should the particular condition you have defined be met.

When you combine this same approach with agents, you are able to further extend the capabilities of what you can accomplish with GenAI. Furthermore, as we will dig into later in this chapter, we will be able to leverage GenAI to orchestrate which actions your agent takes based on what it believes is closest to what the user is looking to accomplish. First, let's walk through the initial use case for our agent.

Autonomous Agent Use Case

For our autonomous agent, let's consider that you work for an organization that attends various trade shows and conferences throughout the year. During those conferences, your sales and services team works a booth, inviting attendees to fill out a simple form if they would like someone to follow up after the event to speak in more detail about your company's products or services. Typically, your sales team leverages a QR code at the booth that takes attendees to a simple form where they fill out their basic contact information for follow-up after the conference. One of the challenges is the back-end workflow to support attendee follow-up, including registering the lead into a CRM platform, creating a new contact record if one does not exist, and informing the sales representative responsible for that account to initiate the follow-up.

Chapter 8 ▪ Building an Autonomous Agent

If you have ever worked in a sales role, you have probably heard the phrase, "Time kills all deals." Therefore, it is important to capitalize on opportunities where someone is interested in your company's products or services and follow up before one of your competitors does. To help streamline this lead follow-up process, we will configure an agent who will assist with the back-end administration tasks to reduce the time between the event, the lead capture, and the follow-up with the attendee.

Microsoft Form Configuration

To replicate this process, let's quickly create a Microsoft Form that you can use to replicate the capturing of an attendee lead. Navigate to `forms.office.com` and walk through the process of creating a new form. To keep it relatively simple, we will only include three fields, all of which will be required to complete the form. This approach will hopefully encourage attendees to complete the form in its entirety. Once you have completed your Microsoft Form, it should look similar to Figure 8.1, with the following fields:

- **Name:** The attendee's name.
- **Company:** The attendee's company name.
- **Email:** The attendee's email address; you can choose to implement a restriction in Microsoft Forms to have it validate that the input is in the format of an email address.

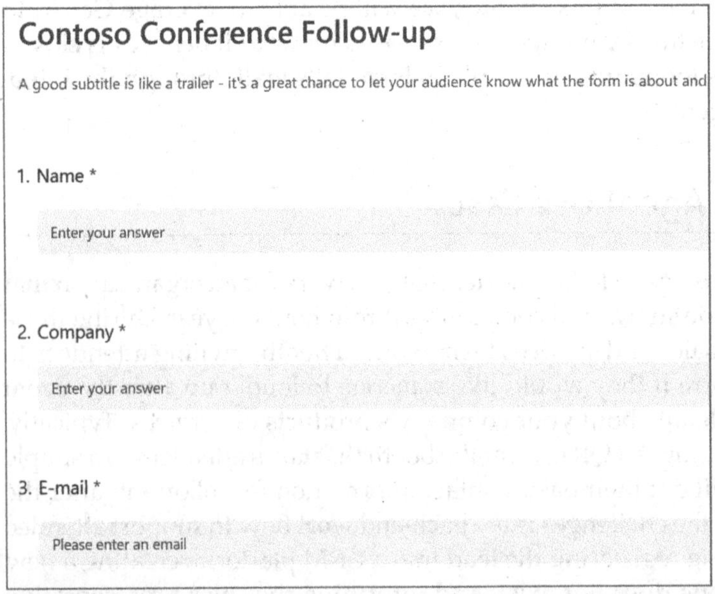

Figure 8.1: Conference follow-up form

To complete the process, click the Collect Responses button in the upper-right corner to open the Send and Collect Responses window, as shown in Figure 8.2. From here, you will want to adjust the form to allow anyone to respond so you can share this form with users outside of your company. Additionally, a QR code generator is built in to Microsoft Forms that will create a PNG file that you can include with your sales material. You can also have it create a shortened URL that you can share in case there's an issue or someone is uncomfortable scanning an unknown QR code. Now that you have a form, we will make sure that your customer relationship management (CRM) platform is ready for this use case.

Figure 8.2: Send and collect responses

Salesforce Sales Cloud Setup

For this use case, we will leverage Salesforce Sales Cloud as our CRM platform for managing opportunities and contacts. However, you can accomplish this same task with Dynamics 365, Zoho CRM, HubSpot CRM, and Pipedrive, all of which have Power Platform connectors available. If a nonproduction environment is available within your company, you can choose to follow along with that instance or sign up for a free developer account directly from Salesforce.com.

Chapter 8 ■ Building an Autonomous Agent

> **NOTE** You can sign up for a free Salesforce developer account, which gives you a fully functioning CRM instance at `developer.salesforce.com/signup`.

You will want to have a couple of Account and Contact objects in place prior to configuring your agent and running tests to simulate different use cases that your agent can assist with. You can reference Figure 8.3, which shows the minimum you need, which is a named account, an owner, and at least one contact record. You should have a couple of accounts, some with contacts and others without. This will help when you are ready to step through a couple of scenarios for your agent.

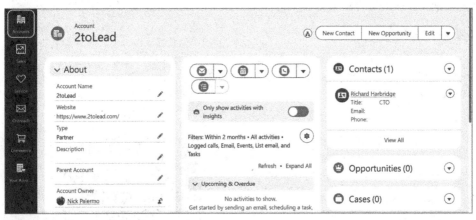

Figure 8.3: Account example

You can also reference Table 8.1 as an example of having a couple of named accounts and contact records associated with each account.

Table 8.1: Account and contacts

ACCOUNT NAME	CONTACT NAME	EMAIL
2toLead	Richard Harbridge	rharbridge1@2tolead.com
Microsoft	Abram Jackson	abrjackson@microsoft.com
Microsoft	Dona Sarkar	donasarkar@microsoft.com
Slalom	Dan Alling	dalling@slalom.com

Configuring Your Agent

Now that you have your Microsoft Form created as an input and your CRM configured with test accounts and contacts, it is time to begin working on creating your agent. Navigate back to `copilotstudio.microsoft.com` and confirm that you are in your developer sandbox environment to begin creating your agent. From the left-hand navigation, click the Create button and then select the New Agent option, as shown in Figure 8.4.

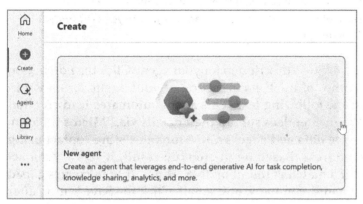

Figure 8.4: Creating a new agent

Enabling Orchestration

Click the Skip to Configure button in the upper-right corner, and then name your agent **Autonomous Amy** or something similar. Click the Create button.

Once your agent has been created, you can begin modifying its properties. In the Details section of your agent configuration, toggle the Orchestration option to Enabled, as shown in Figure 8.5.

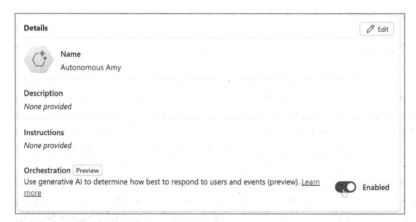

Figure 8.5: Enabling orchestration

Enabling orchestration is what makes your agent autonomous versus declarative. Orchestration empowers the agent to choose the best actions, knowledge, and topics to answer user queries based on their descriptions and inputs. It can also chain together multiple actions or topics, and ask follow-up questions to clarify details before proceeding.

> **NOTE** It is important to note that autonomous agents require very descriptive instructions for each step of the workflow to ensure accuracy, since you are programming through natural language.

Let's go ahead and provide a description for your agent. Click the Edit button in the upper-right corner of the Details section of your agent, as shown in Figure 8.6, and enter the following text: **This agent automates lead creation after a conference. When attendees submit their details via a Microsoft Form, it retrieves the response data and checks CRM for an existing contact using the provided email address. Based on the lookup result, it sets a "Contact Exists" flag to "Yes" if a match is found or "No" if not. It then creates a lead using the attendee's name, company, and email.** Click the Save button after you are done adding the description.

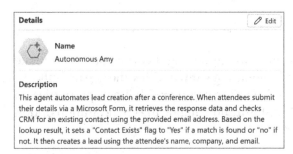

Figure 8.6: Adding an agent description

Creating a Trigger

Now, we are going to configure the trigger for your agent, which is the condition that will cause your agent to start working. A trigger is an event or condition that initiates an action by the agent. Triggers can be based on user inputs, such as specific phrases, or external events, like file uploads, allowing the agent to respond appropriately and perform predefined tasks. An example of a trigger with our previous agents is when a user first sends a message.

For this instance, we will create a trigger that will initiate our agent when an attendee has submitted the form we previously created. Scroll down until you see the Triggers section of your agent, and then click the + Add Trigger button in the upper-right corner, as shown in Figure 8.7.

This will open a new dialog window, as shown in Figure 8.8, which allows you to select from many predefined events. There is a search box available in the upper-right corner that will filter through the list of predefined triggers.

Chapter 8 ▪ Building an Autonomous Agent   205

Additionally, you can pick from custom triggers that you develop in other environments by clicking the Library icon.

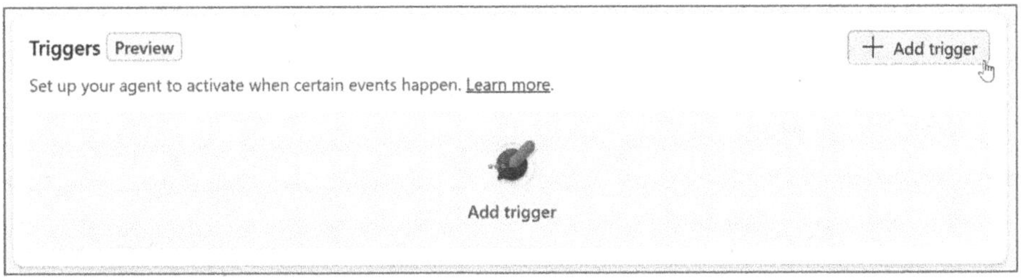

Figure 8.7: Adding an agent trigger

For this example, we are going to have your agent engage when the form you created earlier was submitted. Therefore, you will select the "When a new response is submitted" trigger, as shown in Figure 8.8.

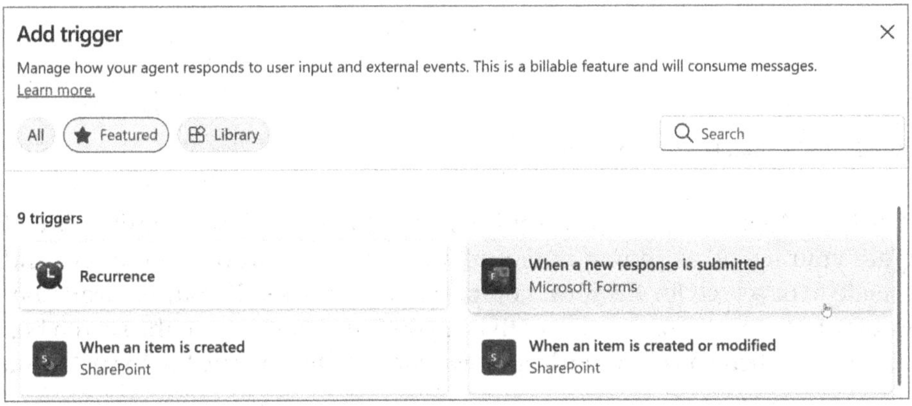

Figure 8.8: Predefined triggers

This will open the Add Trigger dialog box, as shown in Figure 8.9, that allows you to begin configuring your trigger. First, provide a name for your trigger, such as **Microsoft Form Submission**, to help document what is initiating your agent. You can see at the top of the dialog window the following message: "*Manage how your agent responds to user input and external events. This is a billable feature and will consume messages.*" It is important to recognize that when estimating the potential cost of your agent, the trigger event will also count as a message, like if you had sent a chat-based message to it.

Below the Trigger Name input, you will notice two connection references: one to Microsoft Copilot Studio and the other to Microsoft Forms. In this instance, you'll also note that both have a green checkmark next to the connection name, which indicates a valid connection. However, you may find situations where

Chapter 8 ▪ Building an Autonomous Agent

that isn't the case, and you will need to click the ellipsis next to the connection and then build a new connection reference.

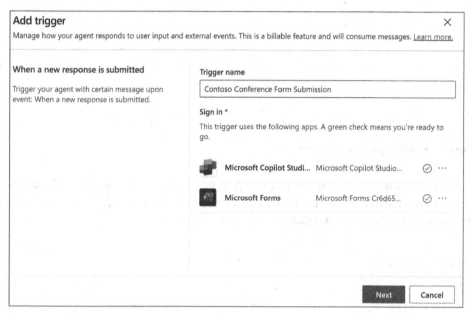

Figure 8.9: Microsoft Form submission trigger

Click the Next button to select the Microsoft Form whose submission will trigger your agent, as shown in Figure 8.10. Click the drop-down menu and navigate to or search for the form you previously created. If your environment has lots of Microsoft Forms, alternatively, you can choose to use the search box that appears when you click the drop-down menu to help locate the correct form.

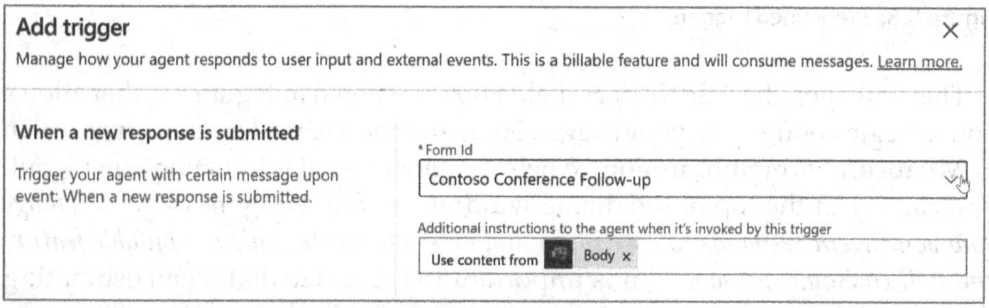

Figure 8.10: Contoso Conference Follow-up form

Select the Contoso Conference Follow-up form and then click the Create Trigger button in the lower-right corner of the window to establish your trigger. For now, leave the existing "*Additional instructions to the agent when it's invoked by this trigger*" input box as is, but note that we'll revisit it later as we continue to configure our agent.

Now, click the Create Trigger button in the lower-right corner of the dialog window and wait for a few seconds until you see a confirmation that your trigger has been created. Click the Close button to return to the agent configuration window.

Configuring your Trigger

You'll need to customize your trigger to ensure the agent can extract the necessary submission information from the form to further progress your workflow. Scroll down to the Trigger section of the agent configuration, click the ellipsis next to the trigger you just created, and then select Edit in Power Automate, as shown in Figure 8.11, to open the back-end Power Automate Flow for your trigger.

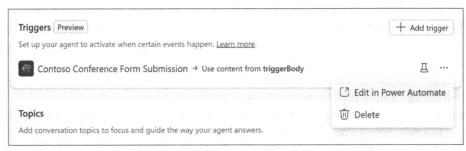

Figure 8.11: Editing your trigger in Power Automate

> **NOTE** If you are unfamiliar, Power Automate is a low-code workflow platform that helps you automate business processes with minimal effort. In the context of Copilot Studio, it integrates seamlessly with other services, making your agents more dynamic and responsive while streamlining your workflows and enhancing productivity.

The next step is optional, but you may want to toggle Power Automate from the new designer experience to the classic experience, as shown in Figure 8.12. At the time of writing, the classic experience is less quirky than the new designer experience, especially when creating connections. Hopefully, Microsoft will ensure that the experiences of the two designers have feature parity and stability before fully deprecating the classic designer experience.

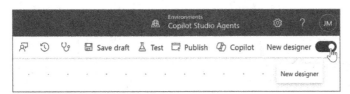

Figure 8.12: The New Designer toggle

Our flow is configured to initiate when a new form submission is made; it then passes the body value back to your agent and continues. What it doesn't do is pull the actual details of the submission, such as the Attendee's name, email, and company name. So, from within the Power Automate authoring canvas, you will want to click the + button between the "When a new response is submitted" action and the "Send a prompt to the specified copilot for processing" action, as shown in Figure 8.13, and then select the Add an Action choice from the menu.

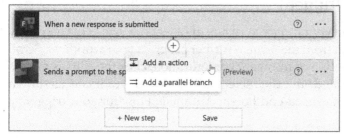

Figure 8.13: Adding an action to your trigger flow

This will open the Choose an Operations menu, as shown in Figure 8.14, which contains various actions you can insert into your flow. The action we are looking for is called "Get response details" and is associated with the Microsoft Forms application. If you enter **Get response details** into the search box, it should filter the actions so that you can easily select the action shown in Figure 8.14 and add it to the canvas.

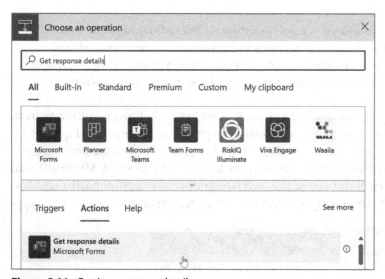

Figure 8.14: Getting response details

Click the Form ID drop-down in the Get Response Details action and select the Contoso Conference Follow-up form, as shown in Figure 8.15. Next, click in the Response ID input and then select List of Response Notifications Response ID from the list of available choices.

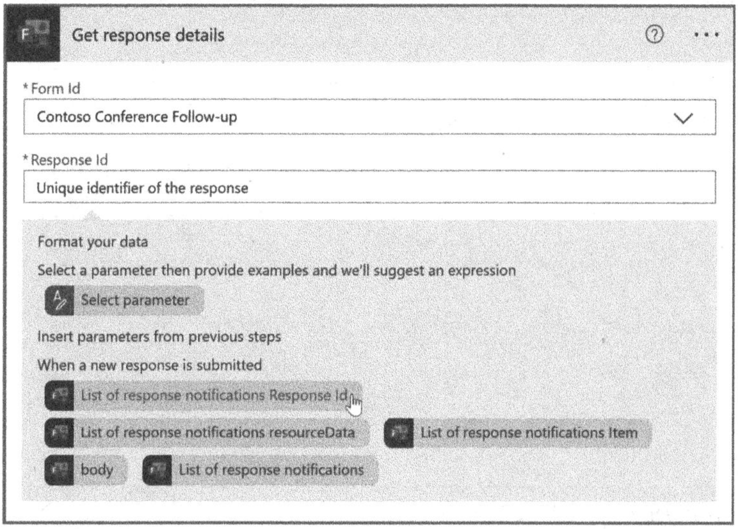

Figure 8.15: Selecting your Microsoft form

This will insert an Apply to Each loop, as shown in Figure 8.16. Typically, this action is used to iterate through a list of results versus a single for submission. However, this is one of those fun quirks you tend to uncover when working in the Power Platform.

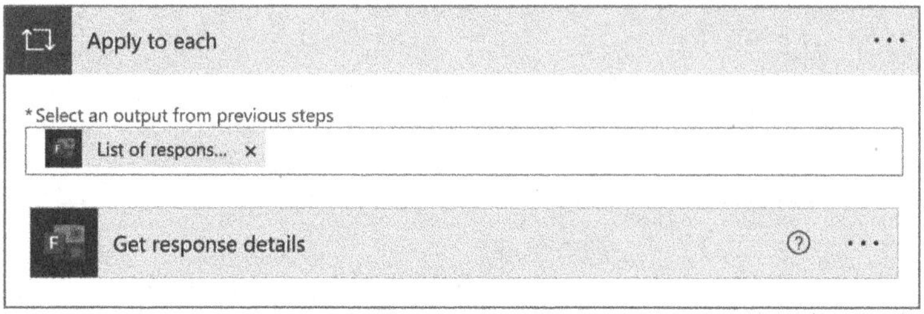

Figure 8.16: Getting response details

Now that you have configured the action to pull the response details from the form submission, you will want to create variables to make it easier to pass the values back to the agent for further processing. You will need to create three Initialize Variable actions to your authoring canvas. Let's put them above the Apply to Each action to keep everything nice and organized.

210 Chapter 8 ■ Building an Autonomous Agent

Again, click the + button above the action you just created and type in **initialize** in the Choose an Operation menu, as shown in Figure 8.17. Select the Initialize Variable action to add it to the authoring canvas.

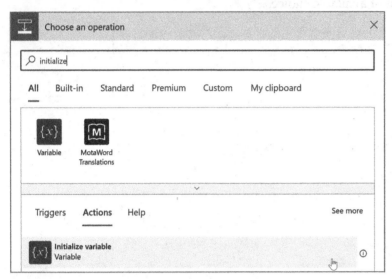

Figure 8.17: Adding an Initialize Variable action

Set the Name field to Attendee Name and then click the drop-down box to set the variable Type to String, as shown in Figure 8.18. Optionally, you can click the ellipsis in the upper-right corner and select Rename and enter a more descriptive name for the action, such as **Create Attendee Name Variable**.

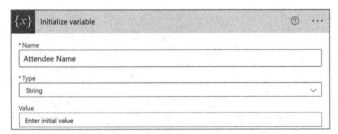

Figure 8.18: Creating the Attendee Name variable

Repeat these same steps two more times to add two more Initialize Variable actions to your canvas so that you'll have a total of three before the Get Response Details action. The other two variables are Attendee Email and Company. All variables should be of type String, and you do not need to set an initial value for any of them. Once you have finished creating your variables, your authoring canvas should match Figure 8.19.

Chapter 8 ■ Building an Autonomous Agent   211

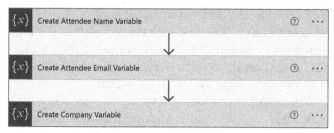

Figure 8.19: The variables list

Now that you have created all the necessary variables, you should set their values as mapped to the Contoso Conference Follow-up Form. Make sure that the Apply to Each action is expanded and then click the + button within that action to add a new action. From the Choose an Operation menu, type in **set variable**, and then select the Set Variable action, as shown in Figure 8.20.

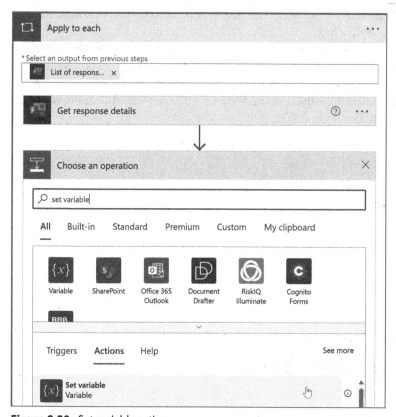

Figure 8.20: Set variable action

When you add the Set Variable action to the canvas, there will be a notification to *"Enable concurrency control for the apply to each loop and set its degree of* parallelization to 1 when using a Set Variable action inside an apply to each loop." By setting the degree of parallelization to 1, you ensure that tasks within the loop are done one at a time, which helps to avoid potential conflicts when updating a variable. For example, if you set the Attendee Name variable to "Sarah Dooley" for the first item in the collection, it could get overwritten to "Tom Gawczynski" on the second iteration of the loop. However, we are okay with proceeding forward as is since this flow will initiate upon the form submission and only pull the information for that one response.

Once the Set Variable action has been added to the canvas, you can click the Name drop-down and pick one of the three variables that you created. The order doesn't make a difference, so go ahead and select the Company variable. Then click in the Value input and select the Company item under the Get Response Details section, as shown in Figure 8.21. Don't worry about performing any formatting just yet; you are only trying to extract the information and provide this to your agent for further processing later. I also recommend renaming the action to **Set Company Variable** or something similar to help others understand the logic you are following.

Follow these same steps two more times to set the values for the Attendee Name and Attendee Email variables. For the Attendee Name, you will want to select the Name value, as shown in Figure 8.21, and for the Attendee Email, select the E-mail value. Finally, rename the two other set variable actions so that your canvas looks like Figure 8.22.

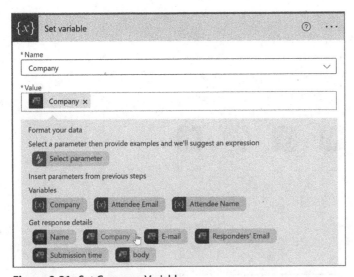

Figure 8.21: Set Company Variable

The last step in the process is to update the "Sends a prompt to the specified copilot for processing" action. You will pass the variables back to the agent so that it can leverage those values in the next steps of your business process. In your Power Automate flow, you'll define both static text labels and corresponding variables to store dynamic values. The format will be: **"Label"**: *Variable*, so you will end up with the following, as shown in Figure 8.23.

- **"Attendee Name"**: *Attendee Name*
- **"Attendee Email"**: *Attendee Email*
- **"Company"**: *Company*

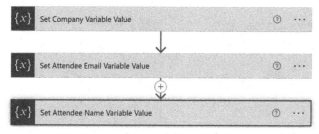

Figure 8.22: Setting variable values

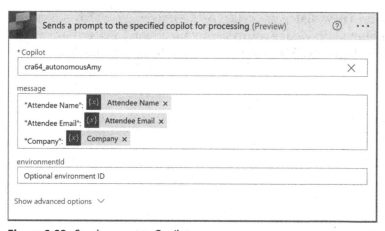

Figure 8.23: Send prompt to Copilot

Just to quickly recap the configuration, you have set the Power Automate flow to grab the actual form submission details after an attendee has submitted the form; you have created three variables and then set the values for those variables based on the form submission. Finally, you have passed those variables back to the agent so that it can continue to be referenced for the rest of the process. Now you can click Save and return to Copilot Studio to continue configuring your agent.

Setting Up Knowledge Sources

Now, you're going to configure your knowledge source by integrating select data from our Salesforce CRM instance. Specifically, you'll be selecting a couple

214 Chapter 8 ▪ Building an Autonomous Agent

of tables to ensure the agent can reference them when looking up account and contact information by creating actions. Scroll down your agent configuration screen until you arrive at the Knowledge section. Ensure that the "Allow the AI to use its own general knowledge" toggle is set to Enabled, and then click the Add Knowledge button, as shown in Figure 8.24.

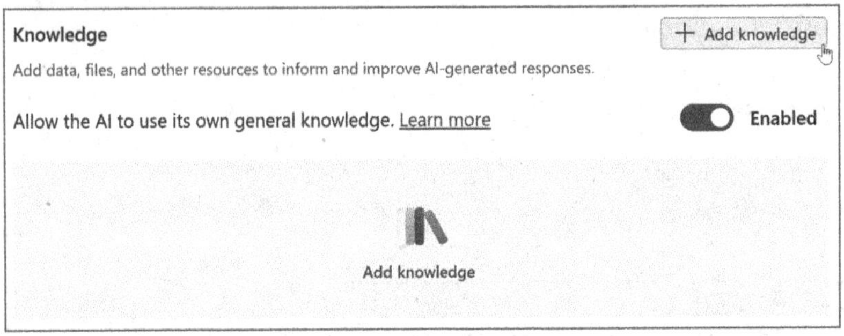

Figure 8.24: Adding a knowledge source

This will bring up a new dialog box called Add Knowledge, which allows you to select form different knowledge sources for your agent. Click the Advanced button, as shown in Figure 8.25, and then select Salesforce from the list of available options.

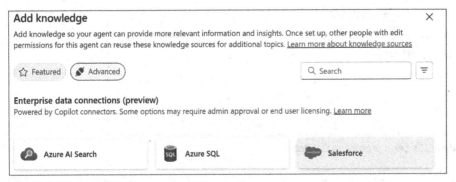

Figure 8.25: Knowledge source advanced settings

You will now need to create the connection to your development `Salesforce .com` instance. For real-world scenarios, you will likely need to work with your Salesforce Administrator to create a service account with appropriate permissions to your Salesforce instance. However, for the purposes of this book, you will use the same login credentials you used to configure your instance earlier. Click the Sign In link in the right-hand corner of the Connect to Salesforce configuration wizard, as shown in Figure 8.26.

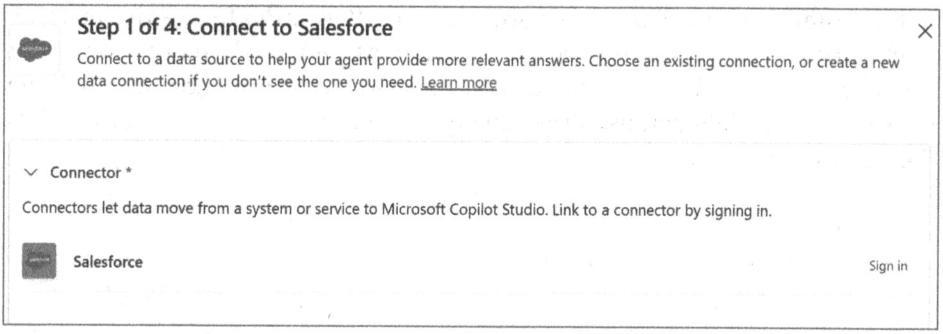

Chapter 8 ▪ Building an Autonomous Agent   215

Step 1 of 4: Connect to Salesforce   ✕

Connect to a data source to help your agent provide more relevant answers. Choose an existing connection, or create a new data connection if you don't see the one you need. Learn more

∨ Connector *

Connectors let data move from a system or service to Microsoft Copilot Studio. Link to a connector by signing in.

Salesforce   Sign in

Figure 8.26: Connecting to Salesforce

This will bring up a new dialog box, as shown in Figure 8.27, that allows you to select the Login URI, the environment you are logging into. Again, for real-world scenarios, you would likely start with connecting to a developer or sandbox environment first and then working your way up. However, for this scenario, feel free to leave the default value of Production. Additionally, you can leave the Salesforce API version to whatever the default value is. The one note you should be aware of is that when Salesforce makes modifications to their APIs, it can sometimes impact the functionality of your agent. For example, if they make certain fields required or deprecate other fields, you may need to make similar adjustments to your agent to accommodate these API-based changes.

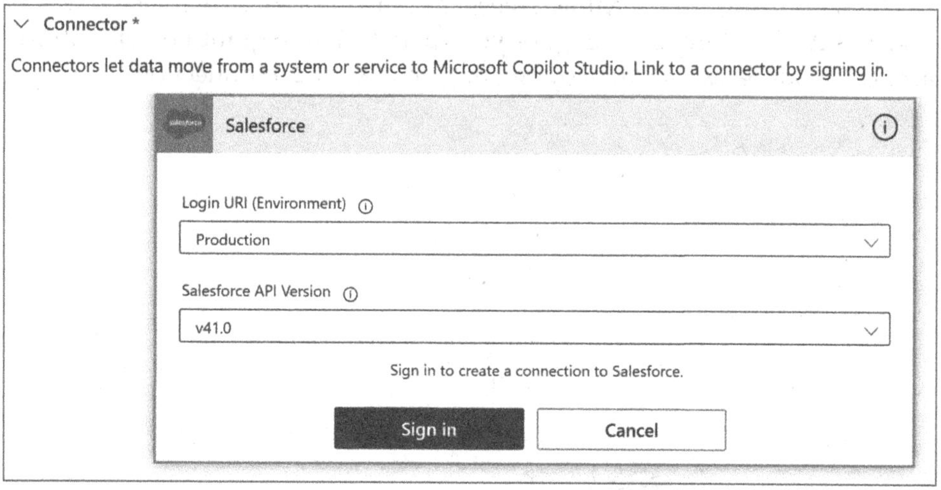

∨ Connector *

Connectors let data move from a system or service to Microsoft Copilot Studio. Link to a connector by signing in.

Salesforce   ⓘ

Login URI (Environment) ⓘ

Production   ∨

Salesforce API Version ⓘ

v41.0   ∨

Sign in to create a connection to Salesforce.

Sign in   Cancel

Figure 8.27: Select your Salesforce environment

Click the Sign In button, as shown in Figure 8.27, which will bring up a login window to access Salesforce. However, there is a chance that you may receive an error message that the connection was blocked by DLP, as shown in Figure 8.28.

Chapter 8 ■ Building an Autonomous Agent

In this instance, you will need to work with your Power Platform Administrator to classify Salesforce as a Business Connector, as previously mentioned. If it's not blocked, you will be presented with a Salesforce admin login screen. Enter the same credentials you used previously to log in to Salesforce and then click the Log In button.

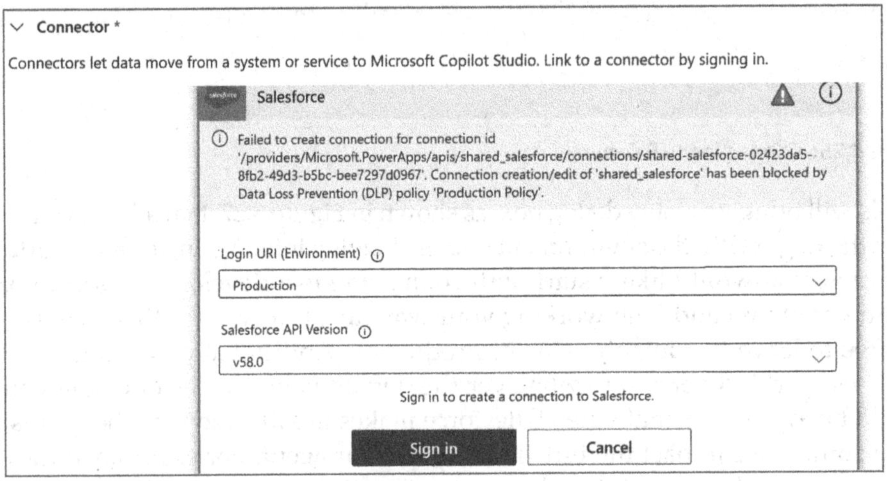

Figure 8.28: Connection blocked by DLP

This will bring up an Allow Access? confirmation screen, as shown in Figure 8.29. Salesforce is asking for your permission to grant Power Platform access to your Salesforce data by creating an OAuth 2.0 connection.

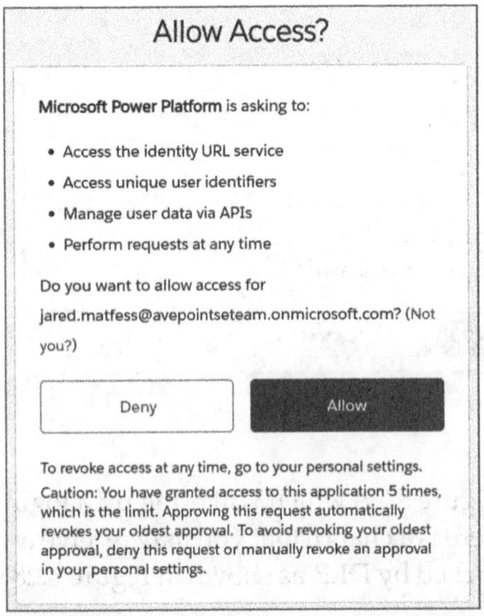

Figure 8.29: Allowing access to Salesforce

Chapter 8 ▪ Building an Autonomous Agent   217

The OAuth 2.0 protocol securely authorizes data sharing between applications through the exchange of tokens. By allowing access, you are enabling Power Platform to interact with your Salesforce account and perform actions on your behalf, such as reading or writing data. Click the Allow button to proceed. You'll arrive back at the first configuration screen, as shown in Figure 8.26, but now with a connection configured.

Click the Next button to advance to the Select Salesforce Tables screen, as shown in Figure 8.30. From here, type in the following one at a time to find the corresponding Salesforce tables: **Account, Contact, Opportunity**. Click each table from the search results list and notice the Selected label will increment each time you select a table.

Figure 8.30: Selecting Salesforce tables

After you've selected all three tables, click the Next button to advance to the Preview Data screen, as shown in Figure 8.31. This will allow you to preview data from each of the tables to ensure you selected the correct ones.

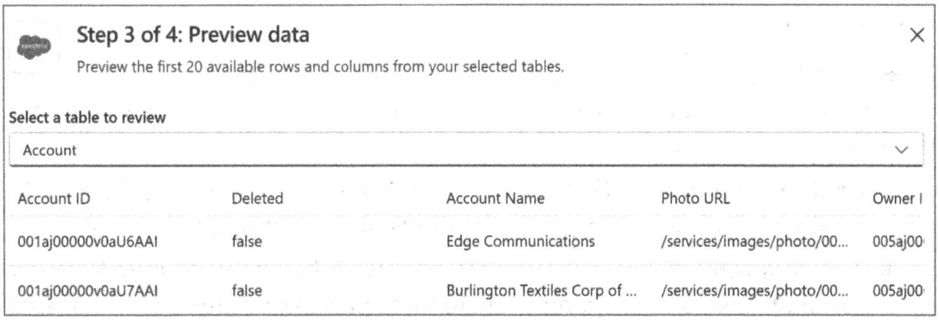

Figure 8.31: Previewing Salesforce table data

218 Chapter 8 ■ Building an Autonomous Agent

Finally, you will end up on the Review and Finish screen, as shown in Figure 8.32. Rename the Knowledge Name to **Salesforce**. For now, you can leave the Knowledge Description as is, but we may further adjust that as we continue building out our agent's capabilities. Once completed, click the Add button to finalize the creation of this knowledge source for your agent.

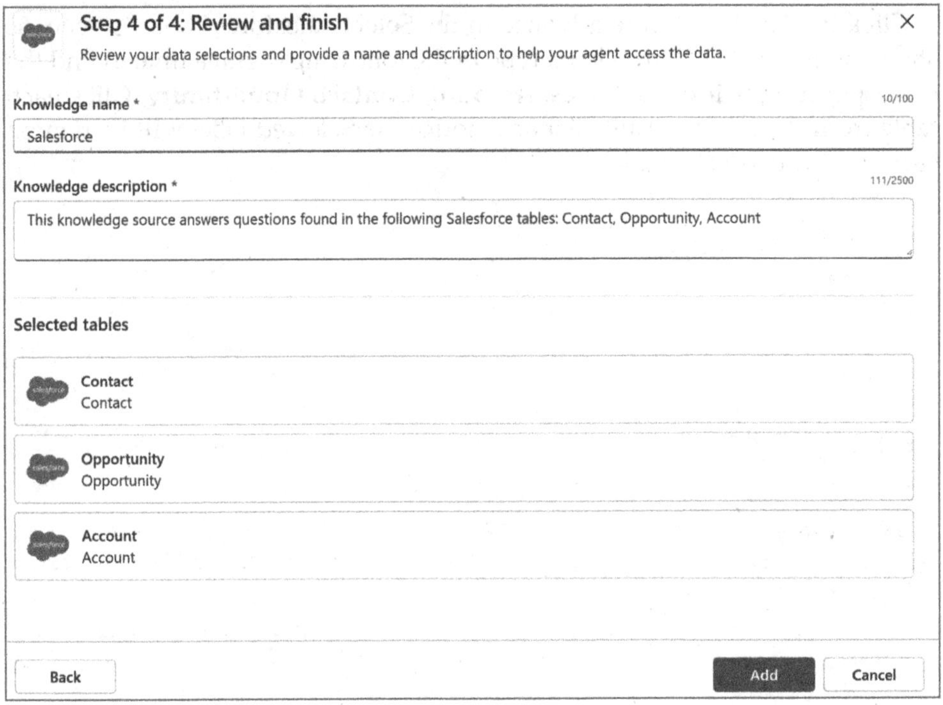

Step 4 of 4: Review and finish ✕

Review your data selections and provide a name and description to help your agent access the data.

Knowledge name * 10/100

Salesforce

Knowledge description * 111/2500

This knowledge source answers questions found in the following Salesforce tables: Contact, Opportunity, Account

Selected tables

Contact
Contact

Opportunity
Opportunity

Account
Account

Back Add Cancel

Figure 8.32: Reviewing the knowledge source setup

Creating Actions

As we briefly touched on earlier, Copilot Studio actions extend the capabilities of your agent, allowing it to complete tasks automatically or through explicit calls within a topic. Here are the core action types that you can build to extend your agent:

- **Prebuilt connector action:** Uses prebuilt connectors to interact with various services such as Salesforce, Dynamics 365, SharePoint, OneDrive, Teams, etc.
- **Custom connector action:** You can create custom connectors for specific needs, such as homegrown applications in your organization.
- **Power automate cloud flow:** Integrates with Power Automate to create automated workflows, connecting to third-party applications and services.

- **AI builder prompts:** Uses AI Builder to generate prompts within a topic that will instruct the LLM for what to respond with in a particular business scenario.
- **Bot framework skill:** Leverages the Microsoft Bot Framework skills to enhance agent capabilities.
- **REST API connection:** Connects to REST APIs for custom integration with third-party platforms.

For this case, we will create an action that will create a new contact if one does not exist in Salesforce. When creating this contact record, we will associate it with the company that the attendee works for, which is also referred to as the Account from a Salesforce perspective. To get started, navigate back to your agent's configuration screen and then scroll down until you see the Actions section, as shown in Figure 8.33.

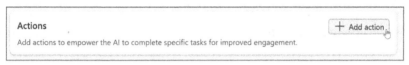

Figure 8.33: Adding a new action

Click the + Add Action button, which will then open a new dialog box. Click the + New Action drop-down menu, as shown in Figure 8.34, and then select the New Power Automate Flow option. Notice that you can see the other types of actions we described earlier in the list of choices.

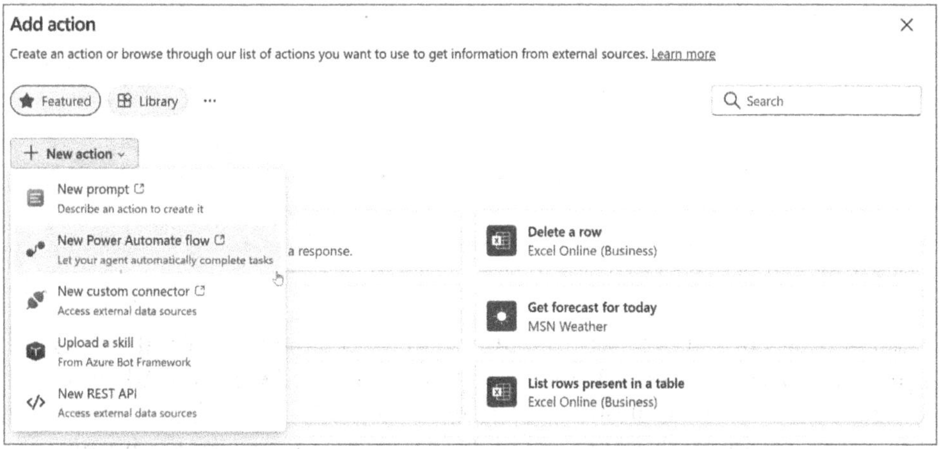

Figure 8.34: The New Power Automate Flow option

From here, you will be redirected to Power Automate in a brand-new flow that will become your action. I again recommend you flip the toggle back to the classic authoring experience and then rename the flow by clicking in the upper-left corner where it says "Run a flow from Copilot" and rename that to **Create Lead**.

Now, you should be looking at an authoring canvas with two actions, as shown in Figure 8.35. The first action is titled Skills, and notice the Copilot logo in the upper-left corner of the action. This means that the trigger for this flow is an agent calling it directly.

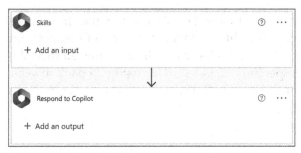

Figure 8.35: The initial Power Automate Flow setup

Creating Inputs

When revisiting your workflow, you will need to have the attendee's name, email address, and company information to see if they exist in CRM. To have access to these details, include them as input to the trigger action. Click the + Add an Input button and select the Text type of user input, as shown in Figure 8.36, and then create an input called **Attendee Name**.

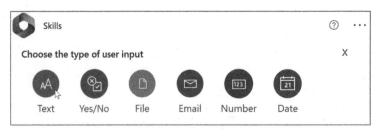

Figure 8.36: Creating text input

Repeat the same step to add a text input called **Company**, create an Email input called **Attendee Email**, and a Yes/No field called **Contact Exists**. When completed, your canvas should look like Figure 8.37.

Now, go ahead and add corresponding variables to match the inputs you just created to make it easier to access those values as part of our workflow. Click the + below the Skills action in the canvas, select Add an Action, and then select the Initialize Variable action, as you did earlier. Set the Name value to Attendee Name, and the type to String. Map the value to the Attendee Name variable from the Skill action. Repeat this same step two more times, to create **Attendee Email** and **Company** variables, both of type String. You should now have three Initialize Variable actions, as shown in Figure 8.38.

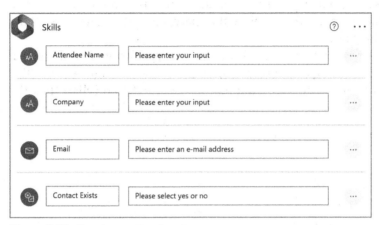

Figure 8.37: Creating contact inputs

Figure 8.38: Initializing variable actions

Formatting Variables

An important note is that Salesforce separates first and last names as separate fields, and your form submission expects attendees to provide their full names in one string. You need to use an expression to extract the first name from a string in Power Automate. This expression will help you identify and isolate the first name from the full string of text provided by pulling all the text before the space in the string, which signifies a breakpoint between the first and last name. The first name is everything before the space, and the last name is all the characters after the space.

First, let's add a new Initialize Variable action of type String, and then click in the Value input. A dialog box should pop up, as shown in Figure 8.39. Click the Expression link, enter the following text next to the fx, and then click the Update button:

```
first(split(variables('Attendee Name'), ' '))
```

Figure 8.39: Initializing the First Name variable

Now, let's go ahead and create a second variable called Last Name with a similar expression to extract the last name from the string. This time, enter the following text into the Expression field, and then click OK:

```
last(split(variables('Attendee Name'), ' '))
```

NOTE In real-world scenarios, you will likely face additional data validation and cleanup activities when designing your agent.

Getting the Account ID

To link the contact to their company, you need to obtain the Account ID for the company's account record. Therefore, the next action to add to your flow is a Salesforce Get Records action. Click the + button after the Initialize Variable action you just created, and then select Add Action.

Start typing **Salesforce Get Records** and then select the action from the list of actions in the menu. You should now see a Get Records action, as shown in Figure 8.40. First, click the Show Advanced Options menu to expand the inputs. Next, in the Salesforce Object Type input, type in **Accounts**.

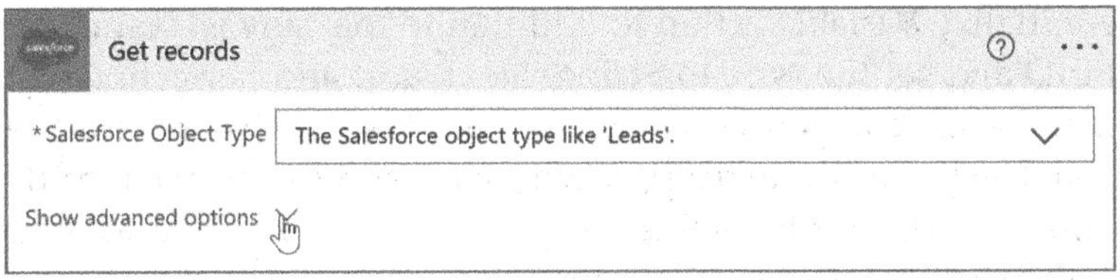

Chapter 8 ■ Building an Autonomous Agent   223

Figure 8.40: The Get Records action

With the Advanced Options menu expanded, you should now see additional fields that can be modified to further refine the results returning from the Get Records action. What we would like to do is find the account record in the Accounts table in Salesforce. We can do so by performing a Filter query in our action.

Click in the Filter Query input field and then type in **Name eq '**, and then select from the Company variable from the Dynamic Content window, as shown in Figure 8.41.

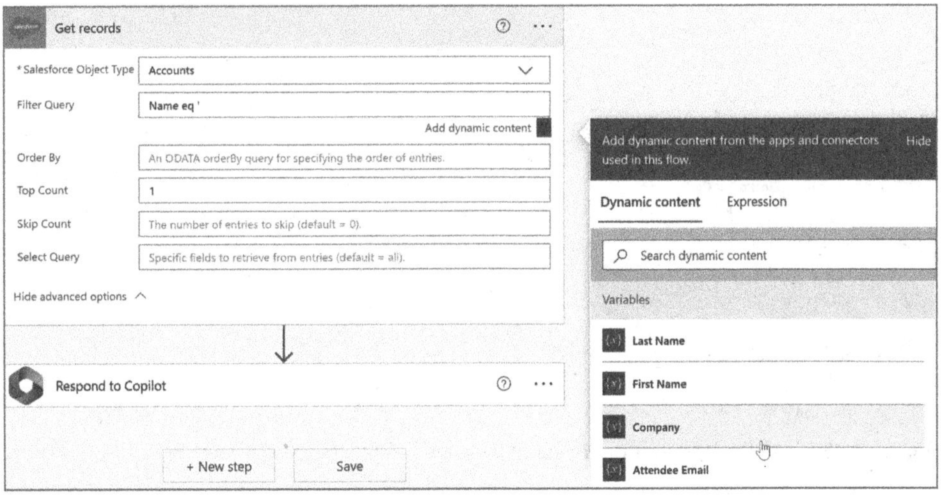

Figure 8.41: Filtering your Get Records action

Then include a closing ' so that your Company variable sits within two quotes, as shown in Figure 8.42. Finally, put the number 1 in the Top Count input field. This ensures that your call only returns a single record to simplify your logic. In a real-world scenario, you might need to perform a combined query that matches the account name with some other attribute, depending on your CRM. However, our solution should work for this development scenario with limited account records.

Next, you will need to create a variable to store the Account ID to reference for when you create the opportunity. Click + Insert a New Step below the Get Account ID, select Add an Action, and then search for the Initialize Variable action. Click the Initialize Variable action to add that to the canvas. Name the variable Account ID and set the type to String. Next, add another action just below the Initialize Variable action you just created. This time, search for the Set Variable action. Click the Name drop-down menu and select Account ID from the list of values. Next, click the Value input field, and then select Account Account ID from the Dynamic Content window, as shown in Figure 8.43.

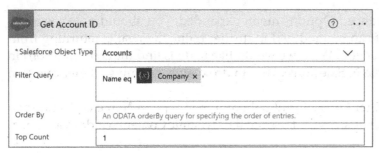

Figure 8.42: Get Account ID Filter and Top Count

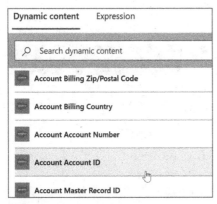

Figure 8.43: Selecting the Account Account ID value

Note that Power Automate will automatically insert an Apply to Each loop, as shown in Figure 8.44, with your Set Variable action within.

NOTE For production use cases, you might need to include additional validation if there are multiple accounts with the same name.

Creating a Condition

For the next bit of business logic, you need to either create a new contact if one does not exist in Salesforce, and then create the opportunity, or, if the contact does exist, you can go ahead and create the opportunity. Remember, one of your inputs for this flow is Contact Exists. If there is already a contact record in Salesforce, this input will be set to true; otherwise, it will be set to false. You can use the value of this input to create two paths for your next section of logic. Click Insert a New Step below the Apply to Each Action. Select the Condition Control action, as shown in Figure 8.45, to add that action to your authoring canvas.

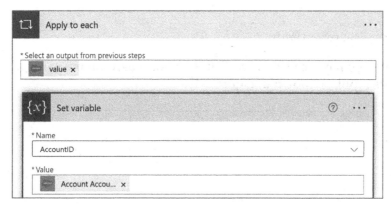

Figure 8.44: The Apply to each loop with the Set Variable action

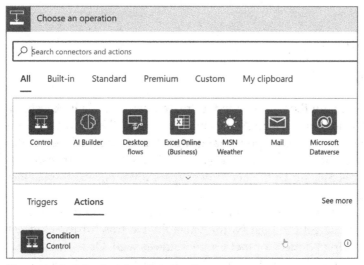

Figure 8.45: Selecting the control action

You are going to use this condition action to check the value of the Contact Exists input. If the contact doesn't exist, you will create a new contact in Salesforce. Otherwise, if the contact does exist, you will proceed forward with creating an opportunity associated with that contact.

Click the Choose a Value input box, and then select the Contact Exists skill from the list of dynamic values. Next, ensure that the drop-down menu is set to "is equal to" and then type in **true** in the third input field, as shown in Figure 8.46.

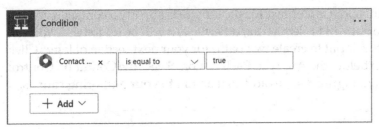

Figure 8.46: Checking if the contact exists

This will create two paths called "if yes" and "if no," based on the value of the Contact Exists input, as shown in Figure 8.47.

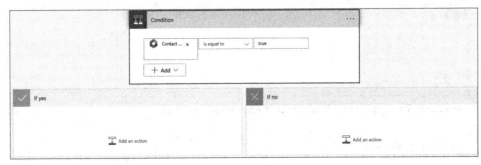

Figure 8.47: Conditional paths

Creating a Contact

Let's go ahead and build out the logic needed to create a new contact in Salesforce if one doesn't exist. Click the Add an Action button in the If No box, as shown in Figure 8.47. In the search box, type in **Salesforce Create Record**. Select the Create Record action from the list of actions provided. Click the drop-down menu next to the label Salesforce Object Type, type **Contacts**, and then select the Contacts Tables.

Next, click in the Contact Last Name field and then from the Dynamic Content window that appears, select the Last Name variable. Do this for the Contact Account ID, Contact First Name, Contact Email fields as well. Once done, your Create Record action should match Figure 8.48. You can also optionally choose to click the ellipsis in the upper-right corner of the Create Record action, and then rename the action to **Create Contact** to help remind you what this functionality does.

Just to recap, we first verified whether a contact exists using a conditional action. If a contact does not exist in Salesforce, we created a new one associated with the account. If the attendee already exists as a contact in Salesforce, we don't need any specific logic in the If Yes box. In both cases, the next step in the process is to create an opportunity in Salesforce associated with both the contact and account.

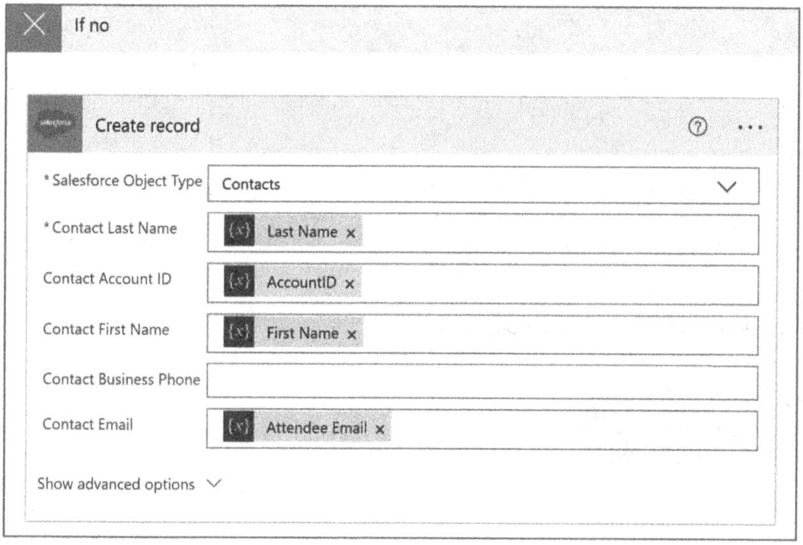

Figure 8.48: Creating the Salesforce contact

Creating an Opportunity

To create the opportunity in Salesforce, click the + Insert a New Step button beneath the If Yes and If No actions. Select the Add an Action choice. Now type **Salesforce create record** into the action search box, and then select the Create Record Action with the Salesforce logo to add that action to the canvas. Click the Salesforce Object Type drop-down menu, type in **Opportunities**, and then select that table from the list of choices. This will expand the action and reveal the required fields to create the opportunity, as shown in Figure 8.49.

For the Opportunity Name field, enter **Contoso Conference Lead**, and for the Opportunity Stage, pick Qualification. For the Opportunity Close date, let's go ahead and create a formula that will calculate 150 days from the current date. Click the Opportunity Close Date field, click the Expression menu, type **addDays(utcNow(), 150)** into the formula input, as shown in Figure 8.50, and then click OK.

> **NOTE** One really helpful benefit of the new authoring experience in Power Automate is that it includes Copilot, which can help with creating formulas.

Click the Opportunity Account ID field and then select the Account ID variable. Next, click the ellipsis in the upper-right corner of the Create Record action,

228   Chapter 8 ▪ Building an Autonomous Agent

and then click the Rename button. Rename this new action to **Create Salesforce Opportunity**, and then confirm that your action matches Figure 8.51.

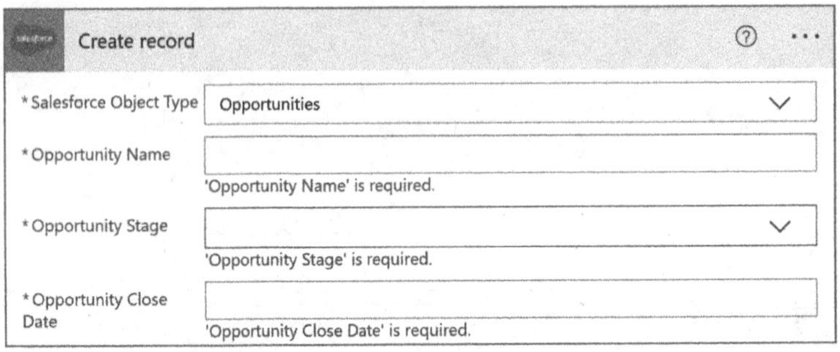

Figure 8.49: The required fields for Create opportunity

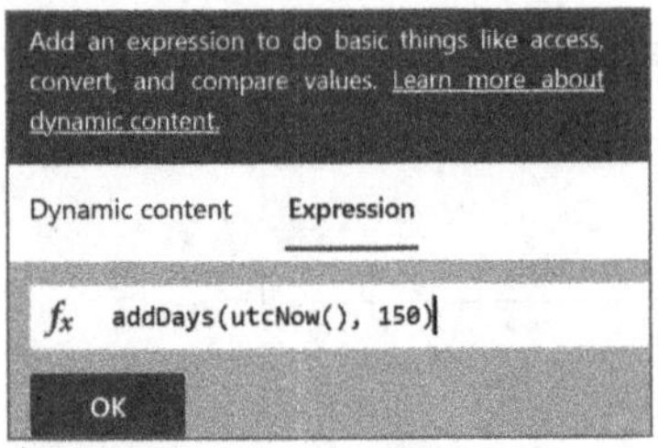

Figure 8.50: Opportunity close date formula

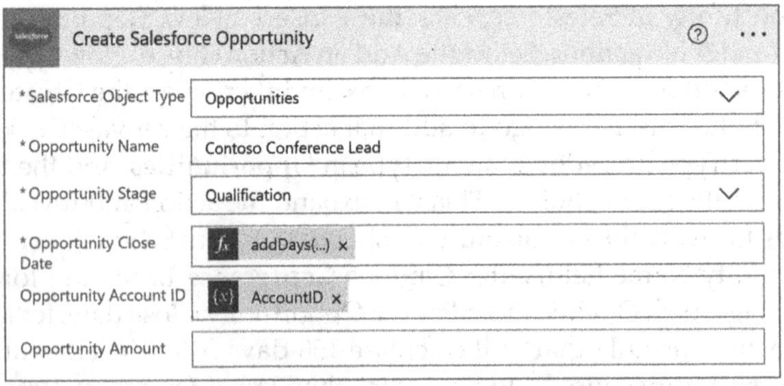

Figure 8.51: Creating the Salesforce opportunity action

Associating Your Opportunity to a Contact

You may be asking yourself, "how do you map the attendees to the opportunity?" If you notice, there was no option to set the contact in the Create Salesforce Opportunity action. This is because Salesforce makes use of a junction object called OpportunityContactRole. A junction object in Salesforce is a custom object that allows for many-to-many relationships between two other objects. For example, if you have objects for accounts and contacts, you can create a junction

Chapter 8 ■ Building an Autonomous Agent   229

object to manage the relationships between them. The OpportunityContactRole junction object has two lookup keys, ContactID and OpportunityID, which are used to associate the contact to the opportunity.

To get started, click Add a New Step above the condition action, select Add an Action, and then type in **Initialize Variable**. Select the Initialize Variable action to add it to the authoring canvas. Click the ellipsis in the upper-right corner and rename this action to **Create Contact ID Variable**. Name the variable **ContactID**, and then select String from the Type drop-down menu, as shown in Figure 8.52.

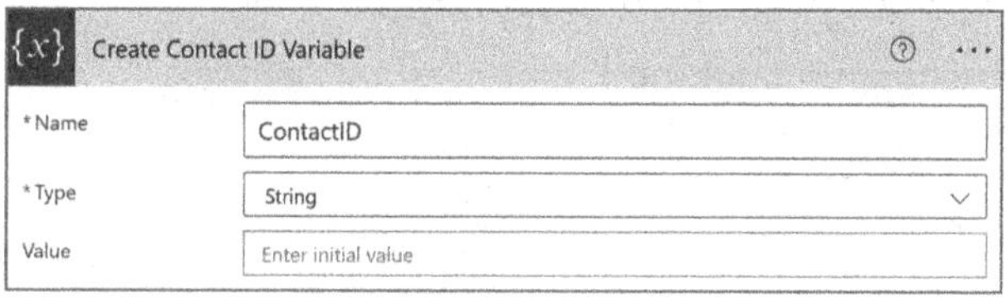

Figure 8.52: Creating a Contact ID Variable action

Setting this variable will differ based on whether the contact already exists. If the contact exists, then you will need to retrieve the ID for that record in the Contacts table. To do this, click the Add an Action button in the If Yes condition box. Type in **Salesforce get records**, and then select the Get Records action to add that to the canvas. Select Contacts from the Salesforce Object Type drop-down menu.

Click the Show Advanced Options link to expand the action configuration menu. Click the ellipsis in the upper-right corner and rename this action to **Get Contact**. In the Filter Query input, type in **Email eq '**, and then select the Attendee Email variable from the dynamic menu. Then type a closing ' so that the Attendee Email variable is between single quotes, as shown in Figure 8.53.

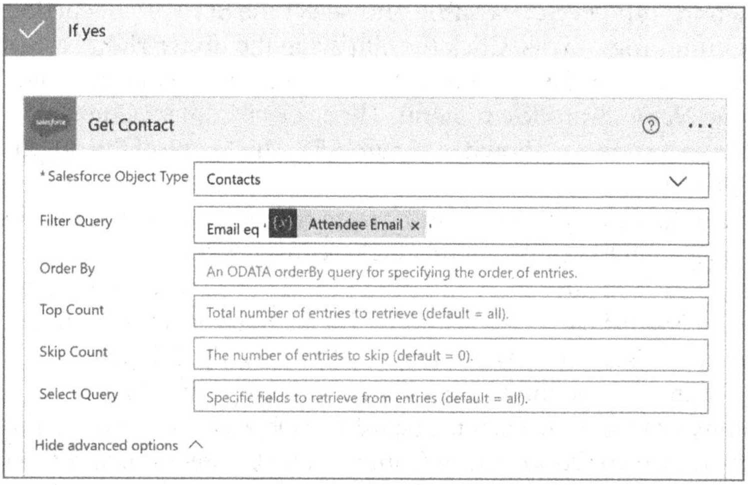

Figure 8.53: The Get Contact action

Next, click the Add an Action link below the Get Contact action. Type in **Set variable** and select the Set variable action to add that to the authoring canvas. Click the ellipsis in the upper-right corner of this action and rename it to **Set Contact ID variable**. Select ContactID from the Name drop-down menu, click the Enter Variable Value for the Value input, and then select Contact Contact ID, as shown in Figure 8.54, from the list of available values. This appears under the Get Contact subheading in the Dynamic Content window. Note that this wraps the Set Variable action in an Apply to Each loop, but we will assume Salesforce data hygiene and that there is only one unique contact record.

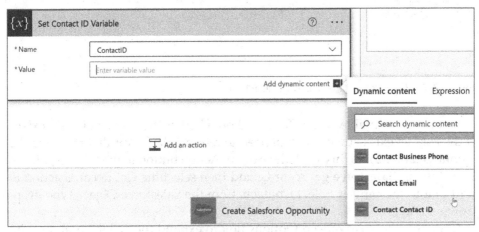

Figure 8.54: Selecting the ContactID value

This solves for the scenario where the contact already exists, but now we need to add a Set Variable Value action in the scenario where we are creating a new contact in this flow. So, click Add an Action in the If No box, underneath the Create Contact action. Type in **Set variable** and select the Set Variable action to add that to the authoring canvas. Click the ellipsis in the upper-right corner of this action and rename it to **Set Contact ID variable for new contact**. Select ContactID from the Name drop-down menu. Then select Contact Contact ID from the Create Contact menu, as shown in Figure 8.55. This is one of the output values from that action.

Now, to wrap up the flow, go ahead and create that linkage between the opportunity you just created and the contact. Click Insert a New Step, below the Create Opportunity step, and then select Add an Action. Once again, type in **Salesforce Create Record**, and then select the Create Record action with the Salesforce logo from the list of actions presented. Click the ellipsis in the upper-right corner and rename this action to **Link Contact to Opportunity**.

Select Opportunity Contact Role from the Salesforce Object drop-down menu. Click the input field next to Opportunity Contact Role Contact ID, and then select the ContactID variable. Click the field next to Opportunity Contact Role

Opportunity ID, and then select Opportunity Opportunity ID from the list of dynamic inputs. Select Other in the Opportunity Contact Role Role, since you don't yet know the role this contact may have for the opportunity. Now select Yes from the Opportunity Contact Role Primary drop-down menu. Confirm that your action looks like Figure 8.56, and then save your flow.

Figure 8.55: Selecting Contact Contact ID value

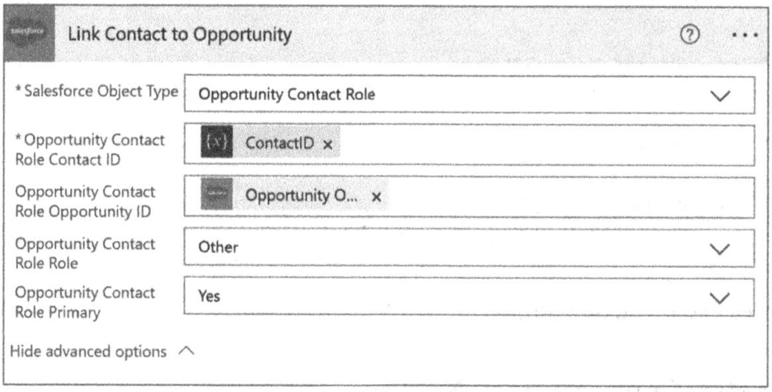

Figure 8.56: Linking a contact to the opportunity action

Configuring "Run as" User

Click the "back" arrow in Power Automate to return to your Create Lead flow's overview page. You need to make one more adjustment prior to moving on, and that is ensuring that Power Automate leverages the connection you established to Salesforce. Scroll down and then in the lower-right corner of your Create Lead overview page, you should see a box titled Run Only Users. Click the Edit link in the upper-right corner of that box, as shown in Figure 8.57.

Scroll down again until you see the Connections Used section. You'll see the connection to Salesforce and note the drop-down menu is set to Provided by

Run-only User. A run-only user is someone who is leveraging your flow but does not have authoring capabilities. The way that this works if it were an interactive session between a user and your agent is that the agent would prompt your user to connect. However, we are building an autonomous agent and there is no user interaction. Therefore, change the value in the drop-down menu to the connection you created, as shown in Figure 8.58, and then click the Save button. This will ensure the agent uses the flow author's connection instead of prompting the user to authenticate to Salesforce.

Figure 8.57: Run-only users

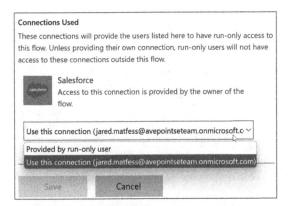

Figure 8.58: The Connection Used drop-down

Configuring the Create Lead Action

We just spent the past few pages building out the Create Lead Power Automate flow, which we now need to wrap within an action. Go back to your agent configuration and click the Actions link in the top navigation menu. Click the + Add an Action button. Search for the Create Lead flow that you just created. Either scroll through the list of actions or use the search box in the upper-right corner, and then select the Create Lead flow, as shown in Figure 8.59.

Next, you can name your action Create Lead to match the name of your flow. Enter the following information into the "Description for the agent to know when to use this action," field, as shown in Figure 8.60:

- Execute the "Create Lead" action only after completing the Salesforce Knowledge check.

Chapter 8 ▪ Building an Autonomous Agent   233

- Map the following inputs to the "Create Lead" action:
  - Attendee Name: Use the value extracted from the submitted form.
  - Company: Use the value extracted from the submitted form.
  - Email: Use the value extracted from the submitted form.
  - Contact Exists: Set to "true" if the Salesforce Knowledge check finds a matching contact; otherwise, set to "false".
  - Ensure that this action is not triggered until the knowledge lookup has provided a result.

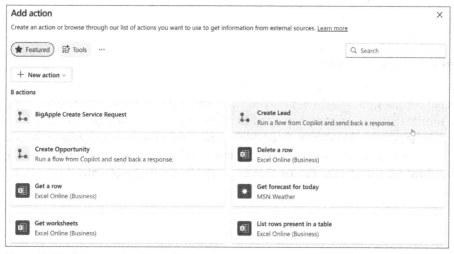

Figure 8.59: Selecting the Create Lead action

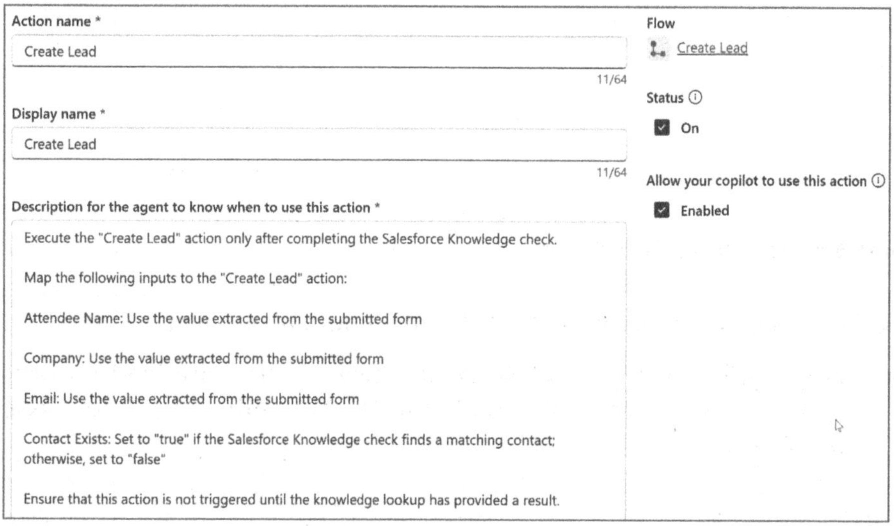

Figure 8.60: Describing the action for your agent

234 Chapter 8 ▪ Building an Autonomous Agent

Click the Add Action button, and in a few seconds, Copilot Studio will finish creating your action. Now, navigate back to Actions and click the Create Lead action, as shown in Figure 8.61, to edit it.

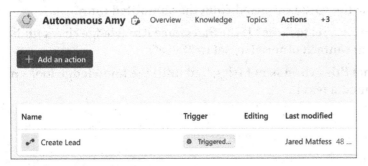

Figure 8.61: Create Lead action

What we are going to do next is provide your agent with instructions for the four inputs that you created as part of the flow. Scroll past the agent instructions until you reach the first input: Attendee Name. Enter the following description, as shown in Figure 8.62: **The attendee's name will be two words such as Cesar Coba, Tom Gawczynski, Taylor Davenport, Madison Siegel, etc.**

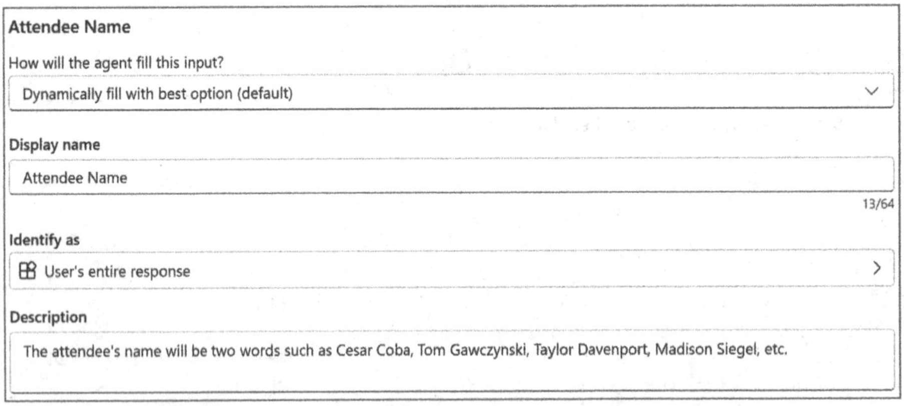

Figure 8.62: The Attendee Name description

Add the following description for the remaining three inputs:

- **Company:** The company will be an organization that the attendee works at, for example, Microsoft, AvePoint, Wiley Publishing, Salesforce, Google, etc.

Chapter 8 ■ Building an Autonomous Agent   235

- **Email:** This is the attendee's email address.
- **Contact exists:** This value is the result of checking Knowledge to see if the contact exists. If you find the contact in Knowledge, then the value should be set to yes. If you don't find a contact in Knowledge, then this value should be no.

After entering the description for your inputs, click the Save button in the upper-right corner.

Configuring Your Agent Instructions

Now, we are going to establish the business logic for this agent by creating a set of instructions for our agent to follow. What is truly very exciting about this is you will see that our programming is all done using natural language. We are going to explain to the agent how it should work, and with the Orchestration toggle set to Enabled, our agent will be empowered to work autonomously.

Navigate back to the Overview screen of your agent configuration. Click the pencil icon in the right-hand corner of the Details section. Enter the following text into the General Instructions input, as shown in Figure 8.63, and then click Save:

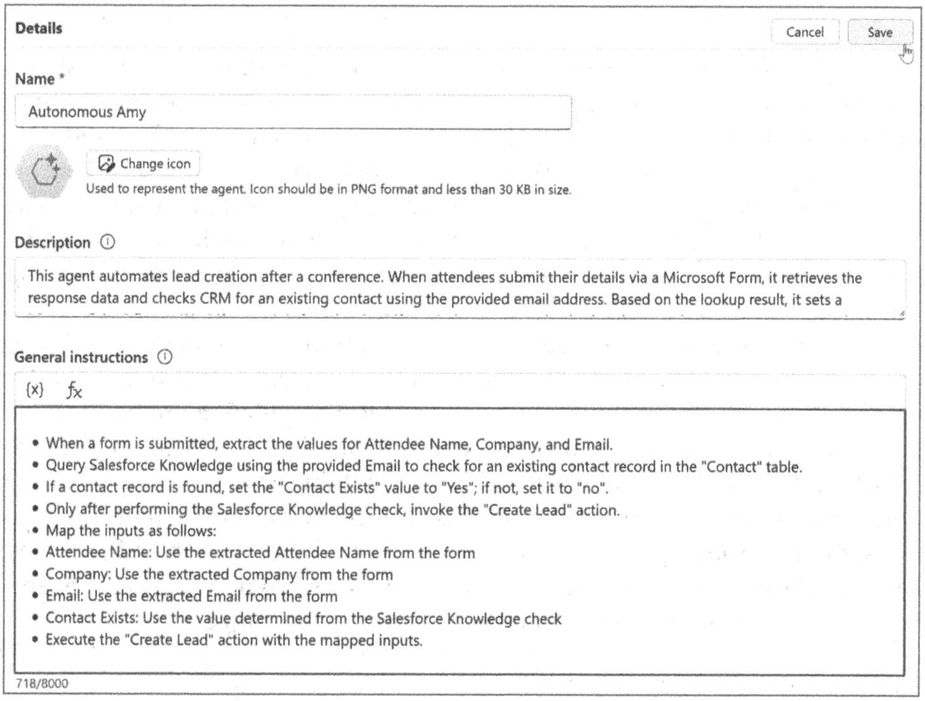

Figure 8.63: Setting general instructions

236 Chapter 8 ▪ Building an Autonomous Agent

- When a form is submitted, extract the values for Attendee Name, Company, and Email.

- Query Salesforce Knowledge using the provided Email to check for an existing contact record in the "Contact" table.

- If a contact record is found, set the "Contact Exists" value to "Yes"; if not, set it to "no".

- Only after performing the Salesforce Knowledge check, invoke the "Create Lead" action.

- Map the inputs as follows:

  - Attendee Name: Use the extracted Attendee Name from the form.

  - Company: Use the extracted Company from the form.

  - Email: Use the extracted Email from the form.

  - Contact Exists: Use the value determined from the Salesforce Knowledge check.

  - Execute the "Create Lead" action with the mapped inputs.

Testing Your Agent

The time has finally come to test our agent to see if it works and adjust any findings that there may be. To start, first you will need to submit a response to your Microsoft Form to help ensure you have test data to work with. Remember that the trigger condition for invoking our agent is "upon new Microsoft Forms submissions." Navigate to the Microsoft Forms application, open your Contoso Conference Follow-up form, and click the Collect Reponses button. Copy the URL to your clipboard and then open a new tab and navigate to the user-facing version of your form.

For the first test, go ahead and enter information for someone who is not yet a contact in your instance of Salesforce. For name, enter in **Ray Loyola**; for company, enter **Microsoft**; and then finally put **Ray.Loyola@microsoft.com** for the email address. Confirm that your entry matches Figure 8.64, and then click the Submit button. Now, navigate back to Copilot Studio.

From within Copilot Studio, click the Test button in the upper-right corner to ensure the Test Your Agent window is open. From there, click the ellipsis next to the Test Your Agent label, select Test Trigger, as shown in Figure 8.65, and then choose the Contoso Conference Form Submission trigger.

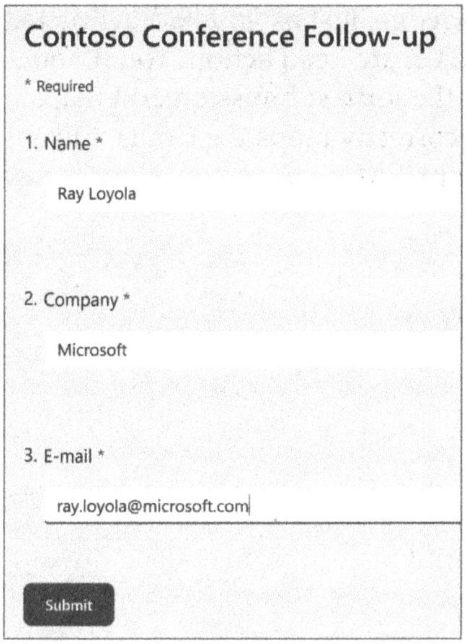

Figure 8.64: Microsoft Form Submission

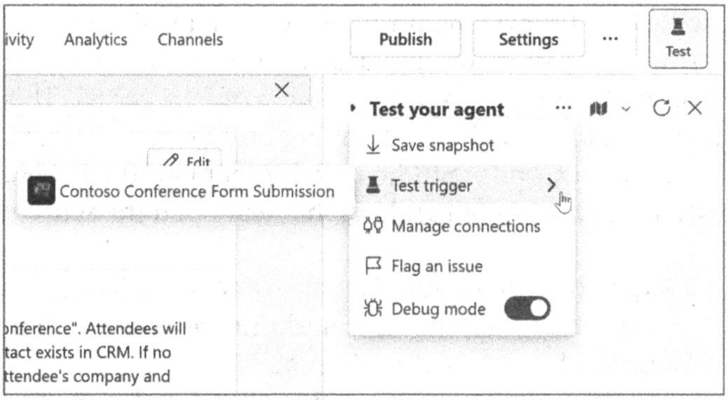

Figure 8.65: Testing your trigger

This will open a new dialog box, as shown in Figure 8.66, that allows you to select which instance of your trigger to test with. This would replicate the same experience of a user submitting your form. Since you only have one instance, you can just click the Start Testing button to begin testing your agent.

This will launch the Copilot Studio Activity Map, as shown in Figure 8.67. You will want to become familiar with this interface because you will likely be spending a lot of time troubleshooting your agent here. You'll notice that it provides a visual step-by-step view of what your agent is doing to process your request. The first step is to check Knowledge, just as you had instructed your agent, and the second step is to call the Create Lead action. You'll notice that the agent extracts the information from the form submission and maps it to the inputs for your flow. You'll see that it correctly maps the Contact Exists input to false, since Ray isn't a contact in your CRM.

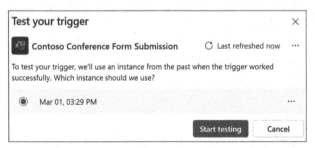

Figure 8.66: Selecting your trigger instance

You can then confirm that your flow ran by navigating back to Power Automate at make.powerautomate.com and then clicking My Flows in the left-hand navigation. You should see a list of flows, including the Create Lead flow.

Click the Create Lead flow to open it. You should see a recent run of your flow, as shown in Figure 8.68, along with a status message of Succeeded. This means that the flow ran successfully without throwing any error messages. Note that, as you continue on your Copilot Studio development journey, there will definitely be times when your flows fail and you have to open them up to troubleshoot.

If you want, you can click the flow run in your 28-day run history to inspect each step of the workflow's run. Just click the date and time to open up that particular run, which, in Figure 8.68, is Mar 23, 04:16 p.m.

You can and should also confirm that you see a new contact and opportunity in Salesforce. Open a new tab and log in to your Salesforce instance at developer.salesforce.com. Open the Sales Console from the App Launcher in the upper-left corner of your Salesforce developer instance. Next, type in **Microsoft** in the top middle of the Salesforce UI and press the Enter key. You should now be taken to the Microsoft account object in your Salesforce instance. In the right-hand side (note Salesforce's UI does change from time to time), you should see a new opportunity, as shown in Figure 8.69. Notice that it has a close date of 8/20/2025 in my example, since that's 150 days after the form submission.

So, there you have it! Your first test ran successfully and not only do you have a new contact in our CRM, but you have also created an opportunity. If you open the opportunity, as shown in Figure 8.69, you will also notice that Ray is set as the Primary contact for this opportunity.

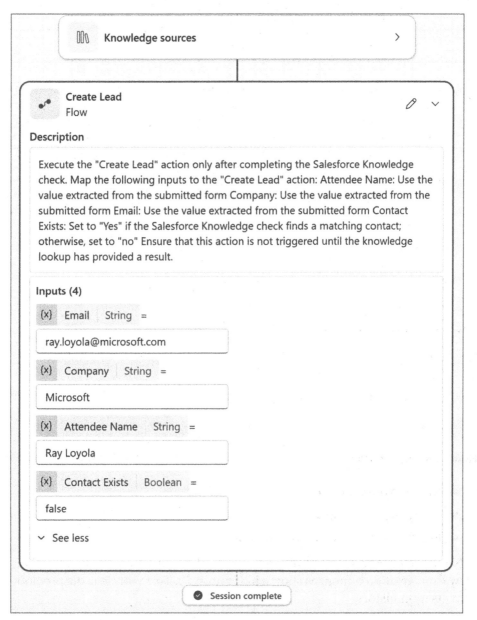

Figure 8.67: Copilot Studio Activity Map

Let's go ahead and try one more test for a contact that already exists. Hopefully you've already created a few contacts in Salesforce as instructed before. Go ahead and click the Submit Another Response link on your Contoso Conference Follow-up form. Enter the following information and then click the Submit button:

Figure 8.68: Recent flow activity

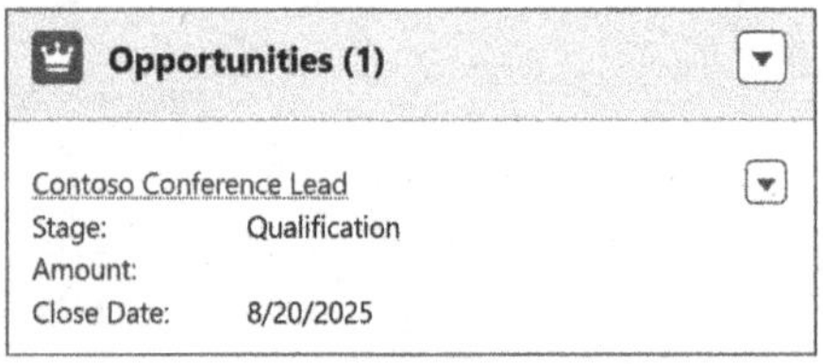

Figure 8.69: Opportunity created

- Name: Abram Jackson
- Company: Microsoft
- Email: abrjackson@microsoft.com

Navigate back to your agent, and then in the Test window, click the Start New Conversation button, as shown in Figure 8.70. This will clear the previous conversation history.

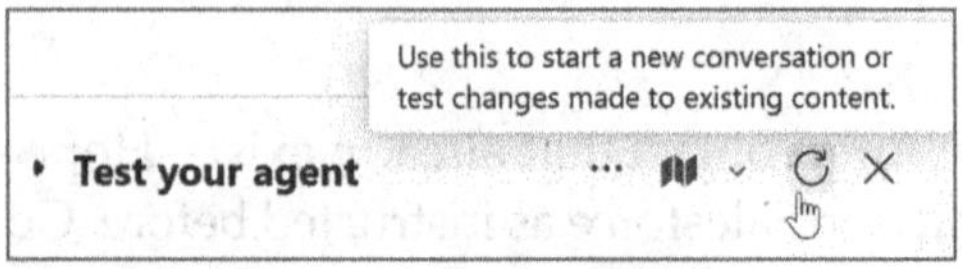

Figure 8.70: Start new conversation

Next, click the ellipsis next to the map element, as shown in Figure 8.65, and expand Test Trigger. Then select the Contoso Conference Form Submission trigger action, as shown in Figure 8.66. You'll notice a second instance of your trigger, as shown in Figure 8.71.

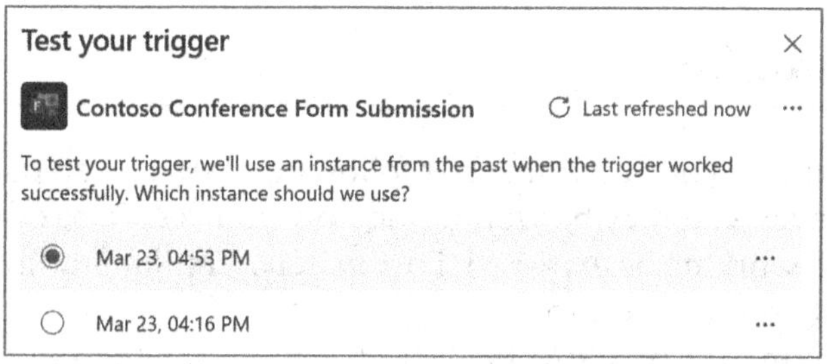

Figure 8.71: Second trigger instance

Click the Start Testing button, and then wait a few seconds for the Activity Map to being populating. You should then see the Create Lead flow, as shown in Figure 8.72.

Figure 8.72: The contact exists

If you click the See More link in the action, you'll be able to see the Contact Exists input is set to True, meaning it found Abram's contact record in Salesforce.

This, of course, means that your flow did not create a new contact but did create an opportunity and set Abram as our primary contact. You can follow the same steps as shown previously in order to confirm that you see this same result in Salesforce.

Publishing and Monitoring

Now that your agent is working, you can publish it following the same steps outlined in Chapter 3. However, you may be wondering how you keep tabs on your agent to ensure that it's working as expected. Fortunately, Copilot Studio includes an Activity log that you can monitor.

From your Autonomous Amy agent, click the Activity link in the top navigation. Once people begin engaging with your agent, you'll see that activity show up as Automated in the Name column, as shown in Figure 8.73. When you are testing your agent within Copilot Studio, you should see your own name in that first column. You can click any of these rows to step through the Activity map to ensure everything is working, just as if you were testing your agent out within Copilot Studio.

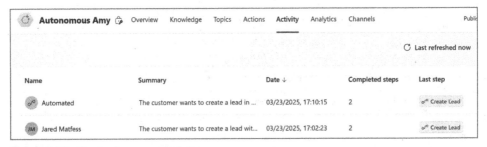

Figure 8.73: Monitoring agent activity

> **NOTE** You can download the full Power Automate flow file, *Ch08_Copilot_Studio_Quickstart.zip*, from the Wiley site at www.wiley.com/go/copilotstudioqs.

Conclusion

In this chapter, we built our first autonomous agent, which represents a significant leap forward in terms of humans and AI working together. We took a common use case of capturing leads from a form and then let our agent perform the heavy lifting of checking the CRM to see if a contact exists, creating a new contact when necessary, and then creating a new opportunity for the sales team to track down.

I am sure you can start to envision expanding this agent further by perhaps notifying the sales representative covering the account, or perhaps having the agent send a follow-up email to the attendee, thanking them for stopping by the booth.

As a reminder, it is crucial to balance the capabilities of autonomous agents with the need for human oversight. Always think about the potential repercussions if AI were to make a wrong decision, and try to put the appropriate guardrails in place to minimize that from happening. In the next chapter, we will start to dig into how you might optimize your agent and measure its effectiveness.

CHAPTER

9

Optimizing and Measuring Your Agent

In previous chapters, we explored the core components of building agents with Copilot Studio. We covered the importance of topics in conversation flow, created triggers, and configured knowledge sources and actions. In this chapter, we are still going to focus on the technical aspects of Copilot Studio, but from a slightly different lens. At the end of the day, agents are yet another "tool in the IT toolbelt" that can be used to help solve business problems. The value of agents doesn't lie in how many connectors you build or the fact that you are leveraging GenAI to help answer complex questions.

The value of agents lies in how they perform in the real world and the impact that they can have on the humans that rely on them. In this chapter, we are going to focus on improving the human/agent interaction experience. By zeroing in on experience, we can ensure our agents are providing value and continue to improve over time. I'll talk about both theory and practice for improving the value of your agents through analytics and development best practices. Let's start by covering some of the prerequisites needed to get the most out of this chapter.

Prerequisites

Before we get started, it will be helpful to have an agent that you have already published and shared with a couple of users. There is no minimum number of users or interactions that need to have occurred with your agent, but the more

245

data you have, the easier it should be to understand the concepts and develop strategies for improving user satisfaction. Just like with any technology project, it is important to receive feedback from real users as a means to improve the product that you are delivering to them.

Feedback is one of the most valuable tools when delivering any IT service to business users. It helps connect the original intent behind a technical solution with the practicality of its application in the real world when applied to a business process. Receiving both quantitative and qualitative feedback regarding your agent is incredibly important, as it will help drive where you take your agent over time.

Consider refraining from providing too much guidance to your users regarding the intent of the agent or the features that it can perform. The idea is, while you do want to encourage usage, you don't want to seed users with too many ideas or biases about your agent's capabilities. Hopefully, you can solicit a few volunteers to test your agent over the course of a couple of days to help populate the backend analytics for your agent and better understand Copilot Studio's built-in reporting capabilities.

Agent Analytics

Copilot Studio includes integrated analytics to help you understand how users are interacting with your agent. As you start to explore the various analytics reports available through Copilot Studio, it's important to have a high-level understanding of the following core concepts:

- **Conversations:** This is a user and agent interaction log that can either be one-on-one or involve a group of users interacting with your agent (e.g., conversations in a Microsoft Teams channel).

- **Analytics sessions:** These track the engagement between the user and the agent and can comprise one or many conversations.

- **Outcomes and engagement:** These track the result of the conversation with your agent. You'll want to focus on this to help identify opportunities for improvement and new features to add.

- **Knowledge source usage:** You can review which knowledge sources are used the most and identify any gaps.

- **Action usage:** You can monitor which of your custom actions are being used the most to help understand the potential impact they may be having.

- **User feedback:** This is an average customer satisfaction score for sessions where the user completes an end-of-session survey.

Chapter 9 ▪ Optimizing and Measuring Your Agent 247

To get started, open your browser and navigate to Copilot Studio (copilotstudio.microsoft.com), and click Agents in the left-hand navigation. Open one of the bots you have recently published and ideally have shared with other users to test. In the top navigation, click the Analytics navigation link, and you will start to see analytics for your agent, as shown in Figure 9.1.

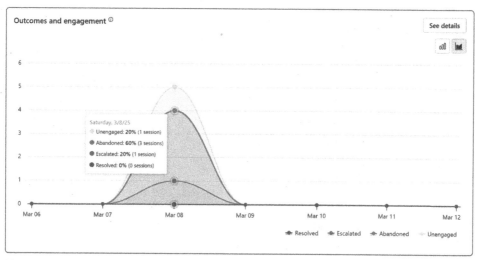

Figure 9.1: Agent analytics

You can also drill into the data further to better understand how users are interacting with your agent. If you click See Details, as shown in Figure 9.1, a new dialog will open from the right, as shown in Figure 9.2. This summarizes the session outcomes with percentages so you can start to pinpoint the effectiveness of your agent. You can also use this to understand the conversation flow for users and then compare the session outcomes with topic outcomes to better pinpoint changes that might drive better session outcomes. For example, if you find a high abandonment percentage on a particular topic, that might be where you start to look for opportunities to better engage the user with "quick replies," which we will cover later.

Additionally, you can dig into the actual user prompts and agent responses by clicking the Download Sessions button, as shown in Figure 9.2. This will initiate an export of the raw data to a *Sessions.csv* file, as shown in Figure 9.3. This will give you the raw data that shows when the user began interacting with your agent, their initial message, the topic that they engaged with, what the agent responded with, the session outcome, and the reason for the outcome. To trace the entire user session, you would want to filter based on column A, which is titled SessionId, to understand the full conversational flow of the user with your agent during that session.

Chapter 9 ■ Optimizing and Measuring Your Agent

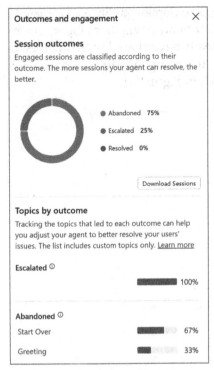

Figure 9.2: Outcomes and engagement analytics

	A	B	C	D	E	F	G	H	I
1	SessionId	StartDateTime	InitialUserMessage	TopicName	ChatTransc	SessionOut	TopicId	OutcomeReason	
2	98541140	3/8/2025 15:07			Bot says: H	Unengaged		NoError	
3	98541140	3/8/2025 16:50	apply for a service	Apply for a ser	User says: ⟨	Abandoned	501e38a5-⟨	UserExit	
4	ab91a19c	3/8/2025 16:50	I would like to apply for assistance	Apply for a ser	Bot says: H	Abandoned	501e38a5-⟨	UserExit	
5	39643be0	3/8/2025 19:10	I would like to apply for assistance	Apply for a ser	Bot says: H	Abandoned	501e38a5-⟨	UserExit	
6	045a670e	3/8/2025 19:25	road closures	Road Closure:	Bot says: H	Abandoned	ea227fea-e	UserExit	
7	8a9525aa	3/8/2025 19:35	are there any road closures in AUstin?	Road Closure:	Bot says: H	Abandoned	ea227fea-e	UserExit	
8	5d0cd056	3/8/2025 19:35	Road closures	Road Closure:	Bot says: H	Abandoned	ea227fea-e	UserExit	
9	c03c8809	3/8/2025 19:58	how do I get a fishing license?		Bot says: H	Abandoned		UserExit	
10	fef6c289-⟨	3/8/2025 19:59	How do I do business with the city of redmond?		Bot says: H	Abandoned		UserExit	
11	87ae7677	3/8/2025 20:30	How do I do business with the city of Redmond?		Bot says: H	Abandoned		UserExit	
12	147b9976	3/8/2025 20:51			Bot says: H	Unengaged		NoError	
13	147b9976	3/8/2025 22:52	what shows are playing now?		User says: ⟨	Abandoned		UserExit	

Figure 9.3: Download sessions

Optimizing Your Agent for Cost

Reviewing analytics about your agent's performance is certainly very beneficial from a user experience perspective, but the second area of evaluation that you will want to consider is cost. AI development and operation are costly due to the complexity of models, large data requirements, and the need for powerful hardware such as GPUs to run. Additionally, ongoing support, maintenance, regulatory compliance, and security measures contribute to these high costs.

Chapter 9 ▪ Optimizing and Measuring Your Agent 249

So, when you consider Microsoft as an AI service provider, it should come as no surprise that they are in the business of making money off their service. When you start to plan for the cost of running your agent, there are a number of different functions to consider:

- **Classic answers:** These events are predefined responses that are manually authored by agent makers. They're statically defined within a topic and do not change unless manually updated. These answers are typically used where precise and controlled responses are the only ones we want the agent to generate—for example, if you want to ensure that the agent only returns a link to the official holiday calendar or a pricing list for your products, rather than potentially sharing outdated or wrong information.

- **Generative answers:** Generative answers are used when your agent responds to user queries based on various knowledge sources at the topic level. For example, in our previous buildouts, when a user's query doesn't match a predefined intent, the agent defaults to the Conversational Boosting topic and uses generative answers as a fallback to provide relevant information from sources like public websites, SharePoint, or custom data sources. It's using AI to both understand the intent of your user's question and to reason over the information provided by querying knowledge, then presenting back to the user.

- **Agent actions:** These events are steps, such as triggers and topics, that appear on the activity map in Copilot Studio when you test an autonomous agent. These events don't include knowledge search, knowledge retrieval, or AI Builder prompts. These include steps such as actions where you call a Power Automate flow to create a task for someone in Jira or create a list item in SharePoint, etc.

- **Tenant Microsoft Graph grounding for messages:** These events provide higher-quality grounding for your agents using retrieval-augmented generation (RAG) over your tenant-wide Microsoft Graph, including external data synced into Microsoft Graph through connectors. This results in more relevant and improved responses and ensures that the grounding information is up to date. This capability is optional, and you can turn it on or off for each agent. Microsoft 365 Copilot users can access tenant Microsoft Graph grounding for messages at no extra cost as part of their license.

- **Agent flow actions:** Actions where the agent calls a Power Automate flow with predefined steps and do not include agent orchestration of reasoning.

- **Text and generative AI tools:** To add just a little more complexity to your cost calculation, the model that you may choose to perform certain actions within your agent will incur different costs. For example, if you were to

Chapter 9 ▪ Optimizing and Measuring Your Agent

use Azure OpenAI 4o-mini model, those interactions would be considered standard, whereas 4o interactions would be classified as premium due to the cost to host that model. Finally, Azure OpenAI o1 prompts are considered a premium feature.

Copilot Studio-developed agents have a billing model that is based on messages. This model is documented in Table 9.1.

Table 9.1: Copilot Studio messages by feature

FEATURE	BILLING RATE	M365 COPILOT AGENT USE	AUTONOMOUS USE
Classic answer	1 message	No charge	N/A
Generative answer	2 messages	No charge	2 messages
Agent action	5 messages	No charge	5 messages
Tenant graph grounding for messages	10 messages	No charge	10 messages
Agent flow actions per 100 actions	13 messages	13 messages	13 messages
AI Tools			
Text and generative AI tools (basic) per 10 responses	1 message	1 message	1 message
Text and generative AI tools (basic) per 10 responses	15 messages	15 messages	15 messages
Text and generative AI tools (basic) per 10 responses	100 messages	100 messages	100 messages

When designing your agent, you should create a high-level conversational flow and balance out the experience you are trying to create along with the cost that you could potentially incur. If you're wondering how you might monitor activity to get a feel for how many messages you are incurring, Microsoft makes this available through the Power Platform admin center. Someone whose Azure Entra ID has been set up as a Power Platform administrator can log in to admin .powerplatform.microsoft.com, then click the Licensing button in the left navigation, and then select Copilot Studio, as shown in Figure 9.4.

From here, you can monitor message consumption by environments to better understand which agents are the most active. You can also create messaging plans and allocate capacity per Power Platform environment as a means of controlling the consumption. We aren't going to go deep into the different strategies for managing and allocating licenses to environments. Just know that Copilot Studio agents are billed based on messages, and there is a joint responsibility between IT and "makers" to help control costs associated with agents. A conversation that should be had regularly is how you might consider optimizing agent message consumption, while also ensuring a positive user experience.

> **NOTE** For the latest information regarding Copilot Studio licensing, please visit `learn.microsoft.com/en-us/microsoft-copilot-studio/billing-licensing`.

Figure 9.4: Power Platform Admin Center – Copilot Studio

Enhancing User-Focused Agent Performance

Next, we are going to walk through three different ways that you can consider optimizing your agents from a user experience perspective. First, we'll talk about "quick replies," which is a technique for providing users with an immediate response within a topic that could be a website link, a message response, or even having the agent call a user. Then, we'll revisit "starter prompts," which we touched on briefly in Chapter 4. Finally, we'll talk through collecting user feedback on the effectiveness of generative answers or your agent overall.

Quick Replies

Quick replies in Copilot Studio are predefined response options that users can select during a conversation with your agent. These replies provide a way for users to quickly and easily interact with the agent without having to type out their responses. They also can help provide context for the capabilities of your agent that might not be obvious. Let's go ahead and add a quick reply to our BigAppleBuddy agent that we created back in Chapter 6. Navigate back to Copilot Studio, and then hover over the Agents link in the left-hand navigation and select BigAppleBuddy from the list of available agents.

Next, click the Topics link in the top navigation. From here, click the System button and then select the Conversation Start topic. Click the conversation bubble in the upper-left corner of the message node, then click the + Add button, and finally click Quick Reply, as shown in Figure 9.5.

Figure 9.5: Adding a quick reply

You have a couple of choices for the type of quick reply that you can initiate when a user clicks on it within the chat window:

- **Send a message:** This will return text that you define if the user clicks this option.
- **Open URL:** This will open a new URL within the active browser session to a website you configure.
- **Make a call:** This will initiate a phone call from the agent to the user.
- **Send a hidden message:** This will send a message to the agent that you can use to configure additional logic depending on the topic context.

For this particular use case, let's go ahead and create an "Open URL" quick reply. From the Quick Reply Properties pane that appears after you select + Add, select Open URL from the Type drop-down menu. Enter `https://www.nyc.gov/events/events-filter.html` into the URL input field. You can then go ahead and enter **Find Local Events** in the Title field, as shown in Figure 9.6. Click the Save button to confirm your changes.

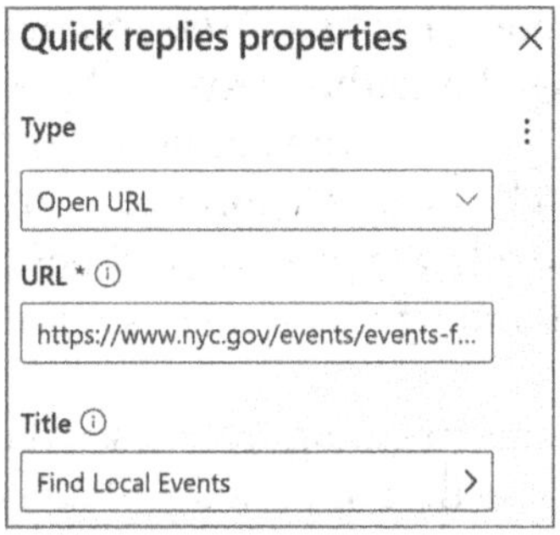

Figure 9.6 quick replies properties panel caption:

Figure 9.6: The Open URL quick action

You can quickly test this functionality by clicking the Test link in the top navigation. Then click the Start a New Conversation button to refresh your agent. You should now see a button labeled Find Local Events between the message "Hello, I'm BigAppleBuddy, a virtual assistant. I can help you navigate government services and information. Just so you are aware, I sometimes use AI to answer your questions." being sent by your agent and the conversation input, as shown in Figure 9.7. If you click the button, it should open a new tab in your browser to a list of events in NYC.

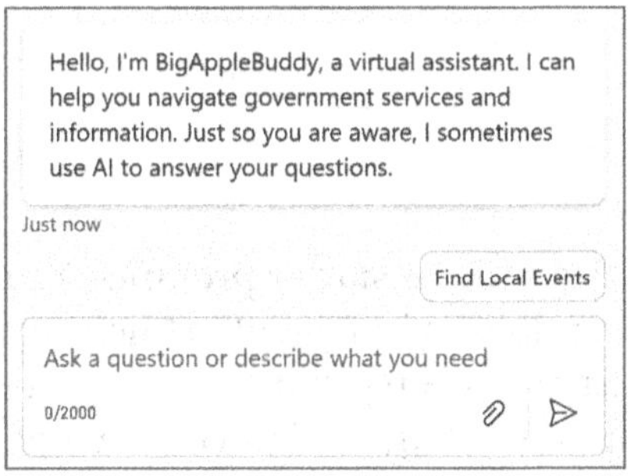

Figure 9.7: The Find Local Events quick reply

While this functionality is relatively basic, think about the number of potential messages it could save by not having to go back and forth with the user about the various events. It can also help steer the user away from assuming that the agent can perform additional tasks around events, like registering for them or sending updates to their email. While this breaks the paradigm of trying to centralize user experience within Copilot, there likely might be situations—such as viewing events—where the user experience would be better on a mobile-friendly website than through a conversation window.

Starter Prompts

Another way that you can enhance your agent's customer experience is through configuring "starter prompts," as we originally covered in Chapter 4. As a refresher, starter prompts are preconfigured suggestions that help users initiate conversations with your agent. Unlike quick replies that either respond back with a message or open a new URL, starter prompts seed the conversation input and serve as a cue for what functionality might be available through your agent. The user could choose to add additional context to the prompt or choose to send it as is. From there, the agent would process the prompt just as if the user typed out the text themselves.

To configure a starter prompt, navigate back to the agent configuration screen and scroll down until you reach the Starter Prompts section of your agent configuration screen. From here, click the pencil icon labeled Edit to start adding your prompts. There are two fields required: the Title, which is a description or category for the prompt, and then the actual Prompt field. For our BigAppleBuddy agent, an example prompt you could consider is "How do I report a noise complaint?" In the Title field, enter **Noise complaint**, and then in the Prompt field, enter **How do I report a noise complaint?**, as shown in Figure 9.8. Then click the Save button.

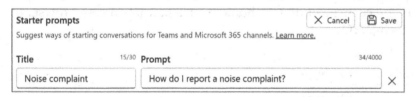

Figure 9.8: Noise complaint starter prompt

Next, you will need to publish your agent to see these starter prompts. You can refer to Chapter 3 for instructions on how to publish your agent to Microsoft Teams or Microsoft 365 Copilot. Once your agent has been published, you may need to wait a few minutes before it shows up in your agent. However, when it does, you should see a View Prompts link next to a book icon, as shown in Figure 9.9. You will notice the Noise Complaint title is above the actual prompt, "How do I report a noise complaint?" If you click that prompt, you will then see it added to the chat window. From there, you can either send it directly to the agent or append additional context based on your use case.

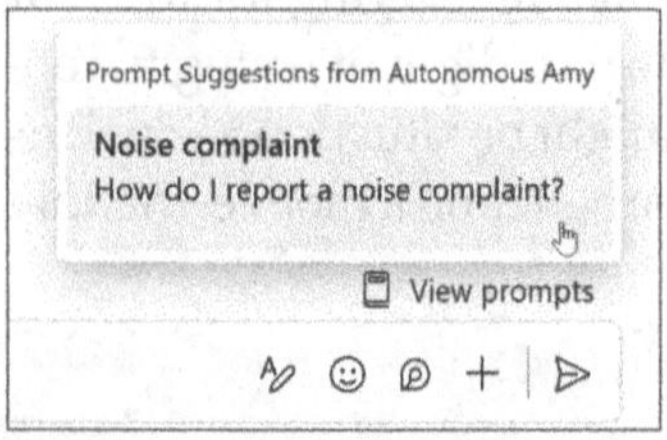

Figure 9.9: Selecting a starter prompt

Capturing User Feedback

Finally, one additional step that you may want to take to further understand how your agent is being used is to expand the logging of activity using Azure Application Insights (App Insights). App Insights is a cloud-based service designed by Microsoft to help you monitor your applications. App Insights helps you gain insights into the performance, availability, and usage of your applications. Included in the service are tools for diagnosing and troubleshooting issues, identifying performance bottlenecks, and tracking how users interact with your applications. You can also leverage App Insights to track custom events or activities in your agents to further identify opportunities to improve knowledge or actions that serve your customers.

For this scenario, we will create a feedback loop for when the agent searches available knowledge and then shares a response with the user. We want to gauge how accurate these responses appear from the user's perspective to decide if the knowledge source needs curation or if additional topics and actions are required. By gathering this feedback, we can refine our approach and ensure we are truly supporting our users. The next section will cover extending our BigAppleBuddy agent to support this feedback loop.

> **NOTE** To follow along, you will need an instance of Application Insights provisioned in your Azure subscription. You can find more information, including how to provision an instance of App Insights, here: learn.microsoft.com/en-us/azure/ azure-monitor/app/app-insights-overview.

We're going to override the default agent response and introduce feedback buttons along with the response. Click the Topics top navigation link, and then click the System button to filter to system topics. Next, click the Conversational Boosting topic, and then click the ellipsis in the upper-right corner of the Create Generative Answers node. Click Properties and then scroll down to the Advanced section of the menu that just appeared. Expand Advanced, and then in the Save LLM Response field, change the value to Complete (Recommended), as shown in Figure 9.10. Also, be sure to uncheck the Send a Message checkbox. Then click the Save button.

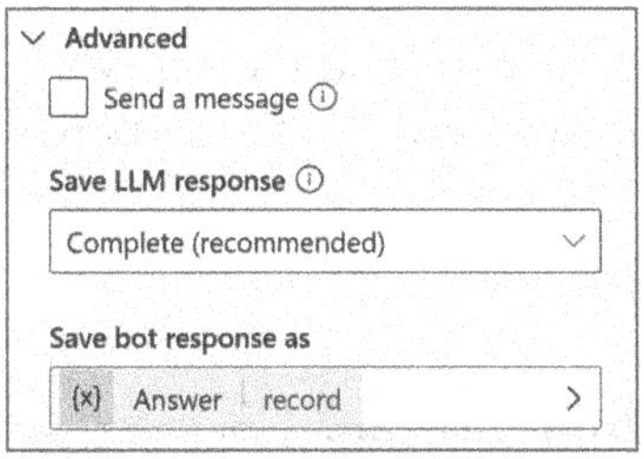

Figure 9.10: Saving the LLM response

Next, click the + Add Node button directly below the Condition node, as shown in Figure 9.11. This node is confirming that the response being returned from the LLM is not blank, meaning that it found an answer in knowledge and is presenting that back to the user. Select Send a Message from the list of available actions to add that node to the authoring canvas.

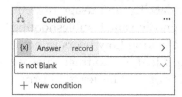

Figure 9.11: Condition node

In the text area of the node, click the "{x} Insert variable" button, type in **Answer.Text.MarkdownContent**, and then select that variable to add it. This variable is the full response provided back from the LLM. Since we previously unchecked the Send a Message from the Create Generative Answers node, this is where we are sending the response back to the user. Next, we want to add an Adaptive Card to enable the user to provide feedback if the response back is helpful. Click + Add in the upper-left corner of the Messages node that you just inserted that variable in, and then select Adaptive Card. Click the Adaptive Card in the messages node and select Edit Formula from the drop-down menu, as shown in Figure 9.12.

Figure 9.12: Editing the Adaptive Card

Enter the JSON presented in Listing 9.1 into the text box, and then click the X button in the upper-right corner to close the Adaptive Card Properties panel:

Listing 9.1: Ch09_Response_Feedback_Formula.json

```
{
  type: "AdaptiveCard",
  '$schema': "http://adaptivecards.io/schemas/adaptive-card.json",
```

```
version: "1.4",
body: [
  {
    type:"ColumnSet",
    columns: [
      {
        type:"Column",
        width: "stretch",
        items:[
          {
            type:"ActionSet",
            actions: [
              {
                type:"Action.Submit",

                title: "Great response ☺",
                style: "positive",
                data:{
                  MessageEvent: "AgentFeedback",
                  Like: true,
                  Prompt: System.Activity.Text,
                  Response: Topic.Answer.Text.MarkdownContent
                }
              }
            ]
          }
        ]
      },
      {
        type:"Column",
        width: "stretch",
        items:[
          {
            type:"ActionSet",
            actions: [
              {
                type:"Action.Submit",

                title: "Poor response ☹",
                style: "destructive",
                data:{
                  MessageEvent: "AgentFeedback",
                  Like: false,
                  Prompt: System.Activity.Text,
                  Response: Topic.Answer.Text.MarkdownContent
                }
              }
            ]
          }
        ]
      }
```

```
                    ]
                  }
                ]
              }
            ]
          }
        ]
      }
```

> **NOTE** You can find the *Ch09_Response_Feedback_Formula.json* file in the downloadable files for this book at www.wiley.com/go/copilotstudioqs.

Let's do a quick spot check to make sure things are working as expected. First, click Save, and then click Test to open the chat window in your agent. Ask a question such as "**Who is the mayor of New York?**", and then press Enter. You should receive a response resembling Figure 9.13. It will display the agent's reply, along with two buttons beneath the response designed to collect user feedback.

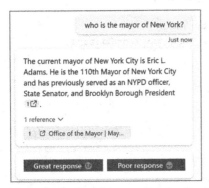

Figure 9.13: The response with feedback buttons

Next, we are going to create functionality that will process that feedback. Click the Topics link, then click the + Add a Topic button, and then select From Blank to create a new blank topic. To rename the topic to Agent Feedback, click the Untitled text in the upper-left corner and type **"Agent Feedback."** Now, we are going to change the trigger for this topic by clicking the arrows pointing in opposite directions. Select the Message Received trigger, as shown in Figure 9.14.

The Message Received trigger means that this topic will be called every time a user sends a message to your agent. However, we only want to invoke the subsequent logic when this topic is being called from the user clicking one of the feedback buttons. Therefore, we will need to understand the context of the conversation.

To do this, click the + Add Node button below the Trigger node, hover your mouse over Variable Management, and then select Parse Value. Let's configure this new node by first clicking Enter or Select a Value underneath the Parse Value

Chapter 9 ▪ Optimizing and Measuring Your Agent

label, and then clicking System in the pop-up menu and selecting Activity.Value from the list of choices. Next, click the Data Type drop-down menu and select From Sample Data. Click the Get Schema from Sample JSON link. Beneath the "Get Schema from Sample JSON" label, enter the following text, as shown in Figure 9.15:

```
{
    "Like": true,
    "MessageEvent": "AgentFeedback",
    "Prompt": "What is Superman's real name?",
    "Response": "Kal-El"
}
```

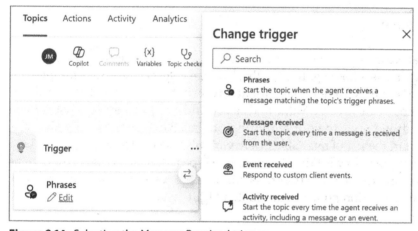

Figure 9.14: Selecting the Message Received trigger

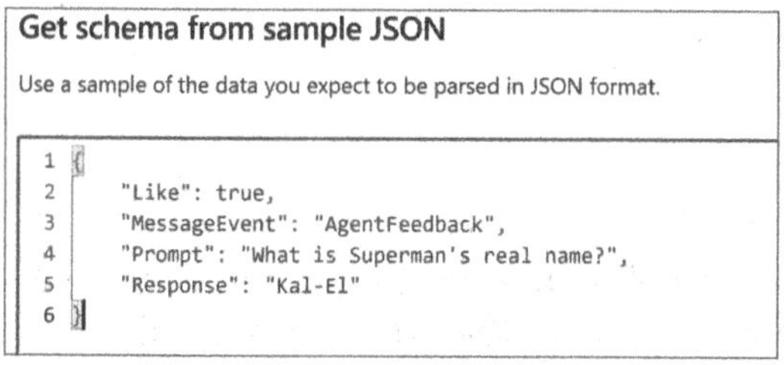

Figure 9.15: Getting schema from sample JSON

Click the Confirm button to continue.

Next, click the Select a Variable input and click Create New to create a new variable. This will create a new variable called `var1` of type record. Click `var1` in the input screen, and then rename the variable to **UserFeedback** in the Variable Properties panel. Click the X button to close that panel. Your Parse Value node should now match Figure 9.16.

Chapter 9 ■ Optimizing and Measuring Your Agent

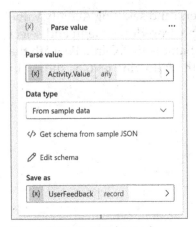

Figure 9.16: Parse Value node

Now that we have the `UserFeedback` variable, we can go ahead and branch our logic so that if a user has negative feedback on the response, we can prompt them to provide what they were looking for and record that response. Let's go ahead and add a node below Parse Value and select Add a Condition. This will add an Add a Condition node to your authoring canvas. Next, click Select a Variable, and then from the list of available Topic variables, select UserFeedback.Like.

Click the input below Is Equal To, and then type in the word **false**. This means we are checking to see if the user does not like the response provided by your agent. Your Condition node should match Figure 9.17.

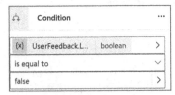

Figure 9.17: UserFeedback.Like is equal to false

Now, click the + Add a Node button below the condition node, and select Ask with Adaptive Card. We are going to prompt the user to provide input for what they were expecting as a response from your agent. Click the node, and then enter the following into the Adaptive Card Node Properties menu:

```
{
    "type": "AdaptiveCard",
    "version": "1.4",
    "body": [
        {
            "type": "TextBlock",
            "text": "Please let us know what you were expecting:"
```

Chapter 9 ■ Optimizing and Measuring Your Agent

```
        },
        {
            "type": "Input.Text",
            "id": "userInput",
            "placeholder": "Enter your text here...",
            "isMultiline": true
        }
    ],
    "actions": [
        {
            "type": "Action.Submit",
            "title": "Submit",
            "id": "submitButton",
            "style": "positive"
        }
    ],
    "$schema": "http://adaptivecards.io/schemas/adaptive-card.json"
}
```

Click the X button to minimize the Adaptive Card Node Properties menu and confirm that your Adaptive Card is rendering to match Figure 9.18. You should also note that it will create a variable called `userInput` that will capture what the user was expecting the agent to return as a response. Click the Save button before proceeding.

Figure 9.18: Collecting user feedback

Before proceeding with the next step, which involves logging user feedback to App Insights, we need to configure our agent. This includes setting it up with the configuration string required to connect to our instance of App Insights. If you have access to your Azure Portal, then you can navigate to your instance of App Insights, and in the Overview tab, copy the Connection String to your clipboard, as shown in Figure 9.19. Otherwise, you will need to work with someone from your IT team to get the connection string.

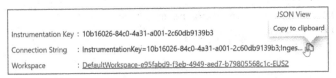

Figure 9.19: App Insights connection string

Once you have your connection string, navigate back to your agent, and then click the Settings button in the upper-right corner of your agent configuration screen. Select Advanced on the left-hand navigation, and then click the > arrow next to Application Insights. Click the input below Connection String, as shown in Figure 9.20, and paste the contents of your clipboard into the box. Click on the X button in the upper-right corner to go back to the agent configuration screen.

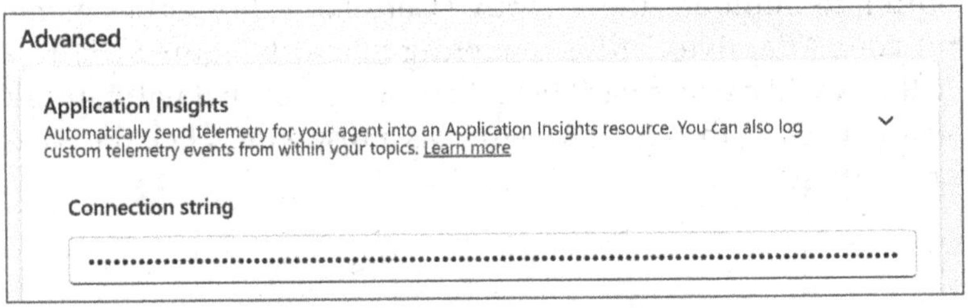

Figure 9.20: Setting the connection string in Copilot Studio

Now, navigate back to the AgentFeedback topic and click the + Add Node button below your Adaptive Card where you are asking the user for feedback. Hover your mouse over Advanced, and then select Log a Custom Telemetry Event to add this node to your canvas. Click the ellipsis in the right corner of the Log Custom Telemetry Event node, and then select Properties. For the Event Name, type in **AgentFeedback**, and then click the > button under the Properties input. Select Formula, and then type in the following information:

```
{
    User: System.User.Email,
    Prompt: Topic.UserFeedback.Prompt,
    Response: Topic.UserFeedback.Response,
    Expected: Topic.userInput

}
```

What we are doing is passing four pieces of information to App Insights:

- **User:** The email address of the user interacting with your agent
- **Prompt:** What the use sent to the agent
- **Response:** The agent's response
- **Expected:** The data collected in the Adaptive Card for what the user was expecting to receive back from the agent

Click the X button to close the formula panel. Then click the X button to close the Log Custom Telemetry Event Properties panel. Now, let's have the agent thank the user for their feedback. Add a "message" node below the Log Custom Telemetry Event node. In the message box, enter the text: **Thank you for your feedback**, as shown in Figure 9.21.

Figure 9.21: Thank you for your feedback

Lastly, to button all this up, let's add a Message node below the All Other Condition node, as shown in Figure 9.22. You can keep it pretty brief—like a "thumbs up" emoji or a simple "Thank you." This condition is met when a user is satisfied with the response provided by your agent. Click the Save button to capture all of these latest changes.

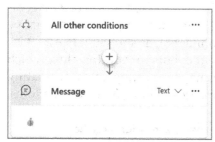

Figure 9.22: Responding to positive feedback

Finally, go ahead and click the Test button in the upper-right corner and refresh the conversation. Try asking your agent "Who is the mayor of New York?", and

264 Chapter 9 ▪ Optimizing and Measuring Your Agent

then press Enter. Select the Poor Response option, and then put some text into the "Please let us know you were expecting:" input. Finally, click the Submit button. You should receive a "Thank you for your feedback!" acknowledgment from the agent, as shown in Figure 9.23.

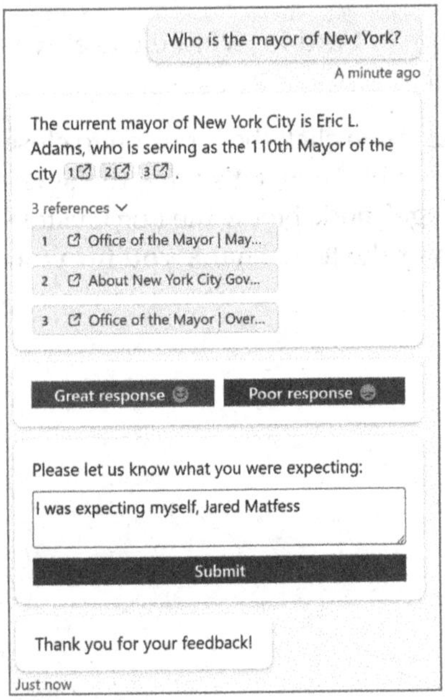

Figure 9.23: Acknowledgment message

Wait a couple of minutes, and then either navigate to your App Insights instance or work with someone from your IT team to confirm that it is collecting messages from your agent. From the Overview screen of your App Insights instance, click Logs, as shown in Figure 9.24.

From here, you can review the logs to ensure that you are seeing events logged to App Insights. The custom event that we created was called "Agent-Feedback," so you should be able to find the event where you provided negative feedback about the response provided by your agent, as shown in Figure 9.25. Congratulations—you are now logging agent events to App Insights, which unlocks a whole range of possibilities in terms of reporting, such as creating custom dashboards to visualize performance metrics, failures, and usage patterns.

> **NOTE** Additional resources for creating reports using App Insights can be found at learn.microsoft.com/en-us/azure/azure-monitor/app/ overview-dashboard.

Chapter 9 ▪ Optimizing and Measuring Your Agent

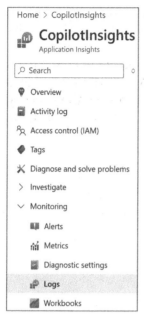

Figure 9.24: App Insights logs

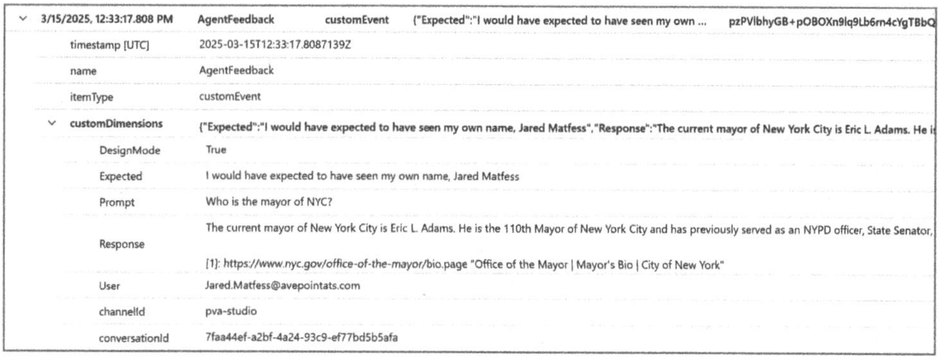

Figure 9.25: AgentFeedback events logged to App Insights

Conclusion

In this chapter, we explored how to optimize and measure agent performance in Copilot Studio. We investigated using the out-of-the-box analytics capabilities to gain an understanding of how frequently users interact with our agent. Then we covered strategies for optimizing the user experience, including quick replies and starter prompts. Finally, we created a feedback loop using Adaptive Cards and App Insights to capture user sentiment about the quality of the AI-generated responses.

In the next chapter, we'll explore Azure AI Foundry and show how it pairs with Copilot Studio to create more robust enterprise AI solutions. We'll also delve deeper into the "better together" story, so you can see the synergy between both tools and how they can drive greater value for your organization.

CHAPTER

10

Copilot Studio and Azure AI Foundry: Better Together

In this final chapter, we will expand our focus beyond Copilot Studio and extend our agent creation capability with the power of Microsoft's Azure AI Foundry. Azure AI Foundry is a SaaS-based AI platform designed to help developers and organizations build, customize, and manage AI applications at scale. The platform offers tools and resources for creating intelligent apps using prebuilt and customizable AI models, APIs, and SDKs. While Copilot Studio is positioned toward makers, Azure AI Foundry is Microsoft's offering marketed toward professional developers and data scientists who have experience with software development. However, the reality is that Copilot Studio and Azure AI Foundry are a better-together scenario.

Agents need access to models and data to help drive business outcomes, and this is possible by leveraging the full power of Microsoft Azure and Azure AI Foundry. We will work through a use case that will replicate using an agent to access data in a custom application that exists within your environment. The solution will utilize Azure AI Search to create a vector index of provider data. Vector database indexing, as we'll discuss later, is the process of organizing and optimizing high-dimensional data into a structured format that enables fast and efficient similarity searches. This blended approach of low-code with Copilot Studio and pro-code with Azure AI Foundry will help you realize the true potential of what's possible when building business solutions.

267

Azure AI Search

Azure AI Search is Microsoft's rebrand of Azure Cognitive Search and the introduction of new capabilities such as improved semantic rankings and vector search. Semantic rankings are used to improve the relevance of search results by understanding the meaning behind search queries and documents. Instead of relying solely on keyword matching, semantic ranking uses advanced models to evaluate how well the search results align with the user's intent. As a very basic example, if you were to search for a "project kick-off deck," Azure AI Search would know that your intent is to locate a PowerPoint presentation that is for a project kick-off.

For our previous examples, we leveraged Copilot connectors built on top of the Power Platform to access Salesforce, Exchange, and SharePoint. We then configured knowledge sources to Azure AI Search, and Copilot Connectors serve different purposes and are ideal in different scenarios. You would use Azure AI Search when your focus is on querying and retrieving content from large datasets, to serve as knowledge for your agent. Copilot Connectors, on the other hand, are for when you are trying to build actions such as integrating external APIs or live systems into your Copilot Studio agent. They are best used for accessing and interacting with real-time data or services, rather than building complex search functionalities.

To get some hands-on experience with Azure AI Search, you are going to build an agent that can help locate a healthcare provider using the "Doctors and Clinicians" national downloadable file. Open a new browser and navigate to `data.cms.gov/provider-data/dataset/mj5m-pzi6`. Click Download Full Dataset (CSV) 659 MB, as shown in Figure 10.1, to download the CSV file to your local computer. (Note that the size of this file may vary.)

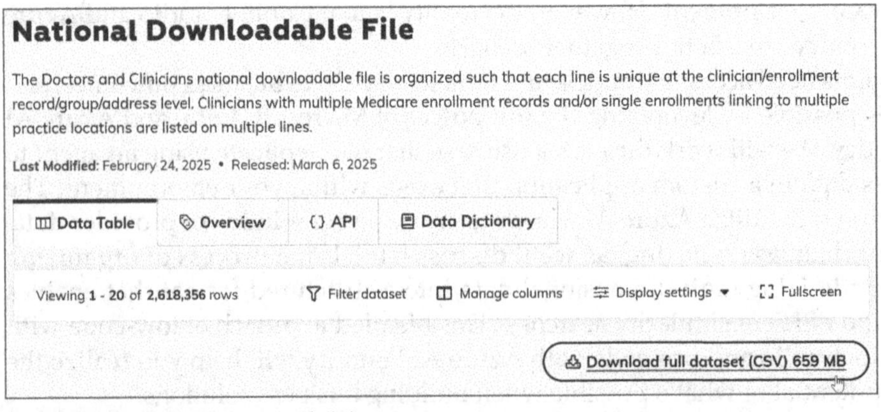

Figure 10.1: Downloading the full dataset

Chapter 10 ■ Copilot Studio and Azure AI Foundry: Better Together   269

For the next steps, you can either work with your company's IT team to provide the necessary Azure resources to follow along, or you can sign up for a free trial of Azure and get $200 in credit to be used within 30 days. I'll walk through some of the core steps for setting this up in case you have less experience with Azure. I won't focus too much on making this solution "production-ready," as many organizations will have different policies and procedures on cloud resources. Rather, I will err on the side of making it all work functionally.

Optimizing for Cost

Before we go too far, I would like to acknowledge that this is a rather large dataset and could potentially run up a high cost. To help reduce that cost, I'll offer an example PowerShell script that can limit the provider data based on state. For this example, you can read in the full CSV and then output a smaller CSV with just providers that operate in Connecticut (CT). You can either follow along with just CT providers or choose to make your own modification to consolidate the data and reduce your cloud costs. Note: To run this script properly you'll need to change the "*C:\Path*" to match your own file system for Mac or Windows.

```
$inputFile = "C:\Path\DAC_NationalDownloadableFile.csv"
$outputFile = "C:\Path\CT_only.csv"

Import-Csv -Path $inputFile |
    Where-Object { $_.State -and $_.State.Trim().ToUpper() -eq "CT" } |
    Export-Csv -Path $outputFile -NoTypeInformation -Encoding UTF8
```

Creating Your Azure SQL Database

As a reminder for this next set of steps, you can certainly solve this same use case through indexing the CSV file directly. However, the intent is to replicate an existing line-of-business application that your organization may have already developed in Microsoft Azure. Most applications have backend databases, and Azure SQL is usually the database of choice for applications.

To get started, log in to Azure by navigating to `portal.azure.com`, and then click the Create a Resource button, as shown in Figure 10.2.

This will present the Azure Marketplace, where you can provision various resources to your Azure subscription. Type **Azure SQL** into the search box in the top left corner, and then click the Create button under the Azure SQL Service, as shown in Figure 10.3.

Next, you will have to select your SQL deployment option. For this example, we want this to be as simple as possible, so click the Create button under the SQL Databases option, as shown in Figure 10.4.

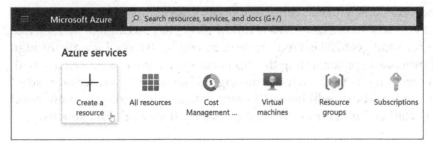

Figure 10.2: Creating an Azure resource

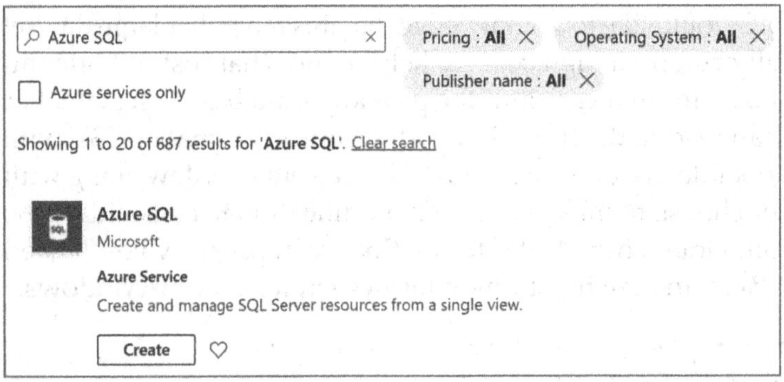

Figure 10.3: Selecting Azure SQL

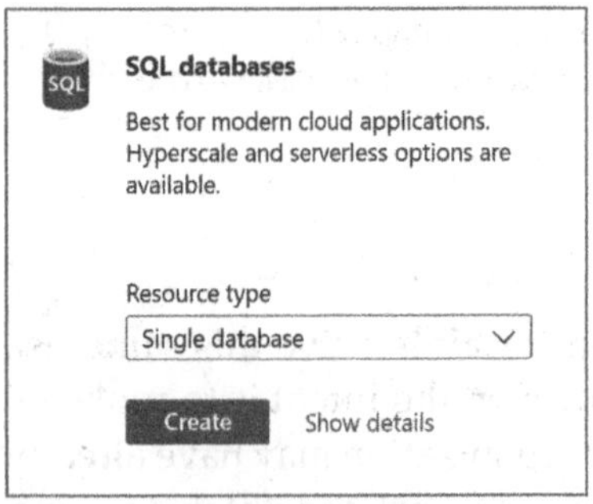

Figure 10.4: Create SQL database

Now you'll need to provide specific configuration information for your database. To start, select either an existing Azure resource group, as shown in Figure 10.5, or create a new one. A *resource group* is a logical container that holds related resources for an Azure solution. It serves as an organizational unit where you can deploy, manage, and monitor resources such as virtual machines, databases, and web apps as a single group. It also serves as a means to control and delegate access. For example, you can have your IT admin create an Azure resource group and delegate you as the owner of that group. That would ensure that your resources are self-contained and provide a means to report out costs incurred for all the Azure resources in that container.

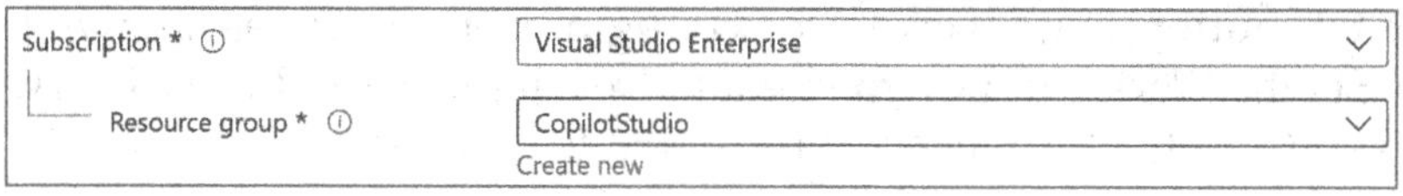

Chapter 10 ■ Copilot Studio and Azure AI Foundry: Better Together 271

Subscription * ⓘ	Visual Studio Enterprise	∨
Resource group * ⓘ	CopilotStudio	∨
	Create new	

Figure 10.5: Configuring an Azure resource group

Scroll down and create a name for your database, such as **HealthCareProvider**, as shown in Figure 10.6. Since you do not have a server to host this database on, click the Create New link.

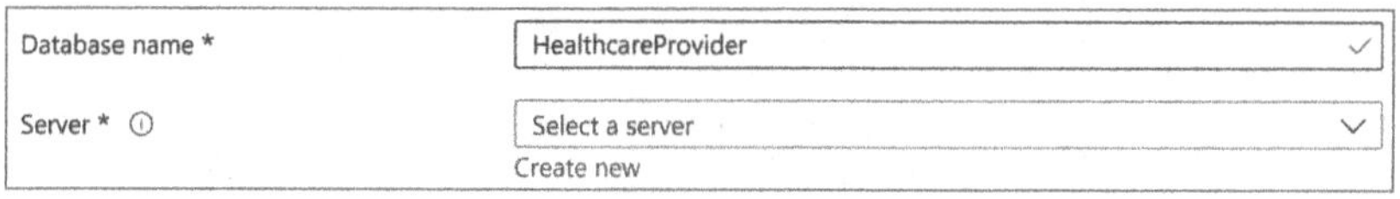

Database name *	HealthcareProvider	✓
Server * ⓘ	Select a server	∨
	Create new	

Figure 10.6: Configuring your database

You will now need to configure the virtual server that will host this Azure SQL database. Provide a server name, as shown in Figure 10.7. For this example, I used my initials, then a hyphen, followed by the name "healthcareprovider." Note that your server name will be prepended with `.datebase.windows.net`. This will be the complete URL for your database server. Additionally, you should be aware of potential naming conflicts and choose a unique name based on your name, initials, etc.

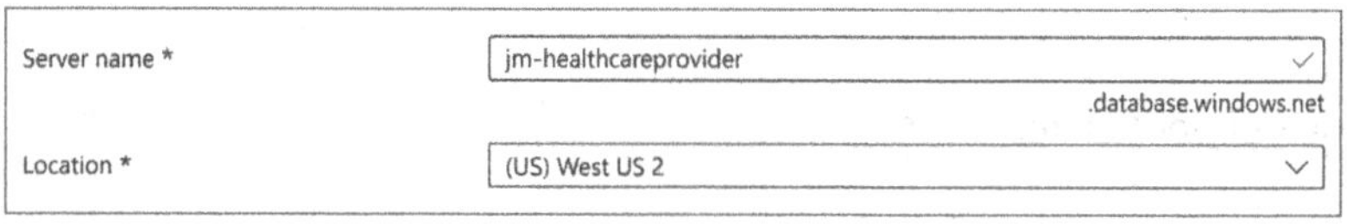

Server name *	jm-healthcareprovider	✓
		.database.windows.net
Location *	(US) West US 2	∨

Figure 10.7: Naming your server

Next, you will need to configure the authentication method for your database server. Your options are Microsoft Entra-only authentication, both SQL and Microsoft Entra, or just SQL authentication, as shown in Figure 10.8. For this example, I'm going to configure "SQL authentication"; however, any of these options should work for real-world scenarios. Create the SQL admin login and password, and keep these somewhere safe for reference later.

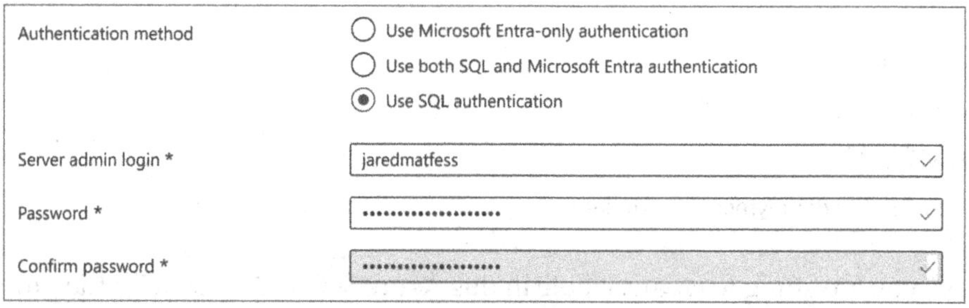

Authentication method	◯ Use Microsoft Entra-only authentication
	◯ Use both SQL and Microsoft Entra authentication
	◉ Use SQL authentication
Server admin login *	jaredmatfess	✓
Password *	••••••••••••••••••••	✓
Confirm password *	••••••••••••••••••••	✓

Figure 10.8: Configuring the authentication method

272 Chapter 10 ▪ Copilot Studio and Azure AI Foundry: Better Together

Click the OK button to go back to the configuration screen, as shown in Figure 10.9. Set the Workload Environment to Development and leave everything else as-is. Click the Review + Create button to proceed.

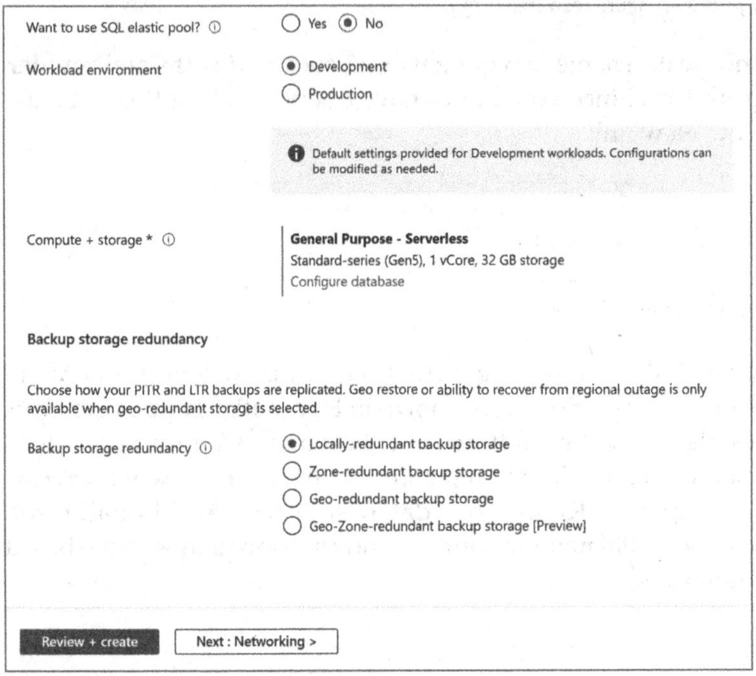

Figure 10.9: Reviewing your configuration

You can perform one last review of your Azure SQL configuration, and then click the Create button to begin provisioning your resources. Keep in mind that this process will take a few minutes to complete. Once it has finished setting up all of your resources, you will see a "Your deployment is complete" message, as shown in Figure 10.10.

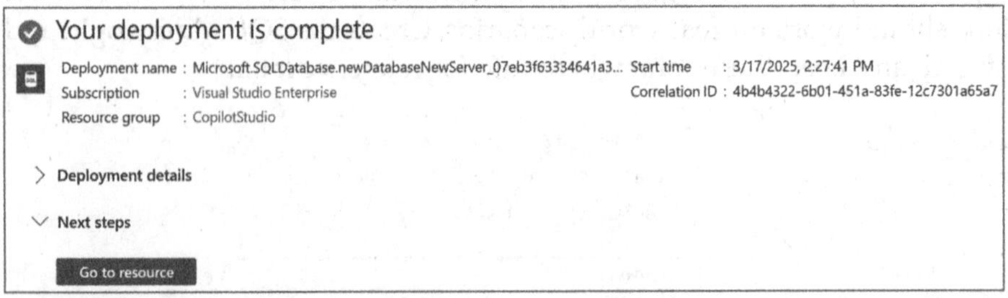

Figure 10.10: The deployment is complete

Next, you are going to create a table in this Azure SQL database with the provider information. Click the Go to Resource button to access your newly created

Chapter 10 ■ Copilot Studio and Azure AI Foundry: Better Together

Azure SQL database. Now, if you try to access your database, you will find that you do not have access to it because you did not configure any networking rules. To remediate that, click the Configure button in the Start Working with Your Database section, as shown in Figure 10.11.

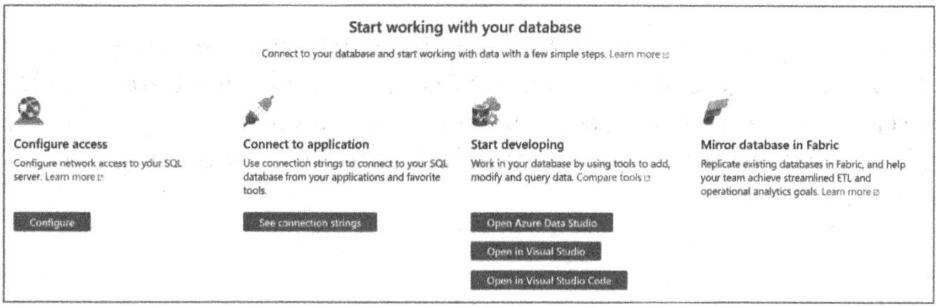

Figure 10.11: Configuring database access

By default, your Azure SQL instance is set up with no Public Network Access. This means that connections to your database are restricted to private endpoints only. This is one of those scenarios where there are lots of ways to securely implement access to this resource. However, for the sake of simplicity, you are going to give your workstation access. First, make sure that under Public Network Access, it is set to Selected Networks, and then scroll down to the Firewall rules section and click the + Add Your Client IPv4 Address button, as shown in Figure 10.12. This allows you to temporarily grant access to your client workstation so you will be able to log in to this Azure SQL instance over the public Internet. Once you're finished with building out your tables, you can turn this off. Click the Save button in the lower-left corner.

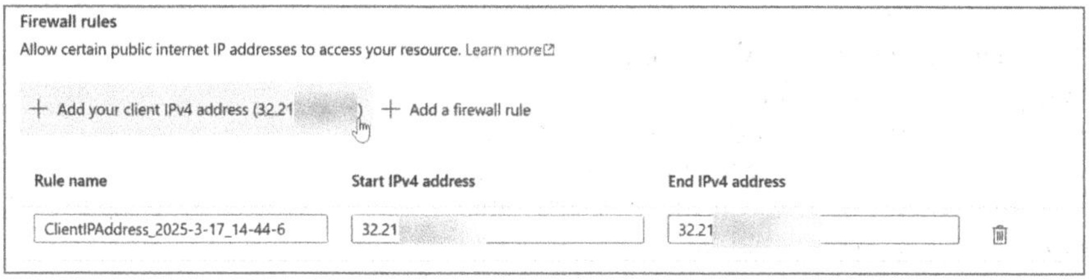

Figure 10.12: Configuring client workstation access

Before you leave, scroll down and check the box next to "Allow Azure services and resources to access this server," as shown in Figure 10.13. Click the Save button again to save this change.

Figure 10.13: Allowing Azure services to access the server

NOTE This configuration will expose your Azure SQL instance to all Azure services and is not ideal for production workloads.

Creating a Table and Loading Data

Next, you are going to create the initial table for your database using "Query editor" in Azure. Navigate back to your database, or type **HealthCareProvider** in the top search menu. This will take you to the Overview screen for your Azure SQL database. Then, click the Query Editor link in the left-hand navigation, as shown in Figure 10.14.

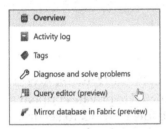

Figure 10.14: Azure SQL query editor

Assuming you also configured your Azure SQL instance with SQL authentication, enter your username and password in the appropriate fields, and then click the Login button. From here, you are going to create the table to store your provider data. Enter the following SQL into Query1, as shown in Figure 10.15, and click the Run button to build your table:

```
CREATE TABLE [dbo].ProviderData (
    [NPI] INT NULL,
    [Ind_PAC_ID] NVARCHAR(MAX)    NULL,
    [Ind_enrl_ID] NVARCHAR(MAX) NULL,
    [Provider_Last_Name] NVARCHAR(MAX) NULL,
    [Provider_First_Name] NVARCHAR(MAX) NULL,
    [Provider_Middle_Name] NVARCHAR(MAX) NULL,
    [suff] NVARCHAR(MAX) NULL,
    [gndr] NVARCHAR(MAX) NULL,
    [Cred] NVARCHAR(MAX) NULL,
    [Med_sch] NVARCHAR(MAX) NULL,
    [Grd_yr] NVARCHAR (50) NULL,
    [pri_spec] NVARCHAR(MAX) NULL,
    [sec_spec_1] NVARCHAR(MAX) NULL,
    [sec_spec_2] NVARCHAR(MAX) NULL,
    [sec_spec_3] NVARCHAR(MAX) NULL,
    [sec_spec_4] NVARCHAR(MAX) NULL,
    [sec_spec_all] NVARCHAR(MAX) NULL,
    [Telehlth] NVARCHAR(MAX) NULL,
    [Facility_Name] NVARCHAR(MAX) NULL,
```

Chapter 10 ▪ Copilot Studio and Azure AI Foundry: Better Together 275

```
[org_pac_id] VARCHAR (50) NULL,
[num_org_mem] VARCHAR (50) NULL,
[adr_ln_1] NVARCHAR(MAX) NULL,
[adr_ln_2] NVARCHAR(MAX) NULL,
[ln_2_sprs] NVARCHAR(MAX) NULL,
[City_Town] NVARCHAR(50) NULL,
[State] NVARCHAR(50) NULL,
[ZIP_Code] NVARCHAR(50) NULL,
[Telephone_Number] NVARCHAR(50) NULL,
[ind_assgn] NVARCHAR(50) NULL,
[grp_assgn] NVARCHAR(50) NULL,
[adrs_id] NVARCHAR(50) NULL
);
```

Query 1 ✕

▷ Run ☐ Cancel query ↓ Save query ↓ Export data as ∨ ▦ Show only Editor

```
1   CREATE TABLE [dbo].ProviderData (
2       [NPI] INT NULL,
3       [Ind_PAC_ID] BIGINT NULL,
4       [Ind_enrl_ID] NVARCHAR(MAX) NULL,
5       [Provider_Last_Name] NVARCHAR(MAX) NULL,
6       [Provider_First_Name] NVARCHAR(MAX) NULL,
7       [Provider_Middle_Name] NVARCHAR(MAX) NULL,
8       [suff] NVARCHAR(MAX) NULL,
9       [gndr] NVARCHAR(MAX) NULL,
10      [Cred] NVARCHAR(MAX) NULL,
```

Results   Messages

▽ Search to filter items...

Figure 10.15: Creating the table to store provider data

NOTE You can find the *Ch10_Create_Table.sql* file at www.wiley.com/go/
copilotstudioqs.

Now that your table is built, you need to populate it with the data in the CSV file. There are many options for how to populate your database; it really comes down to what you are most comfortable with, including but not limited to:

- **Visual Studio Code:** A cross-platform development tool with extensions that can be used to connect to your Azure SQL database.

- **Bulk Copy Program (BCP):** A command-line utility included with SQL Server that can quickly import CSV data into your Azure SQL database.

- **SQL Server Management Studio (SSMS) Import Wizard:** A built-in, GUI-driven tool in SSMS that guides you through importing CSV files into an Azure SQL database table.

276 Chapter 10 ∎ Copilot Studio and Azure AI Foundry: Better Together

- **Azure Data Factory (ADF):** A fully managed, cloud-based data integration service that can orchestrate data movement from CSV in Azure Blob Storage to your Azure SQL database.

- **Azure Data Studio:** A cross-platform tool designed for managing and interacting with databases (being retired in February 2026).

- **PowerShell script:** You can create a PowerShell script to perform a bulk insert of records into your database.

> **NOTE** You can find a PowerShell script (*Ch10_Bulk_Insert.ps1*) included in the downloadable file for this book at www.wiley.com/go/copilotstudioqs.

Pick the approach that you are most comfortable with, or leverage the PowerShell script included with the book, and load your data into your table. You can confirm that your data is loaded by performing a quick spot check in Query editor with the following SQL command:

```
SELECT TOP (1000) * FROM [dbo].[DAC_NationalDownloadableFile]
```

Once you've confirmed that you have loaded all the data from the CSV into your Azure SQL database, you can continue with your configuration.

Provisioning Azure AI Search

Now that you have your Azure SQL database loaded with the national provider directory data, it's time to configure Azure AI Search. A benefit of Azure AI Search is that it can be used to support multiple use cases—meaning you don't have to think about needing Azure AI Search just for building agents. The indexes you create can be leveraged for multiple scenarios across both low-code and full-code solutions. Depending on the AI maturity of your organization, some vector indexes may already exist for certain data sources.

Navigate back to the Azure Portal home (portal.azure.com) and click the + Create a Resource button. This time, type **Azure AI Search** into the Marketplace search box and press Enter. Click to expand the Create drop-down, and then select Azure AI Search, as shown in Figure 10.16.

Next, click the Resource Group drop-down and ensure that you are using the same resource group as your Azure SQL instance. You need to provide a name for this service, such as **copilotstudiosearch**. The Location field, such as West US 2, refers to the Azure region where your Azure AI Search instance will be hosted. Azure regions are specific geographic areas that house Microsoft data centers. Choosing a region determines where your data and resources are physically stored and processed.

Chapter 10 ▪ Copilot Studio and Azure AI Foundry: Better Together 277

Azure AI Search

Microsoft

Azure Service

AI-powered cloud search service for mobile and web app development (formerly Azure Cognitive Search)

Create ⌄   ♡

Azure AI Search

Figure 10.16: Creating Azure AI Search

You'll especially want to keep your Azure AI Search and Azure SQL database in the same region to ensure the highest performance when performing your initial index. Confirm that your configuration screen matches Figure 10.17, and then click the Create button to provision your Azure AI Search instance.

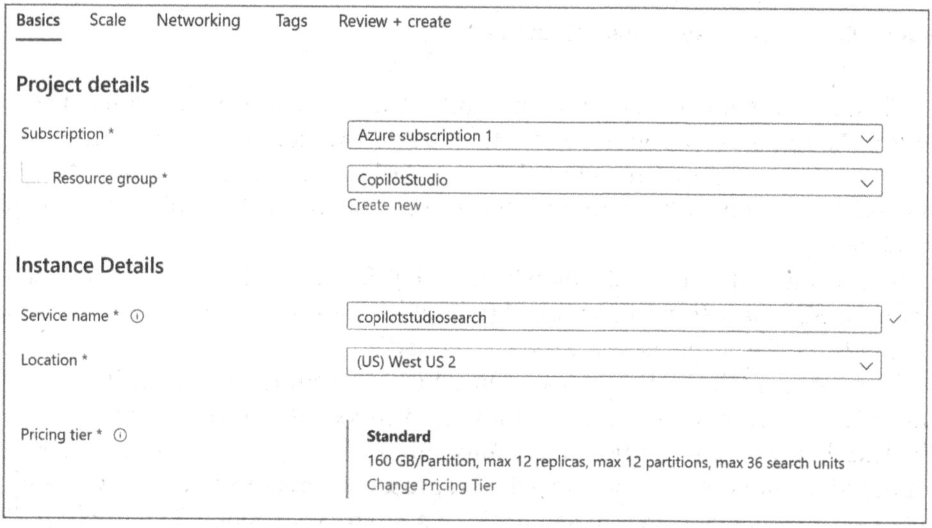

Basics	Scale	Networking	Tags	Review + create

Project details

Subscription *	Azure subscription 1 ⌄
Resource group *	CopilotStudio ⌄
	Create new

Instance Details

Service name * ⓘ	copilotstudiosearch ✓
Location *	(US) West US 2 ⌄
Pricing tier * ⓘ	**Standard**
	160 GB/Partition, max 12 replicas, max 12 partitions, max 36 search units
	Change Pricing Tier

Figure 10.17: Azure AI Search properties

Once your Azure AI Search resource has been provisioned, click the Go to Resource button. From here, click the Import and Vectorize Data button, as shown in Figure 10.18.

Figure 10.18: Importing and vectorizing data

Choose Azure SQL Database as the data source you want to connect to, as shown in Figure 10.19.

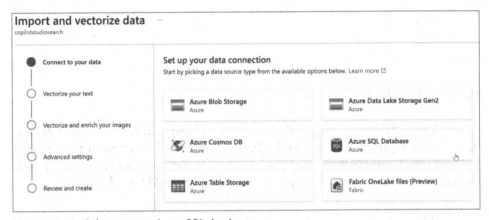

Figure 10.19: Selecting your Azure SQL database

Click the Server drop-down menu and select jm-healthcareprovider. Then, in the Database drop-down, select HealthcareProvider. Select Table from the Table or View drop-down. Select the ProviderData option in the Table Name drop-down. Confirm that your configuration matches Figure 10.20, and then scroll down.

Next, confirm that authentication is set to SQL Server Authentication, and then enter the SQL User ID and Password you set earlier into the fields, as shown in Figure 10.21. Click the Next button to proceed.

Azure AI Search is going to ask you which column to vectorize. If you are unfamiliar with that term, it's asking you to choose the column that contains the text data you want to transform into numerical vector embeddings. These embeddings are essentially numerical representations of your text, allowing the search engine to perform semantic or similarity searches. The intent will be to vectorize the data so that Azure AI Search can calculate similarity scores between search queries and your data, leading to more relevant search results based on context and meaning rather than just keyword matching.

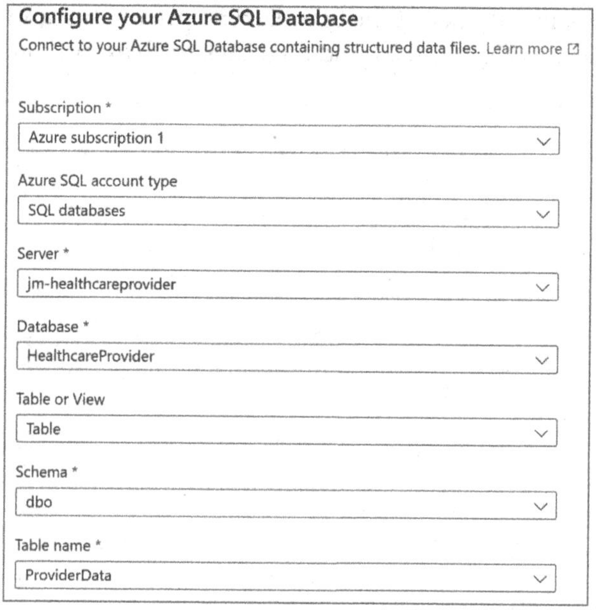

Configure your Azure SQL Database

Connect to your Azure SQL Database containing structured data files. Learn more ☐

Subscription *

Azure subscription 1 ⌄

Azure SQL account type

SQL databases ⌄

Server *

jm-healthcareprovider ⌄

Database *

HealthcareProvider ⌄

Table or View

Table ⌄

Schema *

dbo ⌄

Table name *

ProviderData ⌄

Figure 10.20: Confirming your Azure SQL database

Select an authentication option

◉ SQL server authentication

User Id *

jaredmatfess

Password *

••••••••••••••••••• ◎

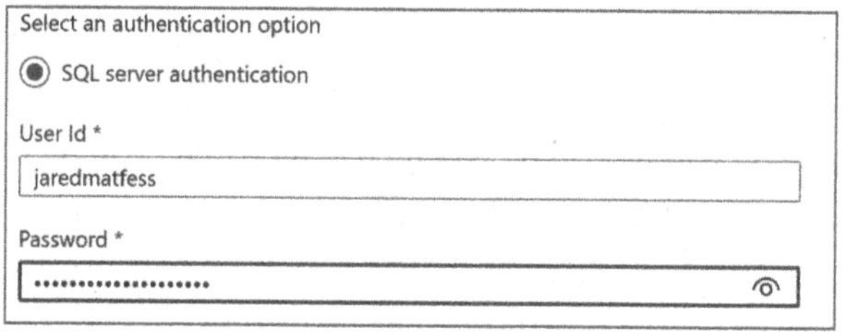

Figure 10.21: Testing your connection to Azure SQL

For example, searching for a "heart doctor" would likely lead to a "cardiologist" since it is performing a semantic search versus a keyword-matching search. As you can see, this approach of vectorizing your data and enabling semantic search can help drive more human-focused experiences. Since this is healthcare provider data, go ahead and select the pri_spec column, as shown in Figure 10.22, which is shorthand for primary specialty.

You are going to need to create an instance of Azure OpenAI service to vectorize that column. Click the Create a New Azure OpenAI Service link, as shown in Figure 10.22, and then select your Copilot Studio resource group from the drop-down menu.

Next, it will ask you for your preferred region for deployment. I'm selecting Sweden Central based on current region availability of resources, which are always subject to change. I'm going to name my instance matfessopenai, but you

Chapter 10 ■ Copilot Studio and Azure AI Foundry: Better Together

should provide a unique name. Finally, select the Standard S0 pricing tier and confirm your configuration matches Figure 10.23, and then click the Next button.

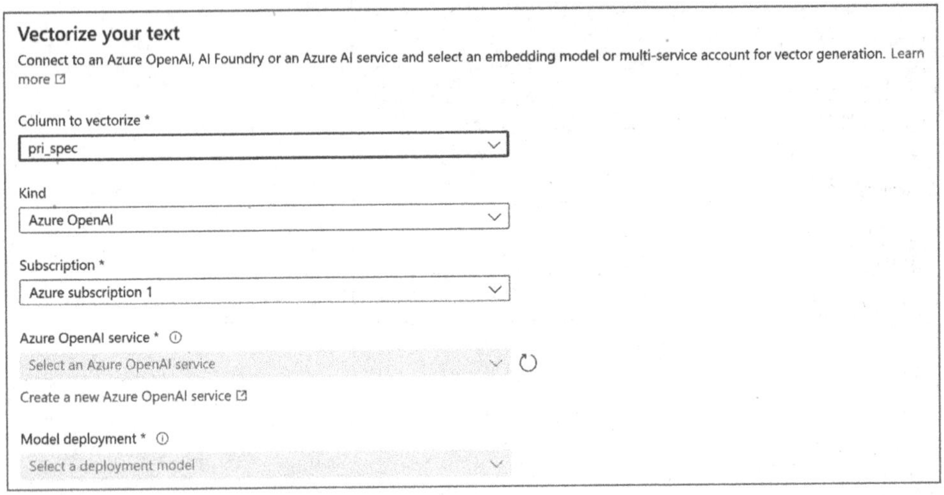

Vectorize your text

Connect to an Azure OpenAI, AI Foundry or an Azure AI service and select an embedding model or multi-service account for vector generation. Learn more ☐

Column to vectorize *

pri_spec

Kind

Azure OpenAI

Subscription *

Azure subscription 1

Azure OpenAI service * ⓘ

Select an Azure OpenAI service

Create a new Azure OpenAI service ☐

Model deployment * ⓘ

Select a deployment model

Figure 10.22: Selecting a column to vectorize

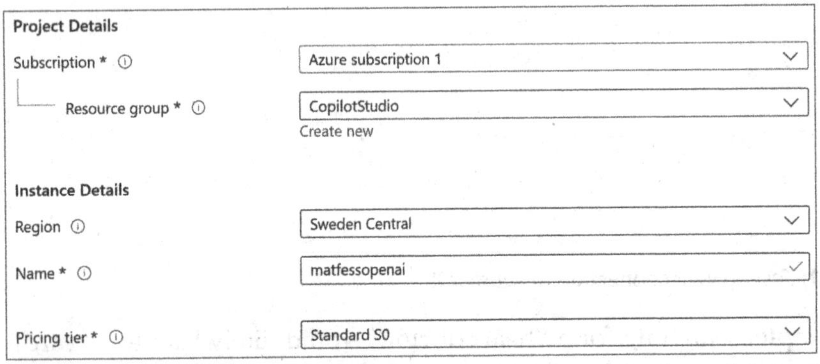

Project Details

Subscription * ⓘ	Azure subscription 1
Resource group * ⓘ	CopilotStudio
	Create new

Instance Details

Region ⓘ	Sweden Central
Name * ⓘ	matfessopenai
Pricing tier * ⓘ	Standard S0

Figure 10.23: Configuring your Azure OpenAI service

You can leave the default setting of "All networks, including the internet, can access this resource," as shown in Figure 10.24. Note again, that your IT team may require additional security configuration for this step. Click the Next button. You can optionally include "tags" if required by your IT team which are just metadata about your resources, and then click the Create button.

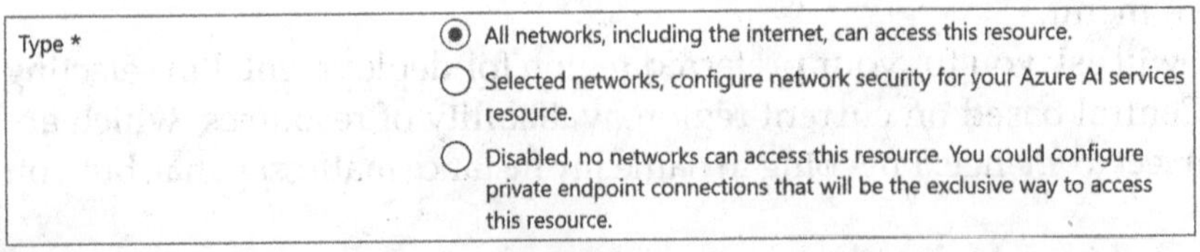

Type *	◉ All networks, including the internet, can access this resource.
	◯ Selected networks, configure network security for your Azure AI services resource.
	◯ Disabled, no networks can access this resource. You could configure private endpoint connections that will be the exclusive way to access this resource.

Figure 10.24: Enabling all networks access

Chapter 10 ■ Copilot Studio and Azure AI Foundry: Better Together

The deployment process will once again start. Once your instance has been provisioned, click the Go to Resource button. As shown in Figure 10.25, this will bring you to your Copilot Studio resource group, as pictured, with a listing of all of your resources.

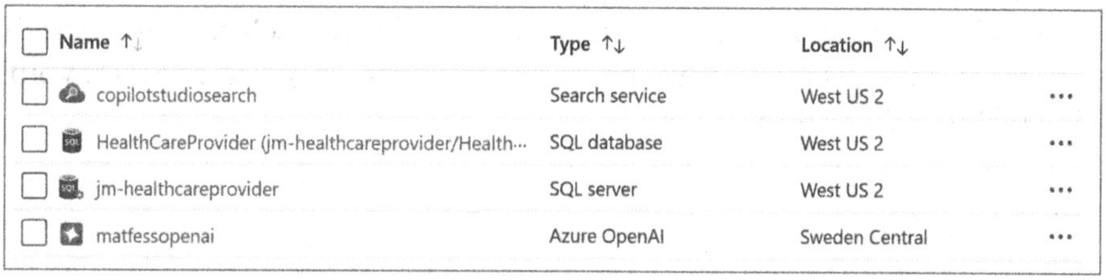

Name ↑↓	Type ↑↓	Location ↑↓	
copilotstudiosearch	Search service	West US 2	...
HealthCareProvider (jm-healthcareprovider/Health…	SQL database	West US 2	...
jm-healthcareprovider	SQL server	West US 2	...
matfessopenai	Azure OpenAI	Sweden Central	...

Figure 10.25: Choosing a Copilot Studio resource group

Click the matfessopenai Azure OpenAI resource, which will take you to the Overview menu as pictured in Figure 10.26. From there, click Go to Azure AI Foundry Portal, which will bring you into your instance of Azure AI Foundry.

matfessopenai
Azure OpenAI

🔍 Search   ↻ «   ↗ Go to Azure AI Foundry portal
⭐ Overview   ∧ Essentials

Figure 10.26: Azure OpenAI overview

From here, a model needs to be provisioned that can be used to analyze the provider data and vectorize the column. Click the Deployments link in the left-hand navigation, underneath the Shared Resources heading, as shown in Figure 10.27.

Figure 10.27: Selecting a shared resources deployment

From here, click the Deploy Model button, as shown in Figure 10.28, and select Deploy Base Model. For this example, you are opting to go with a base model. This means that you will leverage a model with the training data it was originally created with rather than one that you intend to fine-tune. Fine-tuning refers to customizing a pretrained LLM, such as gpt-4.5, gpt-4o-min, o3-min, etc., with additional data. Remember, these models have been pretrained on billions of parameters, which is how they understand and generate language. This approach is used to supplement the LLM's knowledge with domain-specific information to learn new skills and improve the accuracy of answers on subjects on which it was not explicitly trained. The model you select goes through a similar process like its initial training, but with a more targeted focus on your domain-specific information.

Figure 10.28: Deploying the base model

However, in this scenario, we are going to leverage an approach called *vector database indexing*. This involves using an embeddings model to convert data (e.g., text from a column) into vector representations. Each data point is transformed into a numeric vector that captures its semantic meaning or relationships. After the data is vectorized, the resulting vectors are organized into an index. This is what powers applications like recommendation systems or semantic search.

Embeddings models are designed to convert data (like text, images, or audio) into a numerical representation, known as an *embedding*, in a multidimensional space. Think of it as converting words into points on a map, where similar words are closer together. Embeddings are commonly used in tasks like search, recommendation systems, and clustering, where measuring similarity or relationships between pieces of data is important. Therefore, you will need an embeddings model instead of picking a model like o3-mini, which is meant for language understanding and text generation purposes.

Therefore, after you select Deploy Base Model, type in **embedding** in the search box, and then select the text-embedding-3-small model, as shown in Figure 10.29, and finally click the Confirm button. Note that this model might no longer be available; however, there will likely be a newer model that is similar. Just make sure that it has an indication of Task: Embeddings, as the text-embedding-3-small model does, as shown in Figure 10.29.

Now click the Deploy button, as shown in Figure 10.30, to the deploy the model to your Azure AI Foundry instance.

Once your deployment has been completed, you'll be redirected to a page within Azure AI Foundry that has information about how to connect to your model deployment.

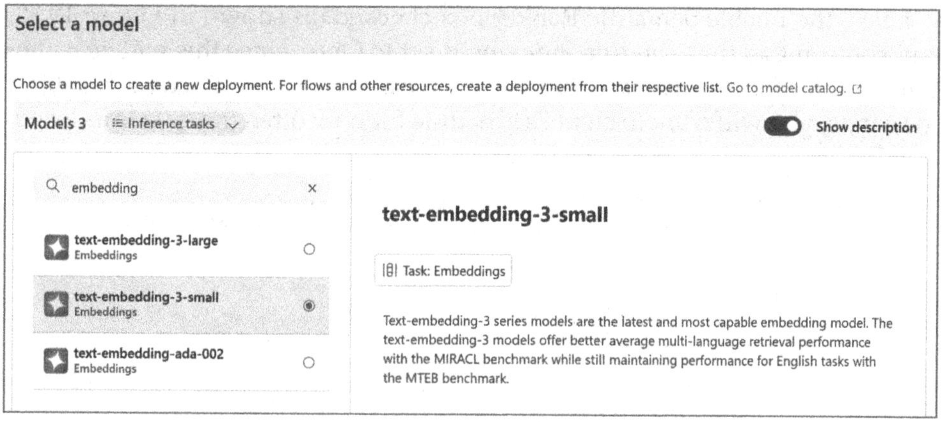

Chapter 10 ■ Copilot Studio and Azure AI Foundry: Better Together   283

Select a model

Choose a model to create a new deployment. For flows and other resources, create a deployment from their respective list. Go to model catalog. ⤢

Models 3   ⋮≡ Inference tasks ⌄   ⬤ Show description

🔍 embedding ✕	**text-embedding-3-small**
⭐ text-embedding-3-large Embeddings ○	⎮θ⎮ Task: Embeddings
⭐ text-embedding-3-small Embeddings ⦿	Text-embedding-3 series models are the latest and most capable embedding model. The text-embedding-3 models offer better average multi-language retrieval performance with the MIRACL benchmark while still maintaining performance for English tasks with the MTEB benchmark.
⭐ text-embedding-ada-002 Embeddings ○	

Figure 10.29: Selecting the text-embedding-3-small model

Deploy model text-embedding-3-small

Deployment name *   👁

text-embedding-3-small

Deployment type

Global Standard   ⌄

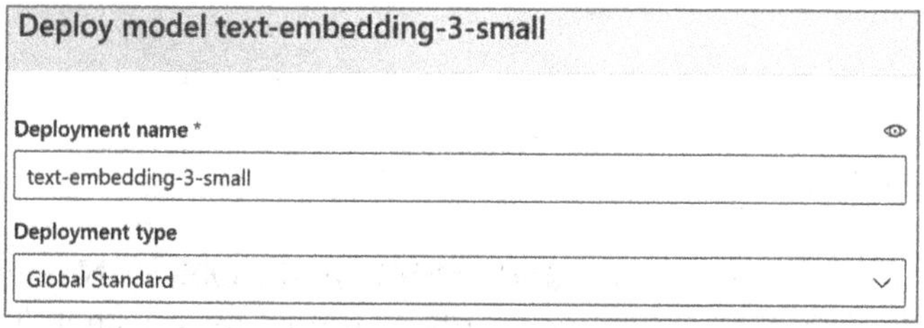

Figure 10.30: Deploying the text-embedding-3-small model

Click back to your open tab that's set on the Azure AI Search configuration screen and click the "refresh" button, as shown in Figure 10.31. Select your newly created Azure OpenAI Service and select your model from the Model Deployment drop-down menu. Select API Key for the authentication type, and check the radio button acknowledging that connecting to an Azure OpenAI service will incur additional costs. Click the Next button to proceed.

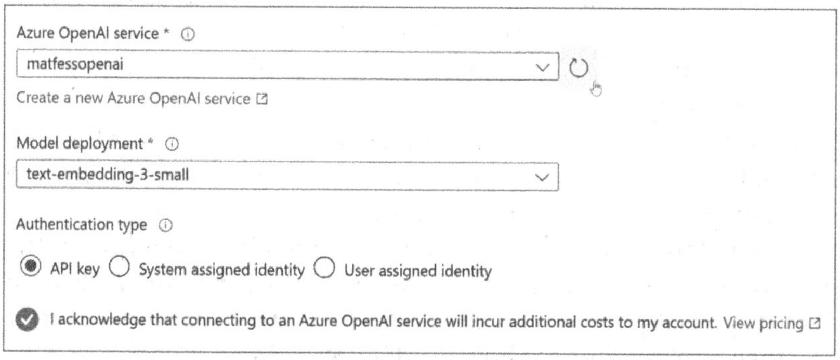

Azure OpenAI service * ⓘ

matfessopenai   ⌄   ↻

Create a new Azure OpenAI service ⤢

Model deployment * ⓘ

text-embedding-3-small   ⌄

Authentication type ⓘ

⦿ API key ○ System assigned identity ○ User assigned identity

✅ I acknowledge that connecting to an Azure OpenAI service will incur additional costs to my account. View pricing ⤢

Figure 10.31: Selecting your Azure OpenAI service

284 Chapter 10 ▪ Copilot Studio and Azure AI Foundry: Better Together

Leave the Enable Semantic Ranker box checked, as shown in Figure 10.32, and confirm that the Schedule Indexing is set to Once, since this will be a one-time activity for this use case. Note that in use cases where the data is subject to change, you will want to create a schedule for how often the data is indexed.

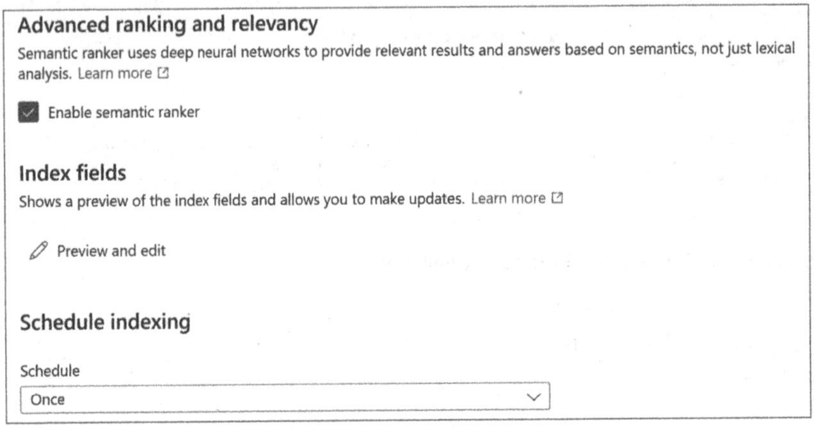

Advanced ranking and relevancy

Semantic ranker uses deep neural networks to provide relevant results and answers based on semantics, not just lexical analysis. Learn more ☐

✅ Enable semantic ranker

Index fields

Shows a preview of the index fields and allows you to make updates. Learn more ☐

✏️ Preview and edit

Schedule indexing

Schedule

| Once | ∨ |

Figure 10.32: Semantic ranker setting

Click the Next button, and then enter **providerhealthdb** in the Objects Name Prefix input, as shown in Figure 10.33. If you recall, when tapping into an agent's knowledge, it will provide a reference for where it found this information. This object name prefix will be included as part of that reference rather than the "vector-" + "string of numbers" that is included by default.

Objects name prefix

providerhealthdb

Figure 10.33: Setting the objects name prefix input

Click the Create button, and you'll be redirected to a Search Explorer, as shown in Figure 10.34. It will take about 20 or so minutes to fully index your content. You can click the Refresh button to see how many documents have been ingested into the index.

You can monitor the actual job by navigating back to your Azure AI Search resource (copilotstudiosearch) and then clicking Indexers under the Search Management heading, as shown in Figure 10.35.

Once the indexer status shows Completed, click the Overview link in the left-hand navigation. You can then look for the URL for your Azure AI Search instance, click Copy to Clipboard, and then paste it somewhere you can refer to in a minute, such as a text file, as shown in Figure 10.36.

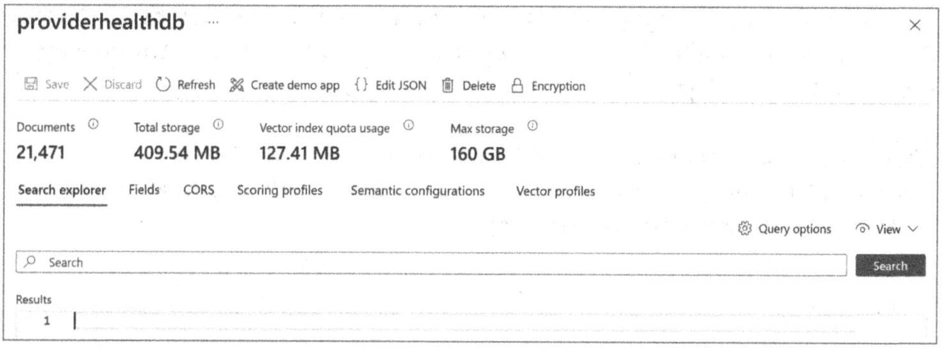

Chapter 10 ■ Copilot Studio and Azure AI Foundry: Better Together 285

Figure 10.34: Copying the endpoint key

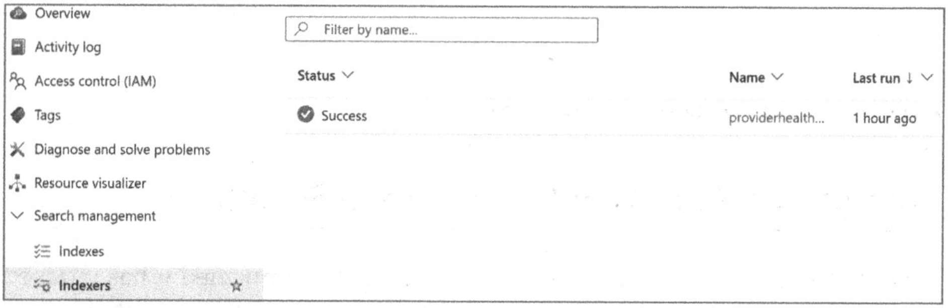

Figure 10.35: Copying the endpoint key

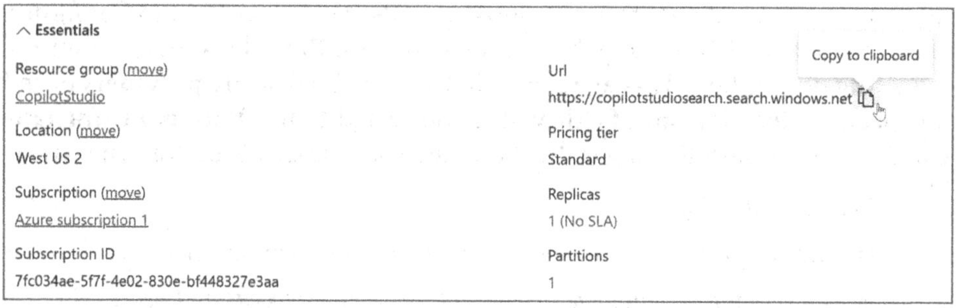

Figure 10.36: Connecting to Azure AI Search

Next, look at the left-hand navigation, and scroll down until you see the Settings section. If it is collapsed, expand it, and then click the Keys link, as shown in Figure 10.37.

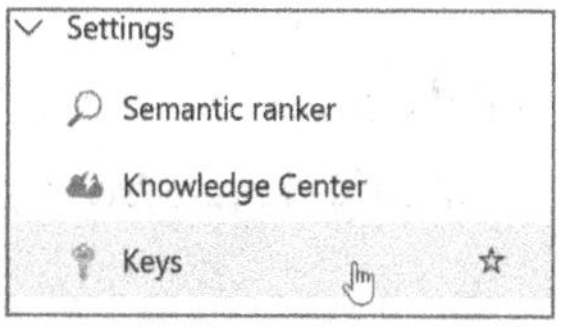

Figure 10.37: Search service keys

286 Chapter 10 ▪ Copilot Studio and Azure AI Foundry: Better Together

Next, in the middle of the Keys configuration screen is a section titled Manage Admin Keys. Click the Copy to Clipboard icon for the Primary Admin Key, as shown in Figure 10.38, and save that as well to your text file.

> **NOTE** Securing the primary search admin key for Azure AI Search is extremely important. This key grants full access to your search service, including the ability to create, modify, or delete indexes and manage data.

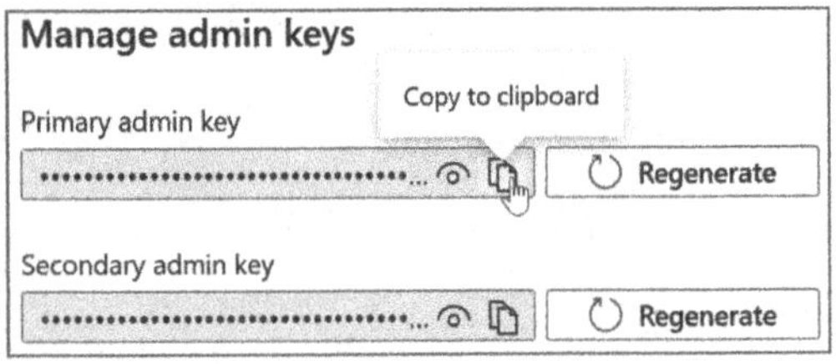

Manage admin keys

Primary admin key

Copy to clipboard

•••••••••••••••••••••••••••••••••••... ⊙ ⧉   ⟳ Regenerate

Secondary admin key

•••••••••••••••••••••••••••••••••••... ⊙ ⧉   ⟳ Regenerate

Figure 10.38: Copying the primary admin key

Configuring Your Agent for Azure AI Search

Now that you have configured Azure AI Search and confirmed it has indexed your Azure SQL database, it's time to create your agent. Navigate back to copilotstudio.microsoft.com and click the Create button in the left-hand navigation. Click New Agent from the subsequent screen. Click Skip to Configure, and then go ahead and name the agent **Healthcare Provider Finder**. Enter the following description: **This agent will help locate healthcare providers based on specialty, location, and facility. It is connected to the National Clinicians Database.** Enter the following instructions and click the Create button when done:

1. *Politeness and Empathy:*
   - *Always greet users warmly and thank them for their patience.*
   - *Use empathetic language to acknowledge their concerns and needs.*

2. *Factual Information:*
   - *Provide accurate information about healthcare providers.*
   - *Ensure that all details, such as contact information, location, and specialties, are correct.*

3. *No Speculation or Diagnosis:*
   - *Do not guess the user's medical condition or suggest a diagnosis.*
   - *Avoid recommending specific specialties unless explicitly requested by the user.*

Chapter 10 ■ Copilot Studio and Azure AI Foundry: Better Together   287

Once the initial agent creation has been completed, scroll down to the Knowledge section and click Add knowledge. In the pop-up window, click Advanced, and then select Azure AI Search, as shown in Figure 10.39.

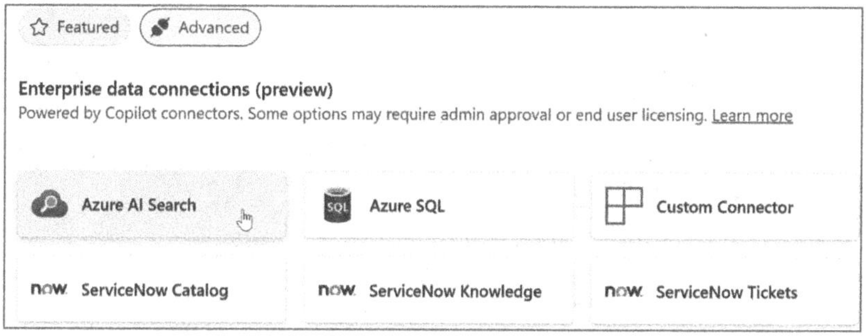

Figure 10.39: Knowledge center search explorer

Next, enter the following into the Knowledge Description field: **This knowledge source provides information about healthcare providers in CT, including name, hospital affiliation, primary specialty, gender, etc.**

Click the ellipses in the lower-right corner, as shown in Figure 10.40, and select Add New Connection.

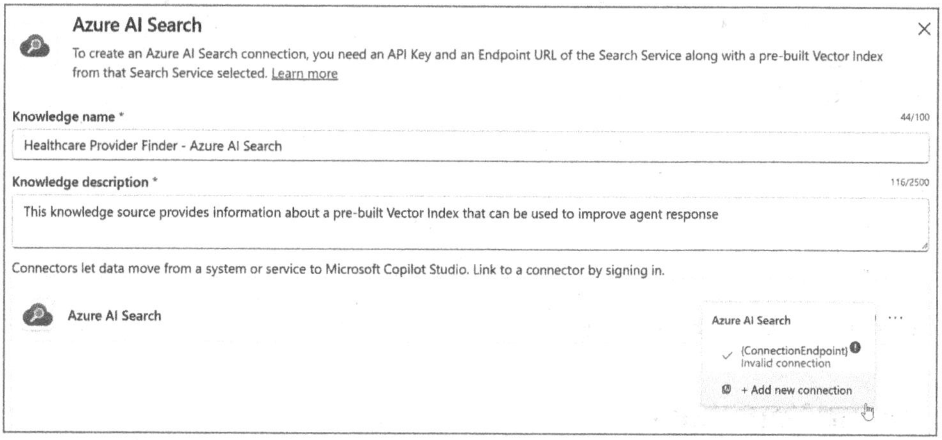

Figure 10.40: Creating a new connection

This will bring up the configuration screen shown in Figure 10.41. The Azure AI Search Endpoint URL is either in your text file that you've been saving or can be copied from the Azure AI Search overview screen, as shown in Figure 10.36. Then you can input the Azure AI Search Admin Key value, which is also in your text file or in the Admin Key section, as shown in Figure 10.37. Click the Create button.

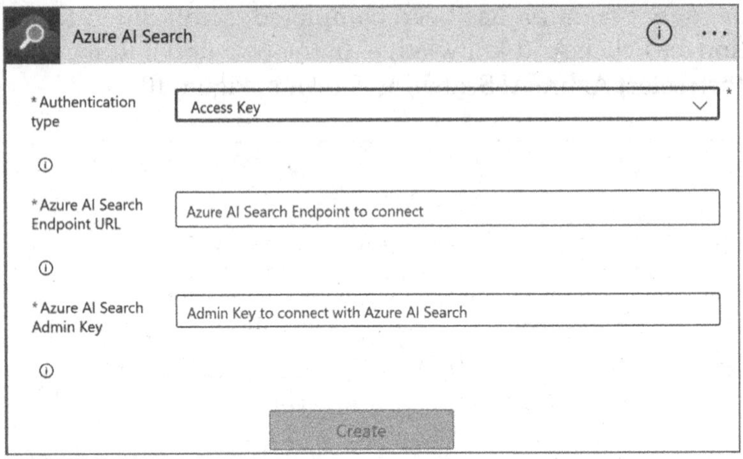

288 Chapter 10 ■ Copilot Studio and Azure AI Foundry: Better Together

Figure 10.41: Connecting to Azure AI Search

Clicking the Next button will take you to the Select a Vector Index screen, as shown in Figure 10.42. If you had multiple vector indices in your Azure AI Search index, you would be able to select those from the drop-down menu. However, you just have the one index, so you can click the Add button to complete the setup of this Azure AI Search knowledge source.

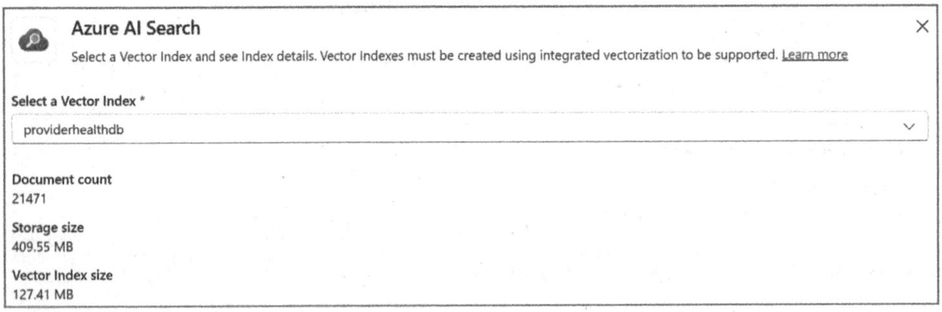

Figure 10.42: Selecting a vector index

Testing Your Agent

Now it's time to test your agent to make sure that you see the full connection from Copilot Studio to your Azure AI Search index. First, navigate back to your agent overview screen. Click the Test button in the upper-right corner, and then type in a very simple prompt of **I'm looking for a male heart doctor**. This will provide an output similar to Figure 10.43.

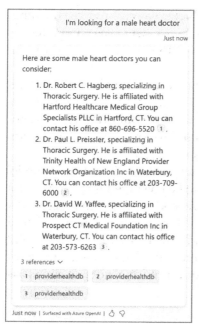

Figure 10.43: Testing your agent

Notice the agent can understand that when a user is asking for a "heart doctor," it can recommend providers that specialize in thoracic surgery. This is the create-vector-index-column step where you leveraged the embeddings model to transform the specified data into numerical representations. This is how you are able to capture the semantic meaning of the text or data. Additionally, the agent response includes both the provider contact information and the reference to where it found that information in your Azure AI index. Note that the reference has "providerhealthdb," as you configured in Figure 10.33.

You now have a fully working end-to-end solution that can leverage the data in the Azure AI Search index and return those values back to the user. You can try additional queries, or you can modify the output using the same approach as we did in Chapter 9 to override the Conversational Boosting topic. What's more, you can also work with your data team to further enhance your solution by pulling in additional datasets. For example, you could pull in a research dataset in addition to the Azure SQL database so that not only would your agent be able to find a doctor by location and specialty but also based on research they produce.

Conclusion

In this chapter, we extended our Copilot Studio agent experience into the world of pro-code development with Azure AI Foundry. We built an Azure SQL database and loaded it with healthcare provider data. Next, we had Azure AI Search index our content and create a vector database index. This was completed by leveraging an embeddings model to help derive the semantic intent for the provider specialty.

We then configured that vector database index through Copilot Studio's Knowledge section, and then ultimately surfaced the responses to the users through a Conversational Boosting system topic. More importantly, we demonstrated how you can take a low-code solution developed in Copilot Studio and connect it to the greater Azure AI Foundry ecosystem.

Imagine scenarios where perhaps your data science team fine-tunes a model with company-specific information. That too can be leveraged through Copilot Studio, once again blurring the lines between low-code and pro-code solutions.

Throughout this book, we've explored the full spectrum of agents—from knowledge to task-based to autonomous—and now extending from Copilot Studio into Azure AI Foundry. But always remember that agents are most effective when they're designed to solve the right problems, not just showcase the latest technology.

APPENDIX

Agent Flows

The pace of innovation coming out of Microsoft is hard to keep up with. As we were putting the final touches on this book, a new feature called *agent flows* was released. Agent flows blend the power of Power Automate with the Copilot Studio interface, offering a more streamlined way for makers to connect their agents to external systems and services. What makes this feature notable isn't just the technical integration, but also how it reshapes the builder experience. Instead of jumping between tools or relying on more complex orchestration setups, agent flows allow you to stay within the Copilot Studio user experience throughout your development.

In this appendix, we will touch very briefly on how to leverage agent flows as part of your development process. We'll describe both how to create a new agent flow and how to convert an existing Power Automate flow into an agent flow. This isn't meant to be a full walkthrough, just enough to get you oriented so you know when it makes sense to reach for this capability. Many of the examples we walked through earlier in the book can take advantage of agent flows, since they are essentially a wrapper around Power Automate flows and actions we have already covered.

Appendix ■ Agent Flows

Creating a New Agent Flow

From within the Copilot Studio user interface, you should notice a link in the left-hand navigation called Flows, as shown in Figure App.1.

Figure App.1: The Flows navigation link

Click Flows to bring up the Agent Flows home screen, as shown in Figure App.2. From here, notice that you have the ability to create a new agent flow, either through the natural language in the "What would you like your flow to do" dialog box or through the New Agent Flow button. Additionally, from this home screen, you can either scroll or search for an existing agent flow, and then open it to make modifications.

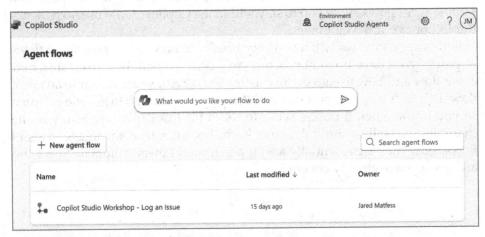

Figure App.2: The Agent Flows home screen

Click the New Agent Flow button, and you will be directed to the new agent flow maker experience within Copilot Studio, as shown in Figure App.3. From here, you can start to build out your flow logic, as you did previously in this book.

Figure App.3: The agent flow maker experience

The first thing you will want to do is define a trigger that will initiate this flow by clicking the Add a Trigger node. This will bring up the Add a Trigger dialog box, as shown in Figure App.4. From here, you can select from the same list of Power Automate flow triggers as before.

Figure App.4: Agent flow triggers

The first option, "When an agent calls the flow," is very similar to when we previously configured Power Automate flows as actions directly within Copilot Studio. However, the benefit of this new authoring experience is that it streamlines the process of making the flow available through Copilot Studio. Once you are done building out your flow, it becomes available within the Agent Flows section of Copilot Studio and will be available to be used by all agents in that Power Platform environment.

Converting an Existing Power Automate Flow to an Agent Flow

Next, let's walk through how you might take an existing Power Automate flow and convert it to an agent flow. The first step you'll need to take is to create a solution for both your agent and Power Automate flow. Follow the same steps as previously outlined in Chapter 5 to create a new Power Platform solution. Then add both the agent that you intend to leverage the flow with, as well as the Power Automate flow itself.

Once completed, navigate to make.powerautomate.com and find the Power Automate flow that you want to convert to an agent flow. Click your flow to navigate to the overview screen, and then click the Set Primary Owner link, as shown in Figure App.5.

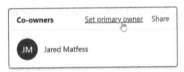

Figure App.5: Setting the primary owner

Scroll down to the bottom of the dialog window that appears, and then select the Copilot Studio radio button, as shown in Figure App.6, to convert the flow from being a Power Automate cloud flow to a Copilot Studio agent flow.

Figure App.6: Setting the Copilot Studio plan for your flow

When you click the Save button, a dialog box will appear, as shown in Figure App.7. At the time of publishing, there is no way to downgrade an agent flow back to a standard Power Automate flow; therefore, clicking the Confirm button is an irreversible step. You will need to re-create your flow from scratch if you need to use it outside of Copilot Studio.

Switch to Copilot Studio plan

Once you change the plan of this flow to Copilot Studio, it cannot be changed back. Please be certain before you select this option.

Confirm   Cancel

Figure App.7: Switching to the Copilot Studio plan

After clicking the Confirm button, you can navigate back to the Flows screen of Copilot Studio, and you should see your flow within the list of agent flows, as shown in Figure App.8.

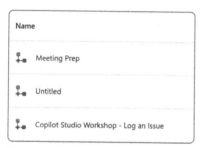

Figure App.8: The list of agent flows

Conclusion

While the examples throughout this book didn't specifically use agent flows, the underlying mechanics are the same. Whether you're triggering Power Automate flows through traditional actions or using the new agent flows experience, the core concepts still apply. Agent flows simply offer a more integrated and streamlined way to bring automation into your agents. And this likely won't be the last update we see, as Copilot Studio is a strategic focus for Microsoft and innovation will continue at a fast pace. Stay curious, stay adaptable, and expect things to keep evolving.

Index

A

action-based events, autonomous agents, 199
actions
  AI Builder prompts, 58
  autonomous, Create Lead, 232–235
  autonomous agents
    Account ID, 222–224
    AI builder prompts, 219
    Bot Framework skills, 219
    conditions, 224–226
    contacts, 226–227, 228–231
    custom connectors, 218
    inputs, 220–221
    opportunities, 227–228
    Power Automate cloud flow, 218–219
    prebuilt connectors, 218
    REST APIs, 219
    variable formats, 221–222
  Bot Framework skills, 58
  connectors
    custom, 58
    prebuilt, 57
  custom, 64–65
  optimization and, 249
  outputs, 63–64
  Plugin, 64–65
  Power Automate cloud flows, 58
  Send an Email, 60–69
Adaptive Card node, 149–150
  Conversation Start topic, 153–154
  disclaimer text, 161
  human resources use case, 189–193
  JSON (JavaScript Object Notation), 151
  multi-platform support, 150
  open standards, 150
  outputs, 151–152
  performance, 151
  Properties panel, 150
  Set Variable Value, 152–153
  Type of Assistance input, 152
Admin Approval button, 83–84
agent analytics, 246–248
Agent Builder, 97
  actions, 103
  agent configuration, 98–99
  ALM (application lifecycle management), 116, 119
    deployment, 122–123
    design, 121
    development stage, 121–122
    maintenance, 123–127

Index ■ A–A

requirements, 120–121
retirement, 123
testing, 122
capabilities, 103
Create button, 105–106
data storage, 115–116
declarativeAgent_0.json file, 110–112
document formats, 102–103
instructions, 99–100
knowledge sources, 101–103
manifest.json file, 107–110
permissions, 106–112
sharing, 106–112
starter prompts, 104–105
testing agent, 112–114
updating agents, 114–115
user experience, 116
Agent Builder Experience, 34–35
agent templates
building agents
Knowledge Sources, 158–159
testing, 166–169
topic updates, 159–166
Citizen Services
knowledge sources, 146–147
topics, 147–157
create screen, 145
agents
autonomous, 92, 197–200
action-based events, 199
actions, creating, 218–231
CRM, 201–202
data changes, 199
instructions, 235–236
knowledge sources, 213–218
Microsoft Forms, 200–201, 209
monitoring, 242
orchestration, 203–204
Power Automate, 199
publishing, 242
response details, 208–209
Run Only Users, 231–232
Salesforce Sales Cloud, 201–202
testing, 236–242

time-based events, 199
triggers, 204–213
background color, 99
building, 34–35
from template, 157–169
Copilot chat, 88–89
cost, optimization, 248–251
creating, 39–42
declarative, 93–97
Agent Builder, 97–112
app package, 93–95
configuration, 96
orchestrator, 96–97
testing, 112–114
updating, 114–115
use cases, 117
description, 77
developer information, 78–79
icons, 99
instructions, 100
knowledge sources, 42–47
M365 Copilot, 92
publishing
Admin Approval, 83–84
app uploads, 81–82
availability, 80–81
channels, 71–74
permissions, 80–81
Publish button, 85–86
status, 80
testing, 86–90
to Microsoft 365, 74–79
to Teams, 74–79
retrieval, 92
semi-autonomous, 197–198
task, 92
testing, 47–49, 86–90,
112–114, 166–169
autonomous, agents,
236–242
contact center use case, 175
topics, 50–51
conversational boosting, 52–55
custom topics, 50–51

system topics, 50–51
user experience and, 55–57
user-focused performance
  quick replies, 251–253
  starter prompts, 253–254
  user feedback capture, 255–265
AGI (artificial general intelligence), 33
Agile project management, 121
AI Builder, prompts, 58
ALM (application lifecycle
  management), 116, 119
  deployment, 122–123
  design, 121
  development stage, 121–122
  maintenance, 123
  Power Platform, 123–124
    environment costs, 124–125
    firewalls, 126
    managed environments, 125–127
  requirements, 120–121
  retirement, 123
  testing, 122
analytical data, 36
  agents, 246–248
APIs (application programming
  interfaces), 33
  ArcGIS API, 154–155
  authentication, 283
  Copilot Connectors, 268
  plugin manifest, 95
  Salesforce, 215
  REST API, 219
App IDs, 82–83
App Insights, 255–265
app package
  app icons, 94
  app manifest, 93–94
  declarative agent manifest,
    94–95
  plugin manifest, 95
apps, uploads, 81–82
ArcGIS API, 154–155
augmentation, 8
authentication

channels, 71–72
Copilot authentication *versus* user
  authentication, 165
author credentials, 72
automation paradox, 32
autonomous agents, 197–198,
  199–200
  action-based events, 199
  actions
    Account ID, 222–224
    AI builder prompts, 219
    Bot Framework skills, 219
    conditions, 224–226
    contacts, 226–227, 228–231
    Create Lead, 232–235
    custom connectors, 218
    inputs, 220–221
    opportunities, 227–228
    Power Automate cloud
      flow, 218–219
    prebuilt connectors, 218
    REST APIs, 219
    variable formats, 221–222
  CRM (Customer Relationship
    Management), 201–202
  data changes, 199
  instructions, 235–236
  knowledge sources, 213–218
  Microsoft Forms, 200–201, 209
  monitoring, 242
  orchestration, 203–204
  Power Automate, 199
  publishing, 242
  response details, 208–209
  Run Only Users, 231–232
  testing, 236–242
  time-based events, 199
  triggers
    actions, adding, 208
    creating, 204–207
    custom, 207–213
    variables, 210–213
  use case, Salesforce Sales
    Cloud, 201–202

300 Index ■ A–C

Azure, 23
  OpenAI RAG pattern, 8–9
Azure Active Directory ID. *See*
  Microsoft Entra ID
Azure AD v1, 79, 83
Azure AI Foundry, 267
Azure AI Search, 268–269, 276–286
  agent configuration, 286–288
  agent testing, 288–289
  optimizing for cost, 269
Azure AI Studio, 1
Azure Application Insights. *See* App
  Insights
Azure Key Vault, 60, 116
Azure OpenAI, 6–7, 48
  RAG pattern, 8–10
Azure OpenAI o1, 250
Azure SQL
  Azure Search, 276–286
  database, 269
    authentication, 271–272
    deployment, 271–272
    resource groups, 270–271
    table creation, 274–276
    virtual server, 271
    tables, 274–276

B
bias in GenAI, 4
BigAppleBuddy agent
  setup, 175–182
  shared mailbox agent,
    182–186
Bing Chat Enterprise, 12–13
Bot Framework, skills, 58

C
channels
  authentication, 71–72
  available, 73
ChatGPT, 4–5
  data leaks, 5–6
  growth, 5
chats, agents, 88–89

CI/CD (continuous integration and
  continuous deployment)
  pipelines, 140
citizen developers. *See* makers
Citizen Services template
  knowledge sources, 146–147
  topics, 147
    Adaptive Card node, 149–154
    Apply for a Service, 148
    Conversational Boosting, 155–157
    Data Collection, 149–154
    Road Closures, 154–155
    summarizing, 157
    topic chaining, 148
    topic linking, 148
CompanyGPT, 7
Connector
  Copilot Author
    Authentication, 60–61
  User Authentication, 60
connectors
  custom, 58
  prebuilt, 57
contact centers use cases, 171
  agent summary, 176
  agent testing, 175
  Contact Center Charlie, 173–176
  Dataverse uploads, 174–175
  policies and procedure
    documentation, 172–173
  setup, 173–175
content creation, 3
Conversation Start topic, 50
Conversational Boosting topic, 155
  Create Generative Answers
    node, 155–157
Copilot
  Bing Chat Enterprise, 12–13
  company persona alignment, 24–25
  Copilot for Finance, 23
  GenAI-as-a-Service, 1
  GitHub Copilot, 22–23
  in Azure, 23
  Microsoft Viva, 19–22

Index ▪ C–G   301

Power Automate, 23
Power BI, 23
Copilot for Finance, 23
Copilot for Sales, 14–16
Copilot for Security, 17–19
Copilot for Service, 16–17
Copilot Studio
  access, 34–35
  audience, 29–30
  declarative agents, 96
  purposes, 25–26
  tenant license, 34
  user license, 34
credentials, 72
CRM (Customer Relationship
  Management), 14–15, 36
  Salesforce Sales Cloud, 201–202
custom topics, 50
  Goodbye, 51
  Greeting, 51
  Start Over, 51
  Thank You, 51
Customer engagement hub, 73

D

data
  analytical data, 36
  data changes, autonomous
    agents, 199
  line-of-business data, 36
  productivity data, 36
  unstructured data, 36
Data Collection topic
  Adaptive Card node, 149–154
  variable assignments, 168
data leaks, 5–6
declarative agents
  Agent Builder, 97
    actions, 103
    agent configuration, 98–99
    capabilities, 103
    Create button, 105–106
    instructions, 99–100
    knowledge sources, 101–103

    permissions, 106–112
    sharing, 106–112
    starter prompts, 104–105
  app package
    app icons, 94
    app manifest, 93–94
    declarative agent manifest, 94–95
    plugin manifest, 95
  configuration, 96
  declarativeAgent_0.json file,
    107, 110–112
  orchestrator, 96–97
  updating, 114–115
  use cases, 117
developer information, 78–79
DLP (data loss prevention), 144
  Power Platform
    environments, 144–145
documents, formats, 102–103

E

e-commerce platforms, 36
EAP (Early Access Preview)
  program, 10
environments
  Microsoft Dataverse, 39
  Power Platform, 35–36
ERP (enterprise resource planning), 36
error handling, knowledge sources, 45
Escalate topic, 187–188

G

GenAI, 1
  bias risk, 4
  ChatGPT and, 5
  Citizen Services template, 146
  conversational boosting, 52
  Conversational Boosting API, 157
  Copilots and, 12–13
  GitHub Copilot, 22–23
  human-in-the-loop, 45–46
  Microsft M365 Copilot, 9–10
  models, 3
  optimization and, 249–250

Index ▪ G–M

orchestrators, 96–97
overview, 2–3
Power Platform, 23
RAG pattern, 9–10
Viva Goals, 19–20
generation, 8
generative answers, 34
  optimization and, 249
GitHub Copilot, 22–23
grounding, 8
GUIDs (Globally Unique
    Identifiers), 112

H

hallucinations, 198
Heidi from HR, 186–187
  Adaptive Card node, 189–193
  Email variable, 191
  Escalate topic, 187–188
  setup, 187–194
  suggested phrases, 187–188
  testing, 194–195
  variable mapping, 193–194
HRBPs (Human Resources Business
    Professionals), 186
human resources use case,
    186–187
  Adaptive Card node, 189–193
  Email variable, 191
  Escalate topic, 187–188
  setup, 187–194
  suggested phrases, 187–188
  variable mapping, 193–194
hyperscalers, 6

I

IaC (Infrastructure as Code), 7
integration, knowledge sources,
    45
ISVs (independent software
    developers), 1, 78–79
IT department
  makers and, 30–32
  roles, 32–33

J

JSON (JavaScript Object Notation), 151
  schema, joining, 162

K

knowledge sources, 42–47
  deleting, 158
  error handling, 45
  integration, 45
  personalization, 44
  updating, 158–159
KQL (Kusto Query Language), 18

L

landing zones, 7
licensing, 34
  contact centers, 172–173
  Microsoft 365, 74
  Microsoft 365 Licensing
      Guide, 172–173
line-of-business data, 36
LLMs (large language models)
  AI Builder prompts, 219
  backend, 96–97
  ChatGPT and, 4
  custom, 9–13
    pretrained, 282
  declarative agents, 93
  description, 3
  external data, 7–8
  freedom, 53
  hallucinations, 198
  OpenAI, 6–7
  RAG pattern, 8
  saving, 255–256
  system prompt, 41
  training data, accessing, 48–49

M

M365 Copilot. *See also* Copilot
  agents, 92
    declarative, 97–98
    testing, 86–90
  architecture, 11

extended first-party Copilots, 25
knowledge workers, 24
messages by feature, 250
Microsoft Viva, 19-20
licensing, 15–16, 33–34
prerequisites, 33–34
release, 10–13
Responsible AI, 97
security, 17–18
sharing permissions, 106
tenant license, 34
testing agents, 86
makers, 30–32
manifest.json file, 107–110
messages, 250
metadata, app package manifest, 93
Microsoft, OpenAI and, 6–7
Microsoft 365
agents, publishing, 74–79
licensing, 74
Microsoft 365 Licensing
Guide, 172–173
Microsoft Dataverse, 36
components, 37–38
environment management, 39
silos, 36
Microsoft Entra, 18
Microsoft Entra ID, 35
Microsoft Forms, autonomous agents,
200–201, 209
Microsoft Graph, 249
Microsoft Intune, 18
Microsoft Power Virtual Agents, 33
Microsoft Purview, 18
Microsoft Teams
agents
publishing, 74–79
testing, 86–90
Teams Administrator, 84
Teams Toolkit, 96
user groups, 82
Microsoft Viva
OKR (objectives and key
results), 19–20

Viva Amplify, 21–22
Viva Engage, 20–21
Viva Goals, 19–20
Viva Roadmap, 21–22
models, 3

N
nodes
action node, 52
condition node, 52
message node, 52
multiple choice node, 52
question node, 52

O
OpenAI, 4–5
Azure OpenAI, 48
o1 model, 250
4o-mini model, 250
RAG pattern, 8–10
service configuration, 280
M365 Copilot, 10–11
Microsoft and, 6–7
orchestration, autonomous
agents, 203–204
orchestrator, 96–97

P
pattern recognition, 3
permissions, agent publishing, 80–81
personalization, knowledge
sources, 44
pipelines, 140
PLM (product lifecycle
management), 36
plugins, app package, 95
Power Automate, 23
autonomous agents, 197–198, 199–200
action-based events, 199
actions, 218–222, 224–235
CRM (Customer Relationship
Management), 201–202
data changes, 199
instructions, 235–236

knowledge sources, 213–218
Microsoft Forms, 200–201, 209
monitoring, 242
orchestration, 203–204
Power Automate, 199
publishing, 242
response details, 208–209
Run Only Users, 231–232
testing, 236–242
time-based events, 199
triggers, 204–213
actions, adding, 208
  cloud flows, 58
  New Designer, 207
Power BI, 23
Power Platform environments, 35–36, 123–124
  adding agents, 130–132
  backups, 126
  catalog, 126
  CMK (Customer Managed Key), 126
  connectors
    blocked, 144
    business, 144
    non-business, 144
  customer lockbox, 126
  data policies, 125
  default environment, 126
  developer/sandbox environment, 124
  environment costs, 124–125
  Export Agent, 128
  exporting data, 126
  groups, 125
  integration, 124
  IP Cookie Binding, 126
  IP Firewall, 126
  managed environments, 125–127
  new publisher, 129–130
  pipelines, 126, 140
  production, 124
  sharing, 125
  solutions, 127–129
    components, 127

creating, 129–132
exporting, 132–135
importing, 135–139
managed, 127
unmanaged, 127
UAT (User Acceptance Testing), 124
usage insights, 125
welcome content, 126
productivity data, 36
productivity paradox, 32
publishing agents
  Admin Approval, 83–84
  app uploads, 81–82
  availability, 80–81
  channels, 71–74
  permissions, 80–81
  Publish button, 85–86
  status, 80
  testing, 86–90
  to Microsoft 365, 74–79
  to Teams, 74–79

R

RAG (retrieval-augmented generation), 7–10
  knowledge sources and, 42, 147
  Microsoft Graph, 249
responsible AI, 198
retrieval, 7
risk detection, 72
Road Closures topic, 154–155
  disabling, 160

S

Salesforce Cloud, autonomous agents, 197–198, 199–200
  action-based events, 199
  actions, 218–235
  CRM (Customer Relationship Management), 201–202
  data changes, 199
  instructions, 235–236
  knowledge sources, 213–218
  Microsoft Forms, 200–201, 209

Index ■ S–U 305

monitoring, 242
orchestration, 203–204
Power Automate, 199
publishing, 242
response details, 208–209
Run Only Users, 231–232
testing, 236–242
time-based events, 199
triggers, 204–213
Salesforce Sales Cloud, 201–202
SCM (supply chain management), 36
semi-autonomous agents, 197–198
Send an Email action, 60–69
SharePoint, declarative agents, 96
silos, 36
SSO (single sign-on), 79
starter prompts, 253–254
summarizing topics, 157
system prompt, establishing, 41
system topics
  Conversation Start, 50, 153–154
  Conversational Boosting, 50
  End of Conversation, 50
  Escalate, 50, 63–64, 66
  Fallback, 50
  On Error, 51
  Reset Conversation, 51
  Sign in, 51

T

Microsoft Teams
  agents
    publishing, 74–79
    testing, 86–90
  Teams + Microsoft 365 button, 74–75
  Teams Administrator, 84
  Teams Toolkit, 96
  user groups, 82
testing
  agents, 86–90, 166–169
    contact center use case, 175
  autonomous agents, 236–242
time-based events, autonomous
  agents, 199
topics, 50–51

Citizen Services template, 147
  Adaptive Card node, 149–154
  Apply for a Service, 148
  Conversational Boosting, 155–157
  Data Collection, 149–154
  Road Closures, 154–155
  summarizing, 157
conversational boosting, 52–55
custom topics, 50–51
editing, 161–162
fields, new, 161–162
formula updates, 161
Message node, 159–160
Message Variations, 159
summarizing, 157
system topics, 50–51
topic chaining, 148
topic linking, 148
Topics Editor, 49
updating, 159–166
user experience and, 55–57
Topics navigation link, 160
training data, 3
  accessing, 48

U

UAT (user acceptance testing), 145
unstructured data, 36
use cases
  autonomous agents, 199–200
  contact centers, 171
    agent summary, 176
    agent testing, 175
    Dataverse uploads, 174–175
    policies and procedure
      documentation, 172–173
    setup, 173–175
  human resources, 186–187
    Heidi from HR agent, 186–195
    setup, 187–194
  public sector, 176–182
    shared mailbox agent
      summary, 185–186
    shared mailbox agent test, 182–185
user experience, topics and, 55–57

306 Index ■ V–X–Y–Z

user feedback capture, 255–265
user-focused performance
quick replies, 251–253
starter prompts, 253–254
user feedback capture, 255–265

V
Viva, 19–22

W
Waterfall project management, 121
website ownership confirmation, 159

X–Y–Z
XDR (Extended Detection & Response), 17